AF413628

SHAPER
OF
GOD

by American Artist

Contents

Media

ARTW	Documentation of American Artist's artwork across various media such as exhibiton images and video stills.
ARCH	Images from The Huntington Library, Jet Propulsion Laboratory, and other archival and research sources.
PHOT	General photographic images, including phone photos, phone screenshots, and professional photographs.
QUOT	External quotes from selected individuals, books, and emails.
RNDR	3D models or AI-generated renders.
SCRN	Screenshots from American Artist's desktop.
SKCH	Hand-drawn sketches.
TXTM	Text message conversations, which may include images sent and embedded within the conversation.

[7]

Introduction

Shaper of God

by American Artist

1   Two years ago, I published a video online declaring my affinity for making sculptures, implying that I had transcended my well-documented origins as a digital artist. ²However, I footnoted this by stating, "My ideas come out of a space of thinking digitally." ³While I have made an effort to create more physical work in the last couple of years, the ethos of networks and hyperconnectivity remains central to my conceptual practice. ⁴What has always fascinated me about digital art, particularly internet-based art, is the omnipresent network through which it flows. ⁵In line with Wendy Hui Kyong Chun's thesis in her 2005 essay "On Software, or the Persistence of Visual Knowledge," there is an analogy between our digital experiences and the way ideology manifests in our material, social, and political lives. ⁶In my multi-year project *Shaper of God*, I considered the life of author Octavia E. Butler, with whom I share a birthplace, as a network of relations to understand how our life experiences might be deeply intertwined.

2   Octavia E. Butler was a prominent science-fiction author, Black woman, and politically conscientious voice, most active in Los Angeles from the 1970s to the 1990s, at a time when the number of widely recognized Black authors in sci-fi could be counted on one hand. ²She continues to influence artists—especially Black, feminist, queer, and politically engaged speculative artists—who are drawn to her empathetic yet stark narratives about humanity's perilous patterns and blindspots. ³Butler's novels depict survival amid geographic alienation, right-wing extremism, wealth inequality, and climate crisis. ⁴Her *Patternist* series questions whether hierarchy and domination are inherent qualities of sentient species, while the *Xenogenesis* trilogy reimagines what forced cohabitation and collaboration with oppressors, who view themselves as benevolent guardians, might look like. [5]The *Parable* series, set in Los Angeles in 2024, suggests that building community is humanity's best chance for survival. [6]It warns that when demagogues and oligarchs hold power and oppose everything you value, you'd better have an escape plan.

3   In September 2020, Butler's 1993 novel *Parable of the Sower* landed on *The New York Times* Best Sellers list. [2]This near-future dystopian novel resonated with readers for its prescient depictions of educational classes held in living rooms and a Trump-like presidential candidate, as they sought guidance on how to navigate life during times of overwhelming crisis. [3]That same year, while quarantined in New York, I re-read *Parable of the Sower* as I began to conceptualize what would become *Shaper of God*. [4]Rather than seeking solutions to the consequences of social distancing, I felt a combination of nostalgia for my familiar landscape of northeastern Los Angeles, now inaccessible, along with a growing interest in speculative fiction as a tool for abolition and social justice. [5]I also felt compelled to pursue a new chapter in my art practice, one that held space for my own fascination, curiosity, pleasure, and excitement, which I had previously been reluctant to indulge.

4   Before this, about a year prior to the murder of George Floyd and the subsequent Black Lives Matter protests, my practice was devoted to interrogating the police and their use of "blue" as an identity politic. [2]The works I created during that time (*I'm Blue I–VI*, *Blue Life Seminar*, and *My Blue Window*, all 2019) were rooted in the material realities of police legislation and technology, while incorporating speculative fiction iconography to emphasize how detached from reality many police practices seemed to be. [3]I used the visual language of *Minority Report* interfaces to satirize the reality that predictive policing technology was nothing new, and the semblance of *Watchmen*'s Dr. Manhattan to exaggerate the absurdity of identifying "blue" as a social or racial demographic. [4]While my work often engages with the subtle design of powerful institutions, I sometimes venture into the visual realm of fiction to reveal just how absurd our reality can be.

5   "Sometime ago I read some place that Robert A. Heinlein had these three categories of science-fiction stories: The what-if category; the if-only category; and the if-this-goes-on category. [2]And I liked the idea. [3]So this is definitely an if-this-goes-on story. [4]And if it's true, if it's anywhere near true, we're all in trouble."

Octavia E. Butler, "'Devil Girl From Mars': Why I Write Science Fiction," speech at MIT on February 19, 1998.

6   Speculative fiction—a broad term encompassing science fiction, fantasy, and narratives that propose scenarios beyond our world—has been highlighted as a tool for radical political imagination in anthologies such as *Octavia's Brood: Science Fiction Stories from Social Justice Movements*. [2]The collected works of Octavia E. Butler, which are always speculative, if not strictly scientific, serve as a powerful foundation for radical political organizing. [3]After my work on policing, speculative fiction appealed to me as a way to approach prison-industrial complex abolition and imagine the type of world I want to live in, one free from the carceral system.

> **7** "Whenever we try to envision a world without war, without violence, without prisons, without capitalism, we are engaging in speculative fiction."
>
> Walidah Imarisha, *Octavia's Brood: Science Fiction Stories from Social Justice Movements.*

8 In 2020, during the protests following George Floyd's tragic passing, Black artists like myself experienced a surge of attention from many onlookers seeking to highlight what we had been saying about the decades-long pattern of state-sanctioned racial violence in the U.S. [2]Emotionally drained from years of trying to understand the mindset behind police violence and disheartened by the praise of my work being tied to Floyd's death, I decided to sunset my project directly engaging the police. [3]Instead, I began a new body of work that I felt was, in the words of abolitionist Mariame Kaba, "life-affirming." [4]Though I've encountered skepticism from some art professionals concerned that I've strayed away from familiar subjects like policing, anti-Blackness, or technology, I don't see *Shaper of God* as a departure from that work, but rather as a continuation. [5]The subjects that have defined my practice for nearly a decade—racial segregation, crime and punishment, surveillance, institutional gatekeeping, and globalization—are also central themes that concerned Butler throughout her career.

9 Octavia E. Butler was born in 1947 in Pasadena, California, a historically segregated town northeast of Los Angeles, with a white middle class and a diverse working class (ARCH253 [164]), and notable institutions and events such as NASA's Jet Propulsion Laboratory and the Rose Parade. [2]This is also where I was born, and I was raised in the neighboring town of Altadena, where Butler also lived. [3]When I discovered that Octavia E. Butler attended John Muir High School in Pasadena, the same high school I attended nearly forty years later, it created a visceral sense of kinship. [4]She attended Muir alongside my aunts, Hermenia Rodgers and Gail Irby (both neé Braden), who were one year older and younger than Butler. [5]This connection inspired a desire to understand what it was about this locale that seemed to nourish important creative work by artists like Butler and myself.

10 "Everyone knows that change is inevitable. [2]From the second law of thermodynamics to Darwinian evolution, from Buddhism's insistence that nothing is permanent and all suffering results from our delusions of permanence to the third chapter of Ecclesiastes ('To everything there is a season'), change is part of life, of existence, of the common wisdom. [3]But I don't believe we're dealing with all that that means. [4]We haven't even begun to deal with it."

Lauren Oya Olamina in *Parable of the Sower* by Octavia E. Butler.

11 As I re-read this passage from the diary of *Parable of the Sower*'s teenage protagonist, I no longer saw these words as abstract religious ideals, as they are framed in the novel. ²Instead, I understood them as an indictment of the ignorance of one's own location—a condition that afflicts the majority of Americans. ³Around this time, I was also reading the essay "Geographical Perspectives on the History of Black America" by Richard L. Morrill and O. Fred Donaldson and I became fixated on a set of diagrams depicting Black American migration from the southern United States to the North and West (ARCH254 [165]). ⁴These diagrams, documenting the Great Migration and lesser-known Second Great Migration, conveyed an intense, compulsory energy that seemed larger than life. ⁵The people mapped during this time were escaping the racial terrorism rampant in the South and seeking industrial employment opportunities. ⁶In *The Books of the Living*, a set of fictional religious texts in *Parable of the Sower*, we are told that "God is Change." ⁷As I tried to identify the artist or geographer behind Morrill and Donaldson's essay, I began to associate this period of Black migration—particularly to the West Coast—with Lauren Olamina's concept of Change. ⁸Could this massive period of change be emblematic of the God that she believes in? ⁹I believe Butler's writing, which often infused autobiographical subtleties into her characters, was reckoning with historical changes like these.

12   "God can't be resisted or stopped, but can be shaped and focused."
The Books of the Living in *Parable of the Sower* by Octavia E. Butler.

13   *Shaper of God* is a three-pronged body of work that attempts to reconcile Butler's lived realities with her fictive portrayals, drawing intimate connections across the geography of her life. ²The title refers not only to Octavia E. Butler as a creator of worlds but also to the racial violence that drove Black migration out of the South. ³It also speaks to the readers of *The Books of the Living*, who embrace their calling as Shapers of God, using their focus to shape their destinies—much like Butler did in her own life. ⁴The three sections of this book and body of work reflect the layers I felt were necessary to show the connection between Butler's life, her work, myself, and the geographical and generational context we share.

14   Octavia E. Butler's maternal legacy is a central theme in the writings and artworks of Section I, which focus on her close relationships with her mother and grandmother. ²This section explores how their material support played a crucial role in Butler's career and traces the family's migration from Louisiana to the California desert, revealing the impact of this journey on her identity and work. ³I spent three years researching and eventually building a sculpture that visualizes Estella Guy Butler's first structure built on Californian land. ⁴As part of my research, I visited the Octavia E. Butler Papers at The Huntington, just outside of Pasadena, where I saw letters, school notes, bus maps, unpublished manuscripts, and other personal artifacts of Butler's. [5]These materials became the basis for drawings I made with pink stationary provided by the library, because you are not allowed to bring your own pen and paper into the archive.

15 Octavia E. Butler's connection to the landscapes of Pasadena and Altadena is explored in Section II, which examines her access to Los Angeles through public institutions like local bus routes and library systems. [2]This section highlights how the unique geography of the region shaped Butler's worldview and is reflected in the vivid settings of her fiction. [3]Butler regularly took the bus from Pasadena to the Los Angeles Public Library to work on novels such as *Parable*, and she often ruminated on the arson attack on the library in 1986. [4]This chapter also traces how Pasadena's native flora and the mid-century architecture of wealthier Pasadena neighborhoods directly influenced the landscapes depicted in her novels.

16 Section III juxtaposes Octavia E. Butler's exploration of space—particularly through the religious community Earthseed in *Parable of the Sower*—with Pasadena's history of rocket science and a contemporary private space race led by figures like Elon Musk and Jeff Bezos. [2]This section draws parallels between Butler's speculative vision and real-world efforts to leave Earth behind, offering a thought-provoking take on the concept of "destiny" and who gets to shape it. [3]Drawing on the origin of Pasadena's storied Jet Propulsion Laboratory and the needs of a community left behind, key works in this section imagine a fiction within a fiction, depicting what early rocket tests by the Earthseed community might have looked like.

17 Though I could spend a lifetime unpacking the 9,062 objects Butler entrusted to The Huntington across 386 boxes, I have spent the last four years learning about Butler's process, and through that, my own. [2]I want to carry that forward, not just by telling "if-this-goes-on" stories, but also by asking "what-if?" [3]Butler was steadfast in her commitment to questioning the reality many take for granted. [4]She taught me that by studying history closely, we can accurately describe the challenges we will face in the future. [5]And the truth must be told, no matter how many people are listening. [6]The evidence is there for the taking, and the audience that will act on it may not even be born yet. [7]You too have the power to "Shape God."

Octavia E. Butler's maternal legacy is a central theme in the writings and artworks of Section I, which focus on her close relationships with her mother and grandmother. This section explores how their material support played a crucial role in Butler's career and traces the family's migration from Louisiana to the California desert, revealing the impact of this journey on her identity and work.

All that you touch
You Change.

Fantasy Is Not Folly, It Is a Lifeline

On the Maternal Lineage of Octavia E. Butler

by Taylor Renee Aldridge

ARTW003b [52]

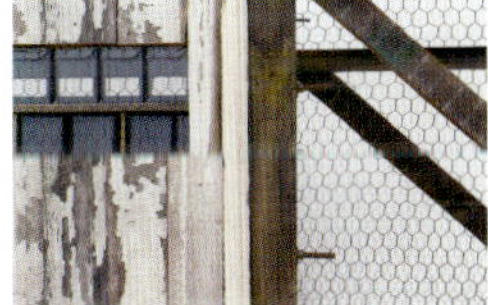

1 When the late science fiction writer Octavia E. Butler was four years old, she experienced her earliest memory. [2]During the early 1950s, at a time when highly flammable kerosene lamps were commonplace, Butler's family home in Apple Valley, California, caught fire. [3]It was the home her family built in the 1930's, after migrating from Louisiana to escape the racial and economic terrorism in the American South. [4]Butler's uncles constructed the property by hand, and it included a chicken coop operated by Butler's grandmother, Estella, enabling autonomous income for her and her family at a time when autonomous labor opportunities for African American women were incredibly limited. [5]In Butler's most well-known novels, the *Parable* series—*Parable of the Sower* and *Parable of Talents*—fires are ubiquitous and formative to the dystopian narrative arc. [6]The series describes great loss, recurring migrations, evidence of what novel faiths may engender, and the inevitability of beginnings and endings. [7]The fires in Octavia's *Parables* directly correlate with the fire she witnessed as a youth in California. [8]The upheaval and precarity she felt during that formative moment of her childhood—marked by the loss of their home and economic security—profoundly influenced her understanding of the human condition and ultimately informed her prolific writing career around faith, fantasy, and survival.

2 Butler's childhood would go on to be characterized by extreme poverty. [2]After her mother, Octavia M. Butler miscarried four times, she birthed Octavia, the only child she would be able to carry to full term. [3]As a single mother working as a domestic in the wealthy areas of Pasadena, Octavia M. Butler witnessed firsthand the class, race, and gender dynamics that shaped their social standing and limited their quality of life. [4]Young Octavia often accompanied her mother to her domestic jobs in affluent neighborhoods, where she observed the stark contrasts between their lives and those of their employers. [5]"Sometimes I was able to go inside and hear people talk about or to my mother in ways that were obviously disrespectful," Butler once shared. [6]"As a child I did not blame them for their disgusting behavior, but I blamed my mother for taking it."* [7]Butler reflected on the resentment of her mother that she developed as a child, and would later recast her mother's tireless laboring as crucial to her own survival, and ultimately, her ability to become a writer: "As I got older I realized this is what kept me fed," Butler admitted. [8]"I started to pay attention to what my mother and even more my grandmother and my poor great-grandmother, who died as a very young woman giving birth to my grandmother, what they all went through."

3 Although men lived in the shared home that was eventually burned down, Butler's upbringing appears to have been significantly matriarchal, reflected even in her naming—she shares her first name with her mother and her middle name, Estelle, comes from her grandmother Estella. [2]When considering labor, the matrix of inheritance, and the loss of land (and thus the loss of potential for material wealth in America), this particular lens illuminates the loss of Estella's chicken coop as even more devastating. [3]As American Artist has noted in their continued reflections on the physicality of that loss, "the chicken coop was a symbolic

ARTW003a [51]

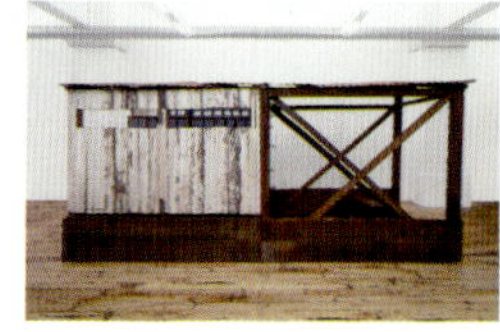

architectural form that represented migration and place-making for them" in the wake of escaping the violent American South, which had few opportunities, if any, for Black economic wealth building.[†] [4]In thinking about Estella's foresightedness in placemaking as a strategy for familial security and eventual wealth, we might also recognize that the method for this strategy began with a vision, and an imagined future. [5]As scholar Katherine McKittrick has noted, "how we make place is a creative and inventive act, and this is especially relevant for communities on the margins."[‡] [6]In this regard, Octavia E. Butler's engagement with speculative and aspirational thinking within her science fiction work can be better understood. [7]If we consider Estella as the origin of speculative and aspirational thinking within and for her own family, we might also view both her and Octavia M. Butler as sowers of a seed for the visionary fiction practice that Octavia E. Butler so masterfully employed throughout her writing career.

4 The history of Butler's family migration from the terse environment in Louisiana to the suburbs of Los Angeles, within the broader context of the Great Migration, exemplifies the enduring aspiration that so many Black folks carried in their movement from the South to northern American cities. [2]What deserves more contemplation and praise is the visionary fiction that our elders employed—and sometimes even required—to place themselves in an environment vastly better than the one they left behind. [3]This is rooted in the Black American impulse to dream beyond our disenfranchised realities that directly correlate with desire, labor, and migration themes depicted in Butler's novels.

ARTW003e [57]

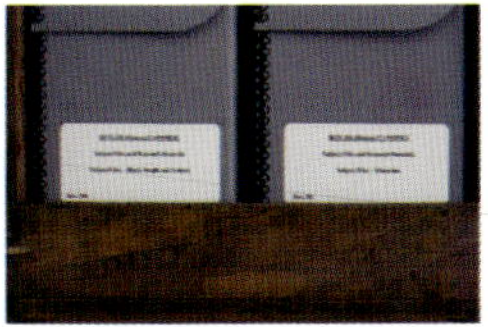

5   In addition to Butler the writer, within the context of the American Artist's *Shaper of God* series, we must also recognize Estella and Octavia M. Butler as practitioners of speculative fiction, enacted through their practices of placemaking, diary entries, inner monologues, and disciplined prayer.

6   During a day-long visit to the library at The Huntington, I found myself peeking into a series of diaries from the 1960s and 70s belonging to Octavia E. Butler and her mother, Octavia M. Butler. [2]In one small, tattered diary, I discovered entries written by Octavia M. from February to March of 1962. [3]Her handwriting had a distinct style—short and stout with a slight slant, rendered in blue ink.

7   On March 2 of that year, she writes:

> [2]second of March I went to get a loan of $200. [3]Paid up my rent which was 150 in rear tax for Victorville also was not paid up... needed school shoes and dress shoes she didn't have no socks. [4]I needed my teeth fixed. But $200. [5]Couldn't Pay all of these Bills so I am praying to God to pleas help me.

8   On March 4, she added:

> [2]We didn't go to Church Because I didn't get any shoes. [3]Need work shoes and dress shoes too. [4]I need some good clothes. We both do.
>
> [5]I bought dress shoes for her but I couldn't get her school shoes
>
> [6]As I don't have no one else to look to but him my God... I thank him for everything."

ARTW004 [45]

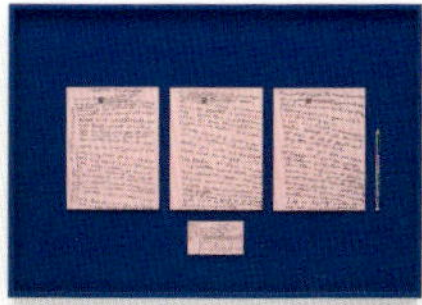

9 These entries by Octavia M. index a poetics of survival, scarcity, and longing. [2]She outlines, with striking clarity, the concerns of debts in tandem with her love and faith in her God. [3]These two brief pages are emblematic of a Black maternal desire for both security and beauty. [4]Even when a loan or dental care could not be obtained, dress shoes for church—to deepen their faith practices—were gratification enough. [5]There is a certain entitlement here: despite precarity and having to do without, Octavia M. obtained what material comforts she could to bring some measure of quality to her life.

10 Born in 1914 in Louisiana, Octavia M. left school early to support her family, returning later only to struggle with feelings of intellectual inferiority. [2]This experience fueled her aspiration for her daughter to achieve a better life, dreaming that Octavia E. might take a stable job as a secretary so that she could sit down as she worked—a luxury her mother never knew. [3]Although Octavia E. disliked the idea of secretarial work, her mother nurtured her interests in literature. [4]Butler's mother is known as an indelible influence in Butler's narratives, but it's worth noting that Butler's writing career was largely made possible by her mother's financial support as well. [5]After a young Butler requested a library card, Butler's mother joyously took her to get one, and her daughter treated the library as a second home.[§] [6]At the age of ten, Butler begged for a Remington typewriter and so her mother saved money to buy one for her.[¶] [7]As Butler continued refining her craft in academia as a young adult, she was advised by mentor Harlan Ellison to attend the Clarion Science Fiction Workshop. [8]Her mother paid more than a month's rent, forgoing money she saved for dental care, to help fund the workshop. [9]The experience proved to be a worthy investment, as Butler sold her first two stories from that convening, changing the course of both of their lives.

11   Octavia E. Butler was raised in a devout Baptist community; Mrs. Butler was particularly religious, as evidenced in her diary entries. [2]Octavia E. admits to despising religion at some point, but later expressed a more nuanced understanding of it, acknowledging its capacity to enhance one's conscious awareness.** [3]Religion often functions as a device in many of her stories, reflecting her rigorous study of society and human behavior; she made it a point to note that there are no human communities without some kind of religion. [4]Butler recognized the sustaining power of faith, particularly within Black communities, stating: "Religion kept some of my relatives alive because it was all they had. [5]If they hadn't had some hope of heaven, some companionship in Jesus, they probably would have committed suicide, their lives were so hellish... They use it to keep themselves alive." [7]This poignant declaration highlights how Black faith, both sacred and secular, engenders a route from struggle toward self-sovereignty.

12   In recalling Butler's ancestors and their experience in migrating from Louisiana in the early twentieth century—to obtain property, build shelter, and even develop a chicken coop that would bore food and economic security— we must also realize how near impossible it was for many Black families to carry out the aforementioned aspirations given the very little resources they had after escaping the harsh and terrorist environments in the American South. [2]Achieving a livable life in such unlivable conditions required detailed organizing, visioning, and conspiring. [3]What may go unrecognized is how crucial it is to vision and speculate about a future before it becomes reality. [4]As activist and author Walidah Imarisha wrote in her introduction to *Octavia's Brood: Science Fiction From Social Justice Movements*, which she co-edited with adrienne maree brown: "Whenever we try to envision a world without war, without violence, without prisons, without capitalism, we are engaging in speculative fiction.... [5]All the organizing is science fiction."

13   Octavia M. and Estella were visionaries. [2]They conspired to build economic security, demonstrating the courage to imagine a world beyond what they knew and what they had access to. [3]Their visions and the eventual materializations of those imagined futures were foundational to Octavia's E. ability to dream as a fantasy writer. [4]Her inheritance was an embodied power of speculative fiction, as a way of calling in the lived experiences one desires to embody, despite unimaginable terror.

* "An Interview with Octavia Butler." *Callaloo* 20:1 (1997), 47–66 © Charles H. Roswell. The Johns Hopkins University Press; Octavia E. Butler, *Conversations with Octavia Butler*, edited by Conseula Francis (University Press of Mississippi, 2010), 78–9.

† American Artist, "Can AI-generated art help us understand the future Octavia Butler saw?," *The Los Angeles Times*, November 20, 2023, https://www.latimes.com/lifestyle/image/story/2023-11-20/american-artist-octavia-butler.

‡ "Katherine McKittrick, a conversation on Black Dreamcatchers," *Dweller*, May 2023, https://dwellerforever.blog/2023/05/katherine-mckittrick-a-conversation-on-black-dreamcatchers.

§ *Callaloo* 20:1 (1997), 47–66 © Charles H. Roswell. The Johns Hopkins University Press; Octavia E. Butler, *Conversations with Octavia Butler*, edited by Conseula Francis (University Press of Mississippi, 2010), 80.

¶ "Black History Month: Octavia Butler," Colorado State University English Department, last modified February 13, 2017, https://english.colostate.edu/news/black-history-month-octavia-butler/.

** "Octavia E. Butler: Persistence." From *Locus Magazine* (June 2000). The Johns Hopkins University Press; *Conversations with Octavia Butler*, edited by Conseula Francis (University Press of Mississippi, 2010), 186–7.

What did the desert teach me?
One of the first lessons of sentience
—— easily learned, and easily
forgotten: We human beings are
not the Center of the universe.
Each individual learns this lesson
early in life — then rejects,
denys it, forgets it, and has to
learn it again —— and again..

Hey aunty, I have a question for you. I remember my dad describing chickens, I think your parents had. Do you remember anything about having chickens or how they were kept?

Hi American, Yes. When we were very young we had chickens. I don't think we kept them long. I am sure they were kept in some type of chicken coop. What I remember the most was mom in the back yard and wringing their necks to kill them. Once the neck was rung off, the chicken would flop all around the back yard until it's heart stopped. As a kid that part was a bit scary. Once the chicken was dead. She would put it in boiling water, and pick the feathers out, clean it and cook for dinner. I don't think my parents kept chickens for long. Also, in the summers when we were kids, we went to our grand parent's home in Tennessee. They had chickens all the time. I would go with our grandmother and gather eggs from the chicken coops. We would have those eggs for breakfast. I don't remember my grandmother killing them when I was there. That was fun to gather the eggs. Hope this helps.

Illustration of OEB 3046. Octavia E. Butler, Notes for speeches: notecards. ca. 1980–2000.

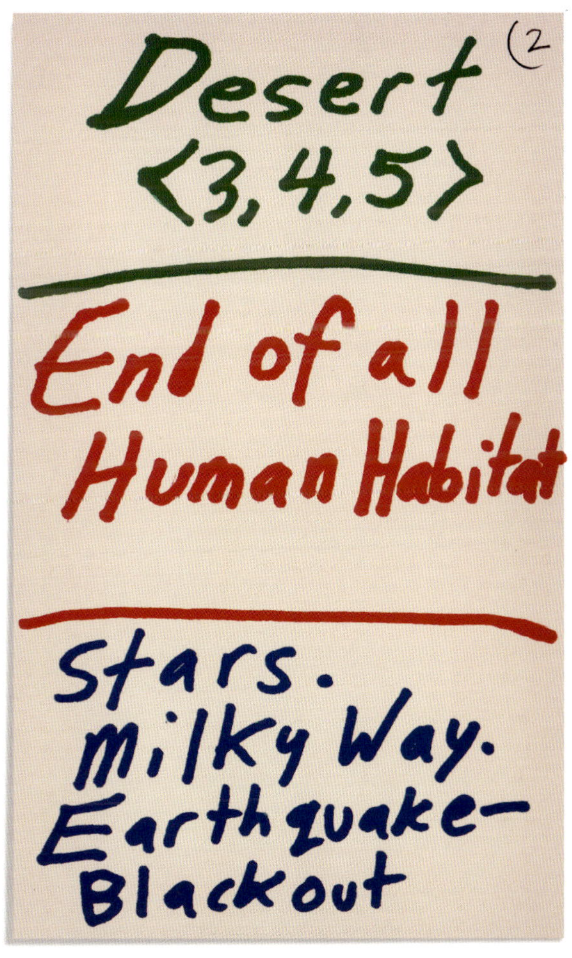

AI image made using Midjourney with reference
photos taken in Apple Valley, CA, 2023.

[34]

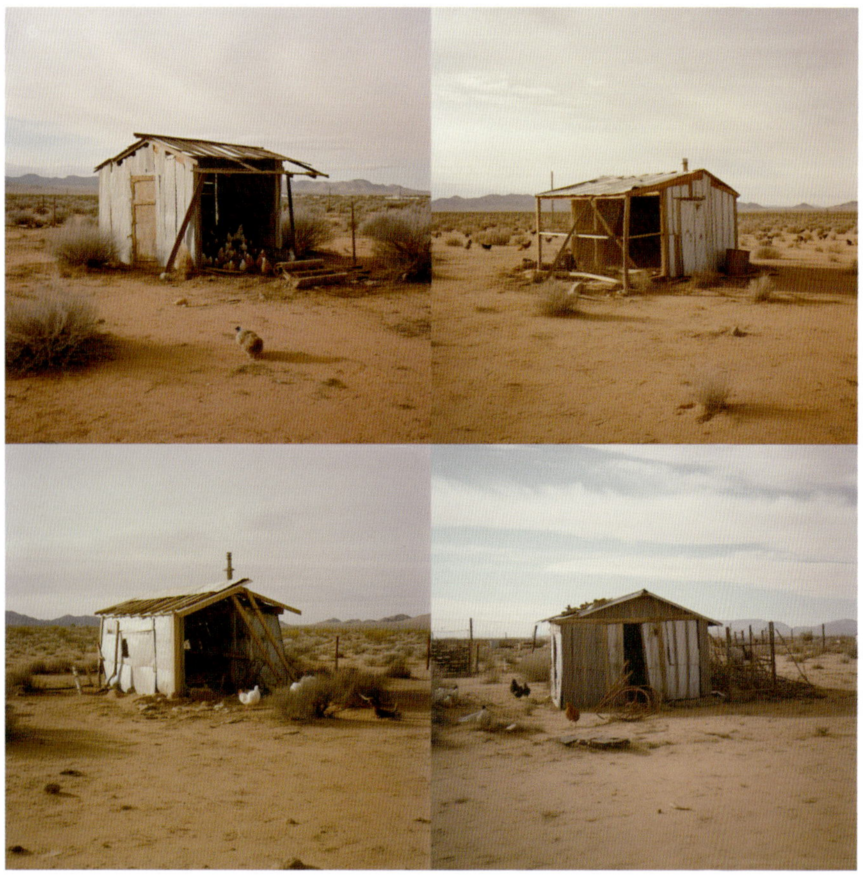

To be honest, in Pasadena, I think my folks only had chickens a short while, only to cook and I don't remember the coop. I remember my grandparent's coop very well. It was wooden posts with screens around for air to come in and there were several like shelves (maybe 2 or 3) where the chickens would nest. It was a nice size where we could go in the door and stand to gather the eggs.

Ok, that's very helpful. The reason I'm asking is because I learned that Octavia Butler's grandmother had a chicken coop in Victorville. I am trying to understand how common it was at the time for black folks in the LA area to have chickens and what type of set up butler's grandmother may have had for the chickens.

Oh, okay. Glad it helped.

Would you be able to make a sketch of the coop your grandmother had?

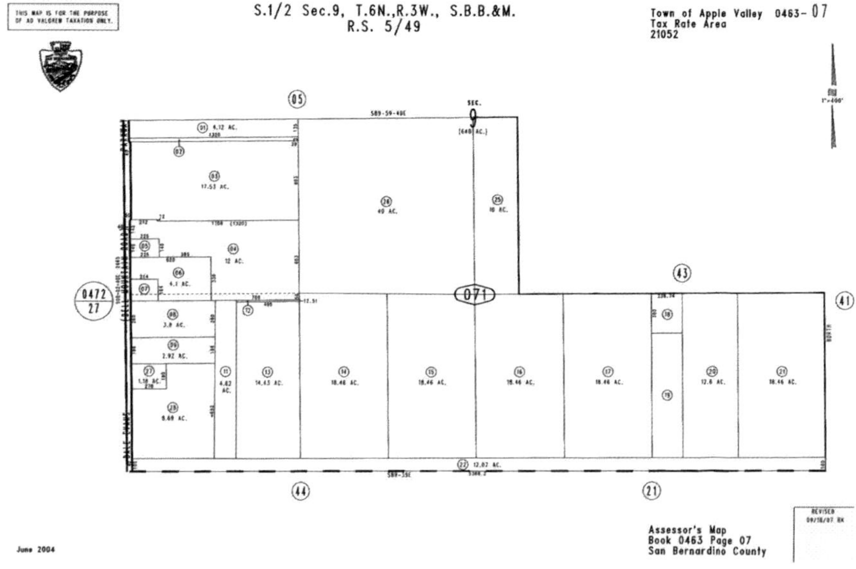
THIS MAP IS FOR THE PURPOSE OF AD VALOREM TAXATION ONLY.
S.1/2 Sec.9, T.6N.,R.3W., S.B.B.&M.
R.S. 5/49
Town of Apple Valley 0463-07
Tax Rate Area
21052
1"=400'
0472
27
0471
June 2004
Assessor's Map
Book 0463 Page 07
San Bernardino County
REVISED
09/18/07 BK

@a_____rtist

Today I went to the desert to see where Estella
Butler's chicken farm was.

5:29 PM · 1/14/23 · **189** Views

Photograph of the estimated location of Estella Butler's ranch in Apple Valley, 2023.

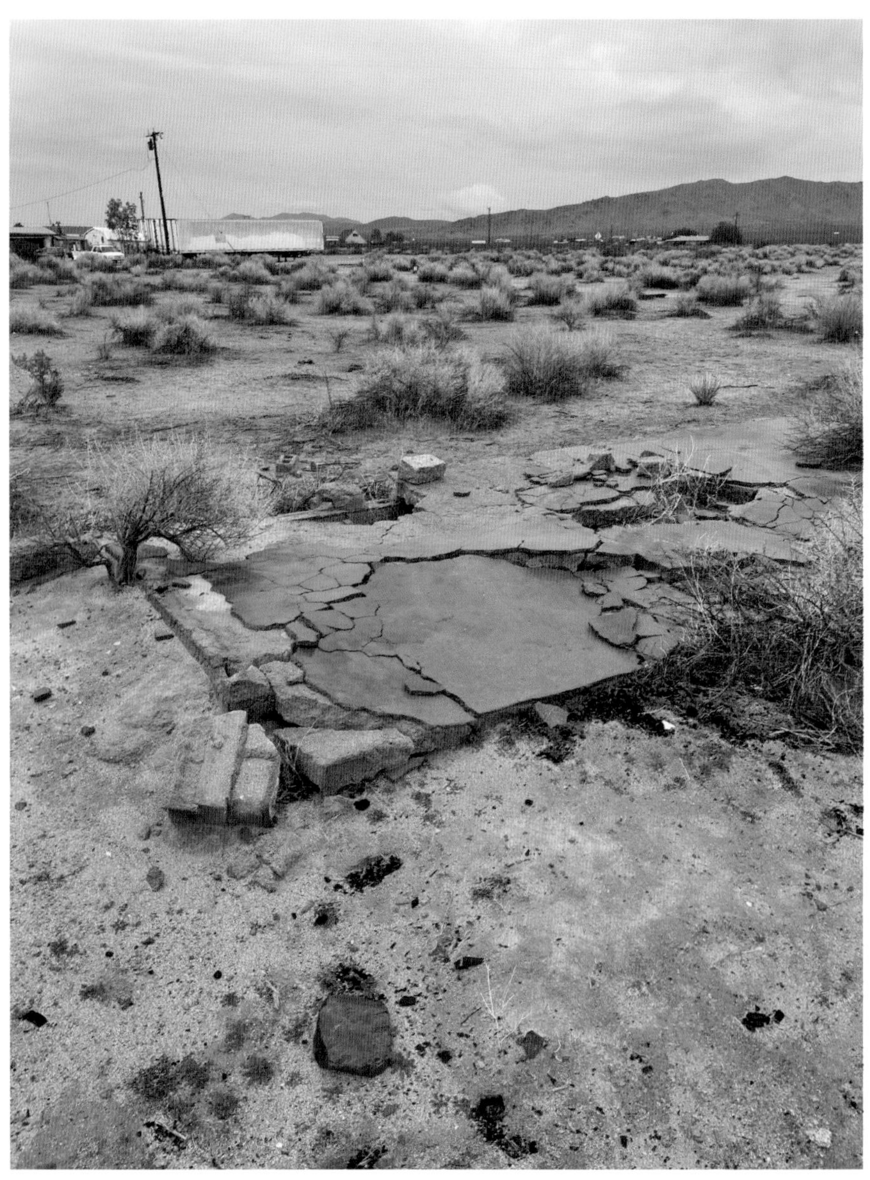

     Photograph of a Joshua Tree in Apple Valley, 2023.

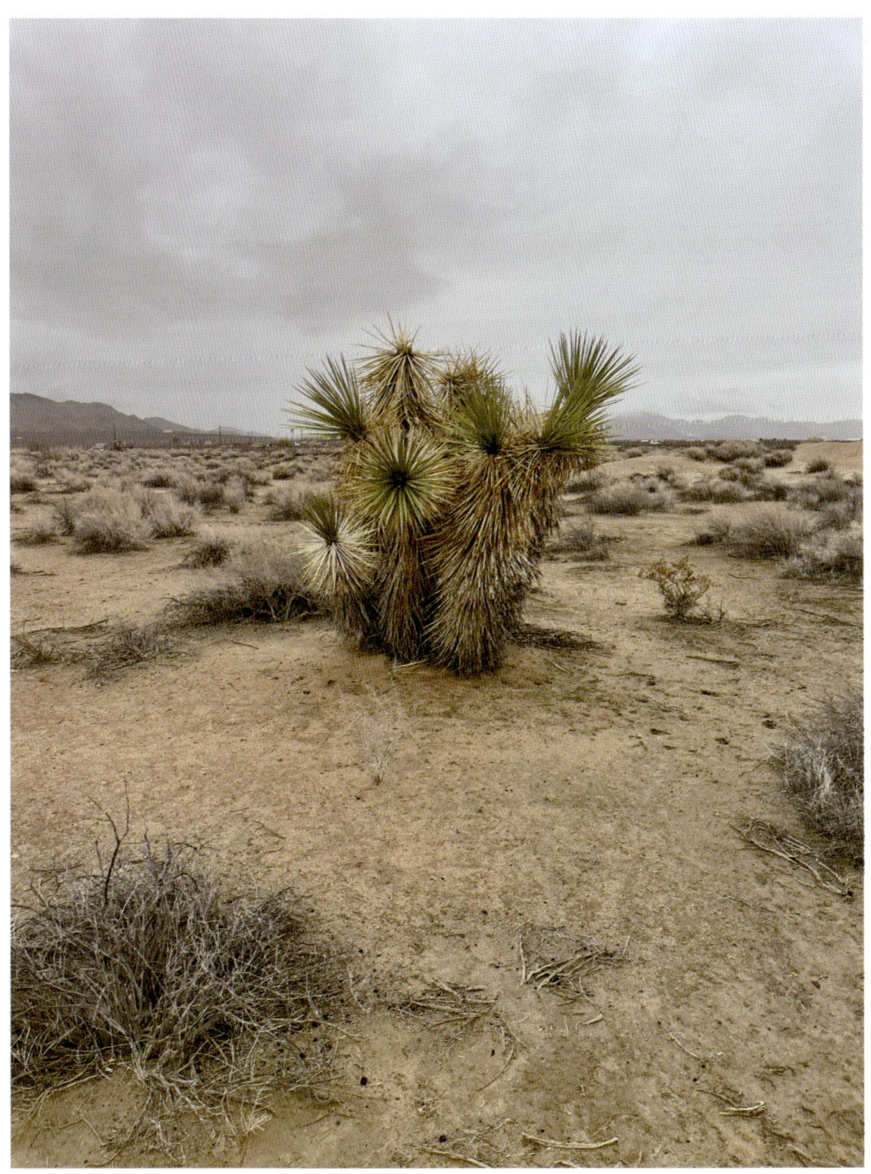

"Hello Nephew, as I mentioned to you in the text, drawing is not my forte. I tried to draw a chicken coop. Attached are some pictures when put together resembles what my memory of my grandparents chicken coop looked like. This is the best I can do. I am sorry, but I did not get you artistic abilities. Hope you can put together my vision.**"**

Sketch of family's chicken coop by American Artist's aunt Hermenia Rodgers, 2022.

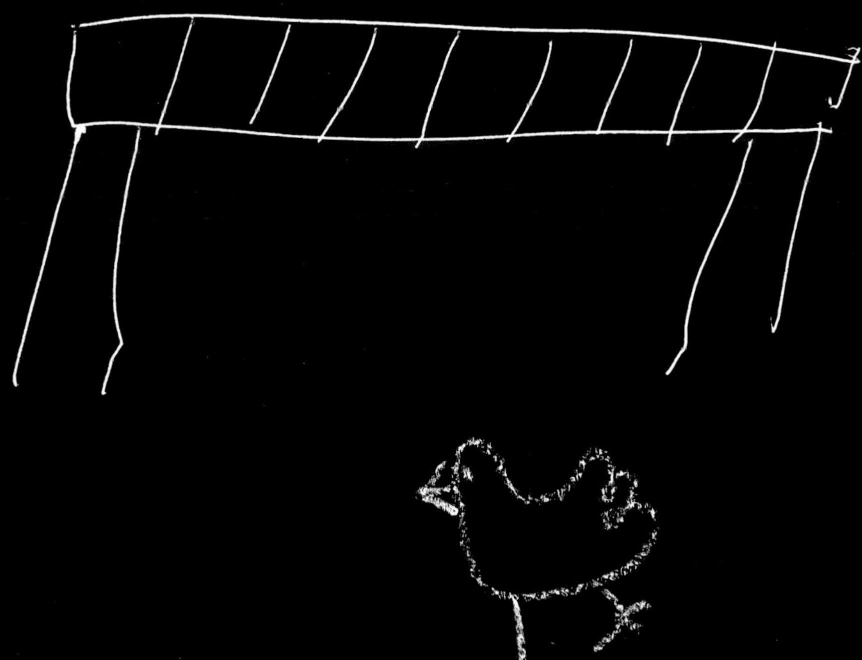

Sketch of a chicken coop and archival storage by American Artist, 2023.

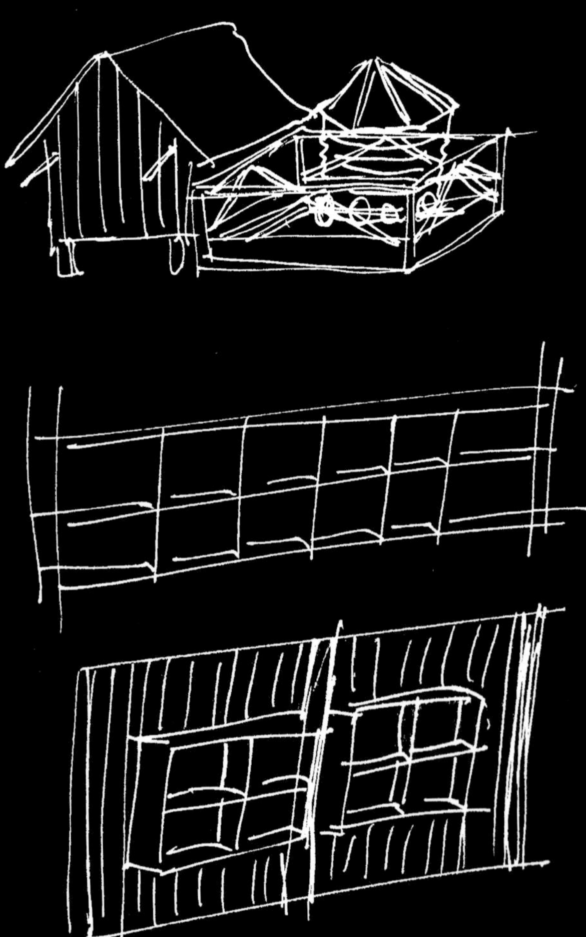

Text message between Ayana Jamieson and American Artist, 2021.

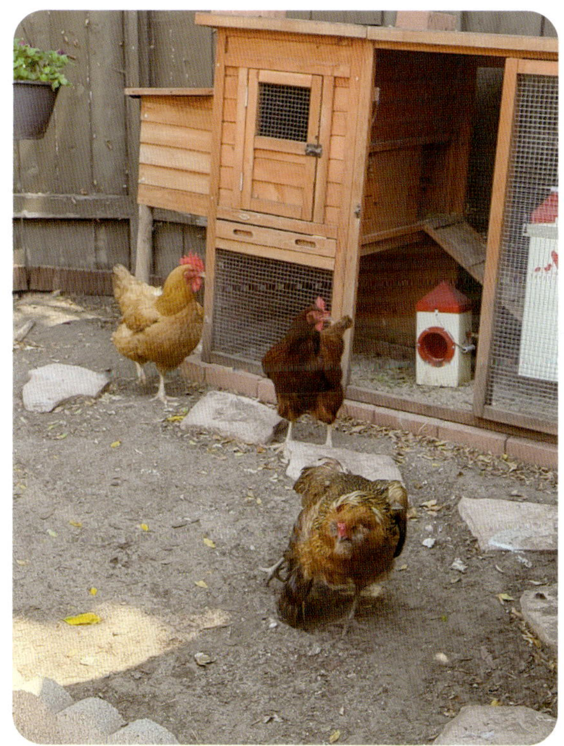

These entries by Octavia M. index a poetics of survival, scarcity, and longing. She outlines, with striking clarity, the concerns of debts in tandem with her love and faith in her God.

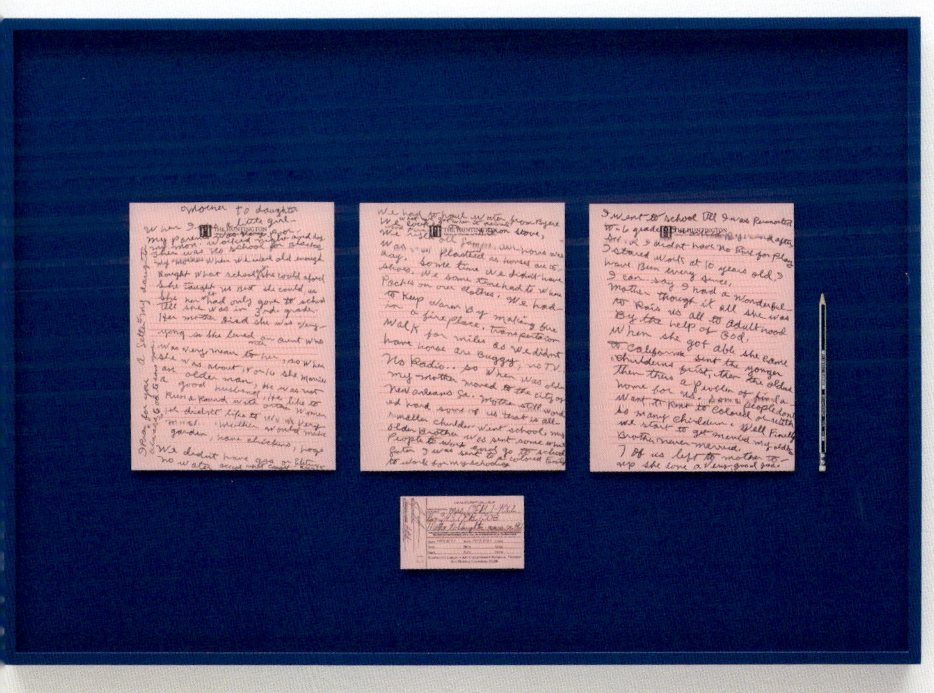

ARTW004
American Artist, *Octavia E. Butler Papers: mssOEB 1-9062 I (Mother to Daughter)*, 2022.
The Huntington stationary, graphite, pencil, felt.
26.5 x 38 x 1.5 in.

AI image made using Midjourney with reference photos taken in Apple Valley, CA, 2023.

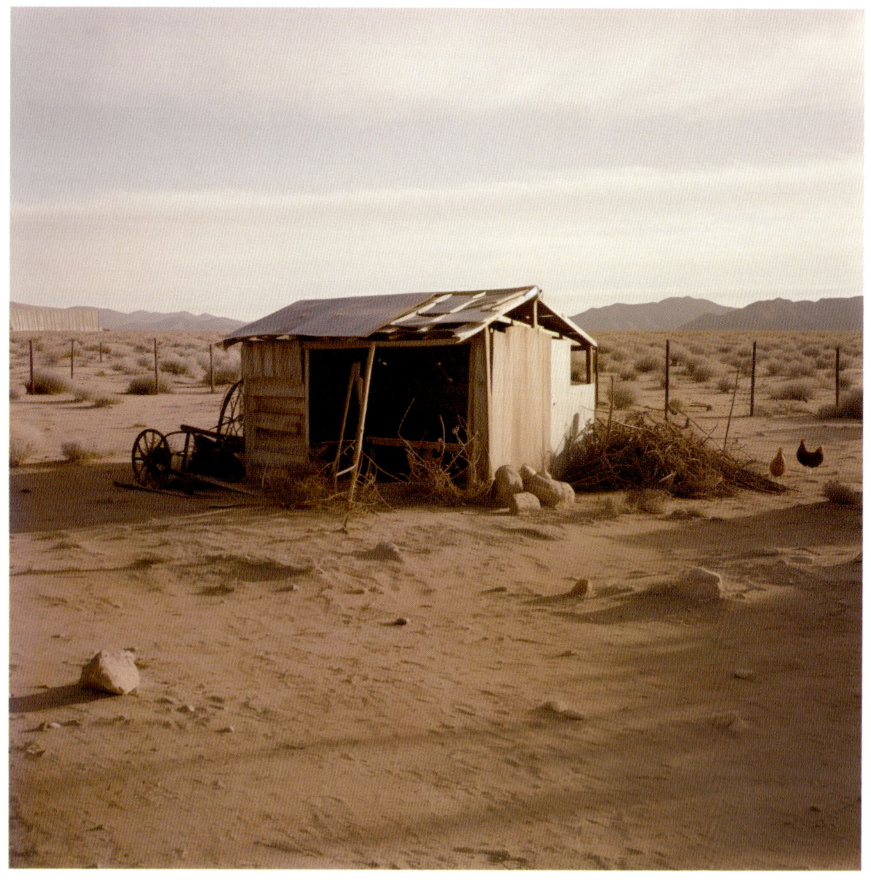

"One of my earliest memories is being carried out of a burning house in the middle of—I guess you could say it was the burning desert, only it was night. My grandmother had a chicken ranch out between Victorville and Barsdale here in California and this was very primitive.**"**

3D model of *Estella Butler's Apple Valley Autonomy* by American Artist.

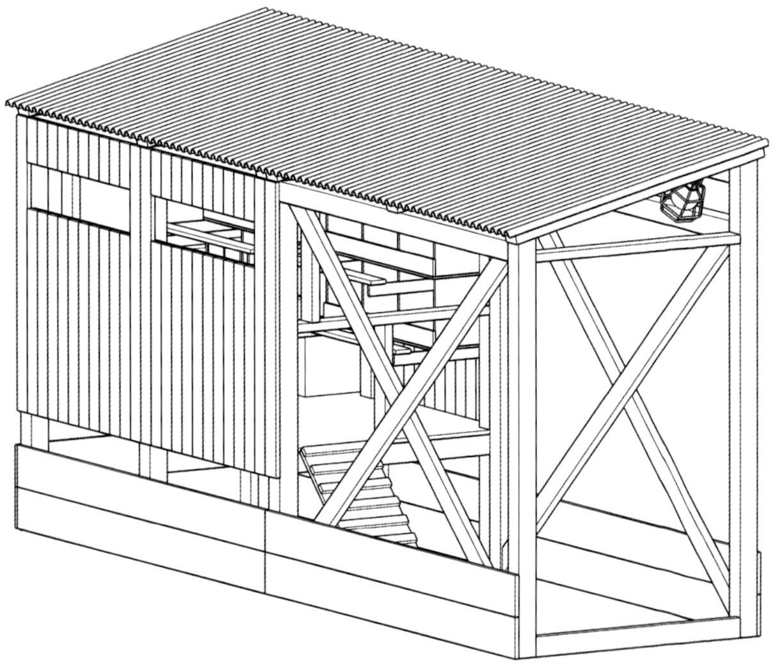

Images collected by American Artist while researching "chicken coop."

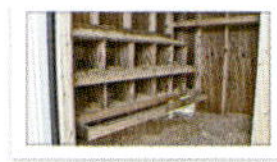

36ff7c4a04a185a19b38a0fd
f8187b29.jpg

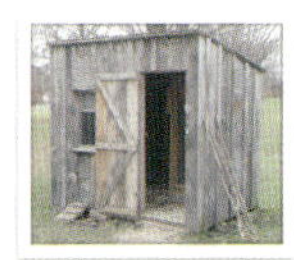

WHHS_Chicken_Coop.jpg

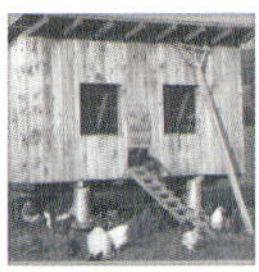

11410_l.jpg

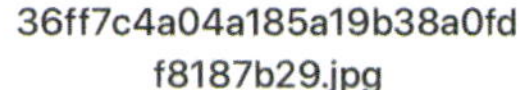

a-woman-farm-worker-
looks-at-her-...2BW8K0D.jpg

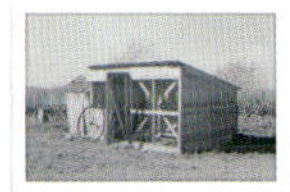

chicken-coop-
e1431525193714.jpeg

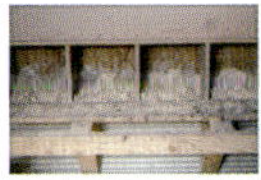

chicken-coop-ideas-7.jpg

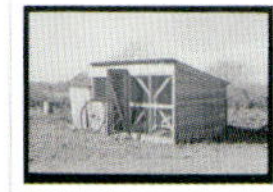

chicken-coop-on-farm-of-
small-vegeta...exas-1024.jpg

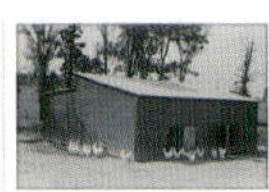

Chicken-coop.jpg

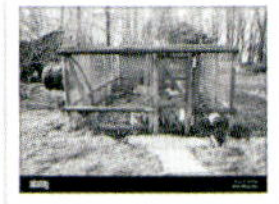

chicken-run-or-coop-
hattingley-me-RNBWJ0.jpg

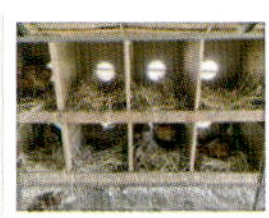

images (1).jpeg

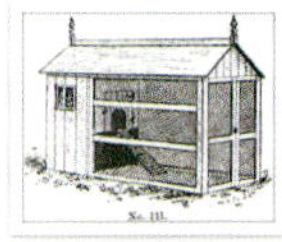

coop2.jpg

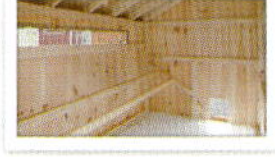

6-inside-the-coop-
smuckerfarms_orig.jpg

As American Artist has noted in their continued reflections on the physicality of that loss, "the chicken coop was a symbolic architectural form that represented migration and place-making for them" in the wake of escaping the violent American South, which had few opportunities, if any, for Black economic wealth building.

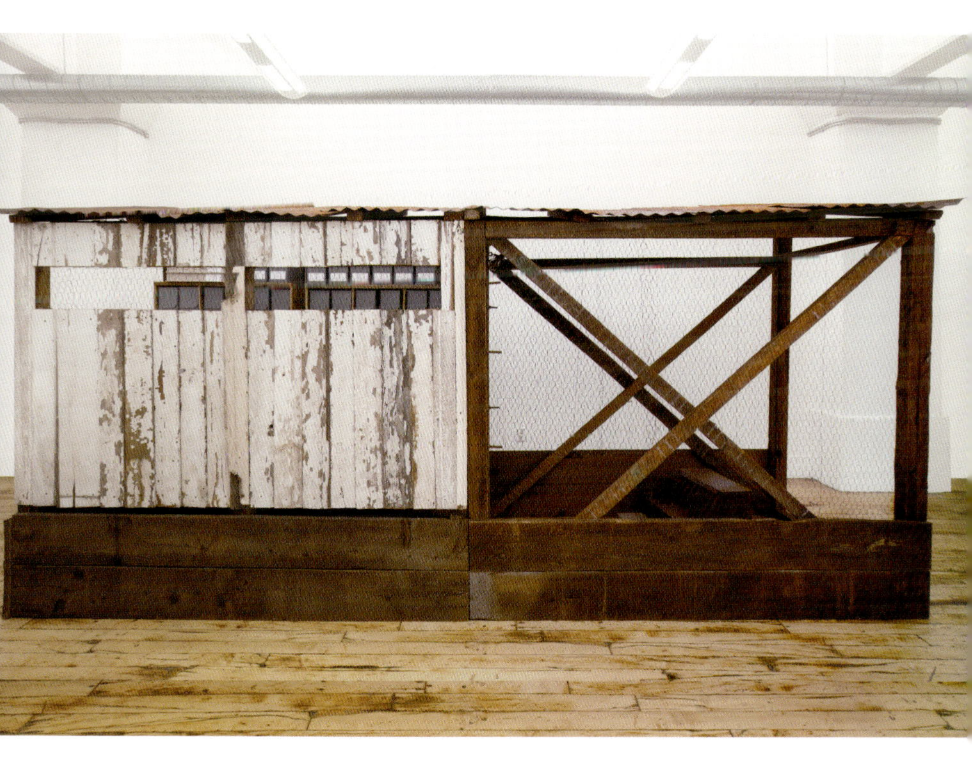

ARTW003a
American Artist,
Estella Butler's Apple Valley Autonomy, 2024.
Wood, paint, rusted steel, archival boxes.
168 x 48 x 84 in.

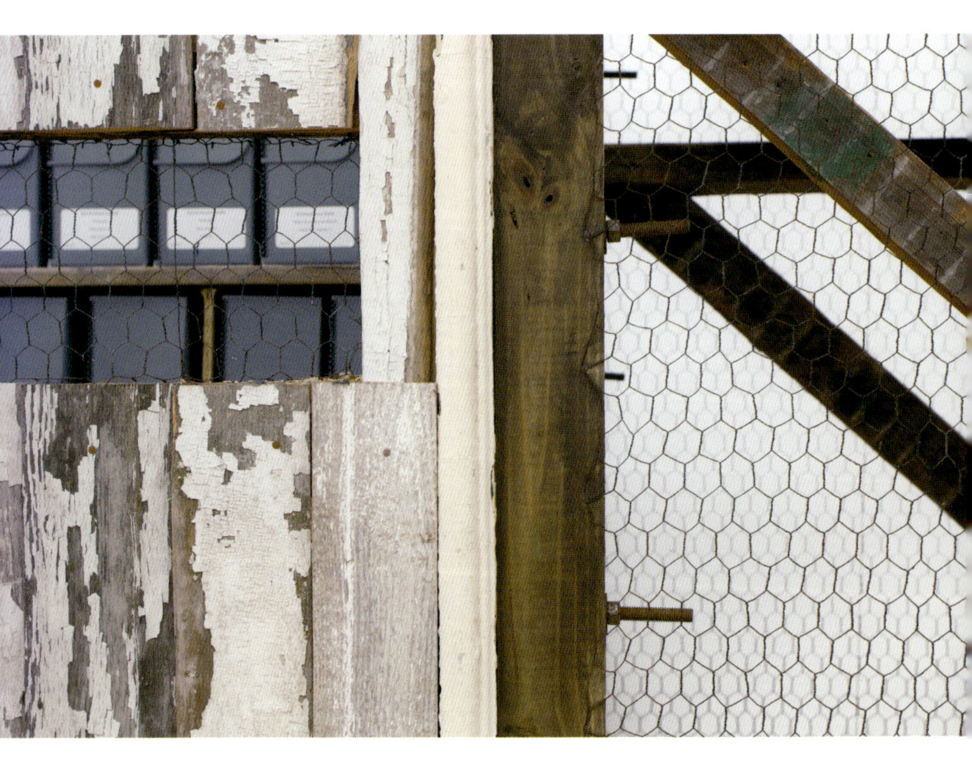

ARTW003b
Detail of American
Artist, *Estella Butler's
Apple Valley Autonomy,*
2024.

Butler's uncles constructed the property by hand, and it included a chicken coop operated by Butler's grandmother, Estella, enabling autonomous income for her and her family at a time when autonomous labor opportunities for African American women were incredibly limited.

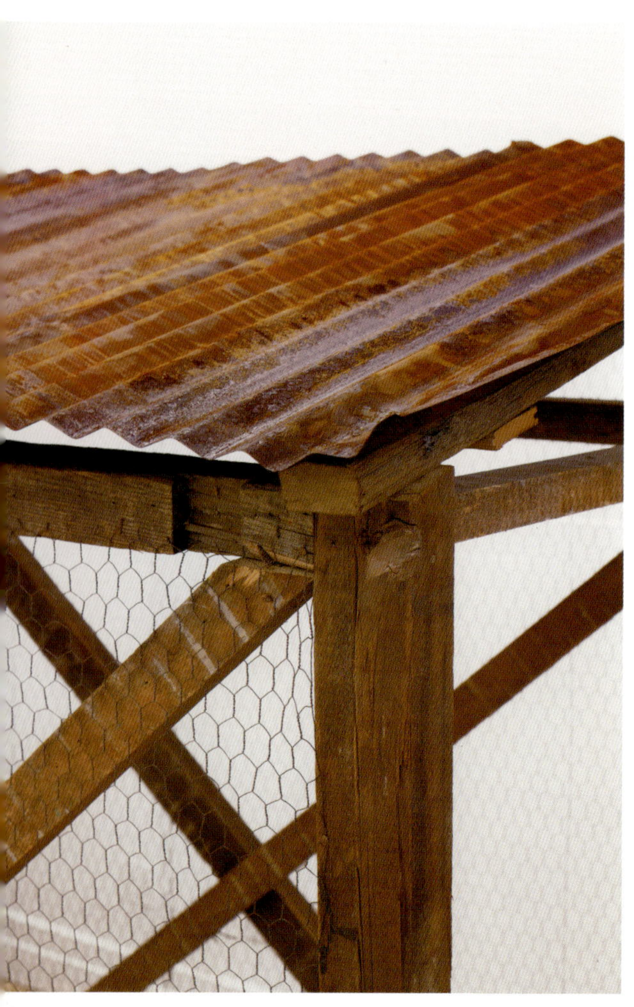

ARTW003c
Detail of American
Artist, *Estella Butler's*
Apple Valley Autonomy,
2024.

ARTW003d
Detail of American
Artist, *Estella Butler's
Apple Valley Autonomy,*
2024.

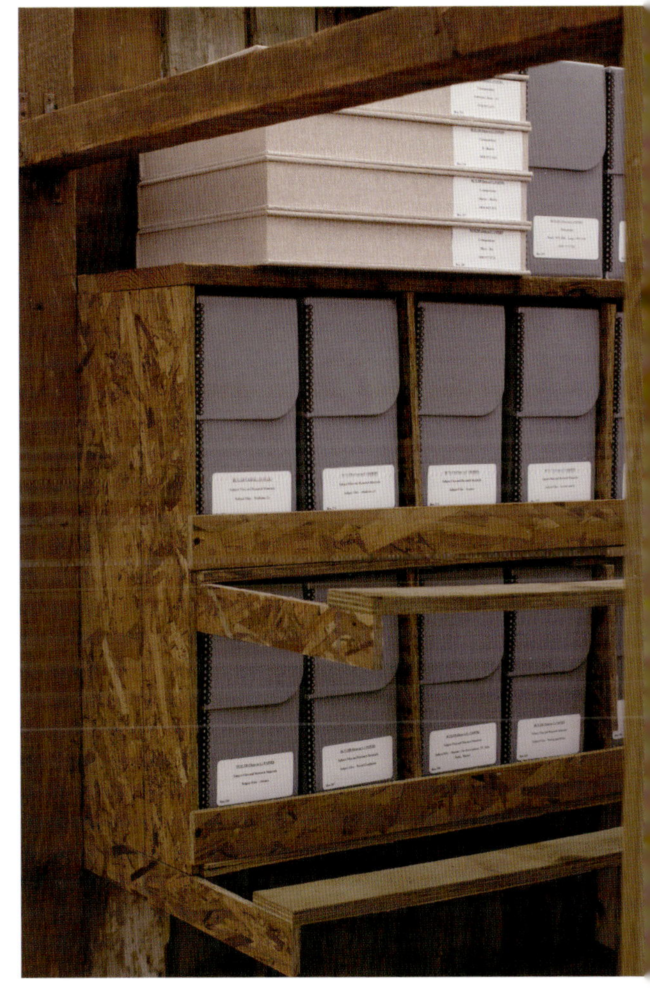

What deserves more contemplation and praise is the visionary fiction that our elders employed—and sometimes even required—to place themselves in an environment vastly better than the one they left behind.

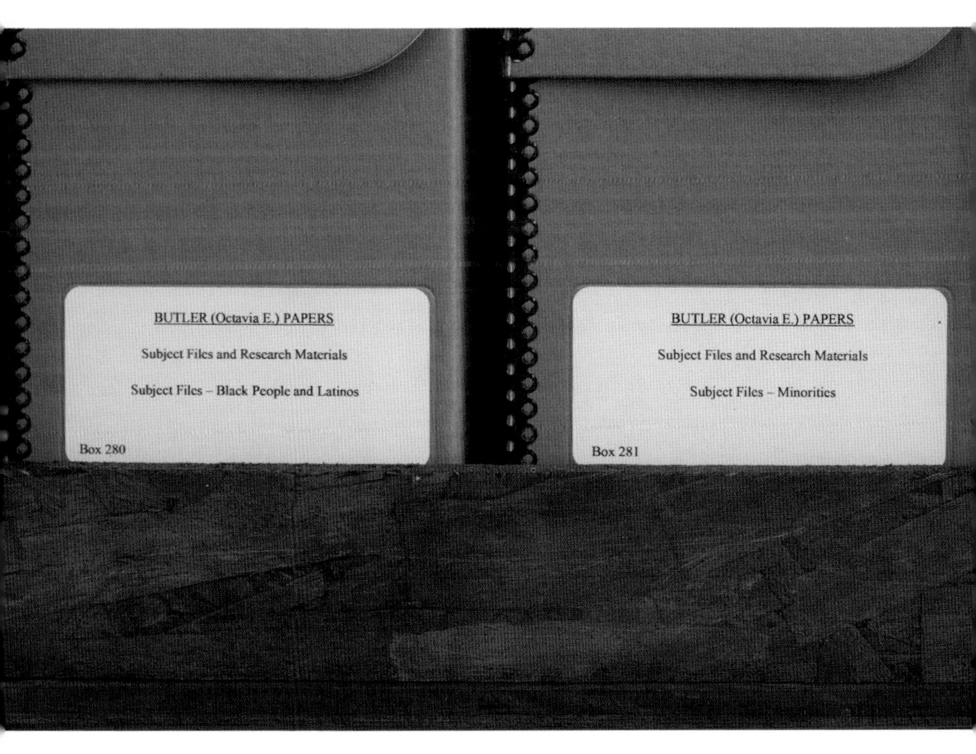

ARTW003e
Detail of American
Artist, *Estella Butler's*
Apple Valley Autonomy,
2024.

What if we were already living in Octavia Butler's 'Parable of the Sower'?

by Tananarive Due

The following conversation between Tananarive Due and American Artist was originally published in the *Los Angeles Times* on May 18, 2022.

1   What face comes to mind when people think of the term "American artist"? Whose stories?

2   The 32-year-old visual artist who took the name American Artist knows that they are not the picture that comes to mind: "I am a little bit of a troll in terms of how I engage with public perceptions of what it means to be an American artist." [2]The renaming was also a way of stepping into the role. [3]"I was making art, but I didn't really know how to create a life for myself around that, professionally and otherwise. And so, part of it was: What if I just say I am that, then would that make it true?"

3   The renaming unlocked a new focus in their art that also closely coincided with their discovery of the speculative fiction of the Afrofuturism pioneer Octavia E. Butler.

4   Dystopia.   [2]History.   [3]Conservation. [4]Memory.

5   American Artist's admiration for Butler's work has led to their creation of the upcoming "Shaper of God" exhibition, which opens on May 28 at REDCAT in downtown Los Angeles. A collaboration with Pasadena's Jet Propulsion Laboratory and the LACMA Art + Technology Lab, the exhibition is a conversation between two very different artists—both of whom lived in Pasadena and attended John Muir High School during very different eras.

6   In Butler's novel "Parable of the Sower," a teenage Black girl named Lauren Olamina becomes an unlikely leader after her gated and fortified community—the fictitious Robledo— is attacked and burned. [2]She must cling to her own philosophy, which she calls Earthseed, to lead displaced survivors toward a better life.

7   The most famous Earthseed parable: "The only lasting truth is Change."

8   Fittingly, American Artist's exhibition is like a road map through Southern California locales inspired by "Parable of the Sower."

9   The fallen wall of Robledo. [2]The vintage bus stops of Butler's life. [3]Butler's journal entries.

10   In this conversation, I talk to American Artist about the imprint of a childhood near JPL, Butler's inspiration and building a better future.

Tananarive Due

11   You grew up in Altadena. What are some of the personally iconic spaces or buildings that come to mind for you when you think about where you grew up?

American Artist

12   The one that really came to mind, and I think it was really key for me in developing this project, "Shaper of God" was the site of this JPL campus that exists right on the perimeter of Altadena and La Cañada Flintridge. [2]When I was young, I would drive by it with my family, and then eventually, when I was driving to high school, John Muir High School, I would drive from Altadena towards the west, and then I would turn south, right on where it overlooks JPL. [3]And it was always this strange, almost sci-fi-ish site, because it's this extremely advanced space institute that's sitting in this canyon, that's kind of on its own, and it's surrounded by these suburbs. [4]It felt like something out of a movie. [5]It wasn't a site that I was ever able to visit when I was that age, so it also had this kind of curiosity about it. [6]And thinking of other institutions like Caltech or PCC [Pasadena City College]—these institutions that have this culture of academic prestige—I think they really informed the culture of Pasadena and Altadena.

TD
13   I'm wondering how included you felt in that culture.

AA
14   I didn't necessarily feel included. I felt like they created this image of what aspiration was meant to look like. [2]I was a creative kid, I liked creating art, but I was also interested in science and technology. [3]And at one point, I imagined the possibility of going to Caltech, but at the same time it seemed elusive to me. [4]But knowing that was there informed my image of what I should aspire to, what I should try to accomplish.

TD
15   Let's talk a little bit about Octavia Butler. [2]What are the biggest ways you would say that her vision dovetails with yours?

AA
16   Octavia Butler was very understanding of the ways in which power operates and how it impacts people differentially. [2]I think also understanding the way that apocalypse is not a singular event but something that we are living in. [3]What I relate to is wanting to speak about these systems that often oppress many people that encounter them, but not in a way that treats it as something spectacular, but rather something that we're continually navigating. [4]Octavia But-

ler understood that because she had a very difficult life herself.

TD

17   All of Octavia's readers have an origin story. ²I'll tell you mine. ³It was in the mid-
1990s, and I was working on my novel "My Soul
to Keep," about an immortal African from Ethi-
opia. ⁵I was talking about it with a friend of mine
who was like, have you ever read Octavia Butler's novel about an immortal African? And I had
a complete panic attack—I had to run out right
away to get "Wild Seed," more out of a sense of
terror that I might be duplicating a book. ⁶But,
of course, "Wild Seed" was nothing like my book.
⁷And then it was joy and wonder—I'd been introduced to this revolutionary writer that I would
soon meet and come to know and love dearly,
both personally and as a reader. ⁸What was your
first Octavia Butler novel, and what was the impact on you?

AA

18   The first novel that I read was "Dawn."
²A friend recommended it to me. ³We were
speaking about some of the most radical ideas
we'd encountered in fiction. ⁴I think this idea
of aliens wanting to regenerate with humans—
it wasn't like an invasion, it was like, "Hey, we
picked you up, and you're hanging out with us."
⁵I think that really stuck with me.

TD

19   When my husband, Steven Barnes, and I
talked to Octavia in 2000—Octavia had known
him for quite some time—we asked her about
her vision and how she was using her art to try to

create what I call real-life world building. ²And she mentioned "Dawn" specifically and "Parable of the Sower" specifically. ³"Dawn" was her way of like, OK, we're really headed to ruin, and we need aliens to come step in and set us on the path. ⁴But in "Parable of the Sower" she wanted to do the same thing but with religion.

20	For Southern Californians, it's particularly disturbing to read "Parable of the Sower," which is the subject of your exhibition. ²Not just because the year when it's set is so rapidly approaching—and really, it already feels so much like here and now—but it's the familiarity of the spaces that we can all imagine. ³Robledo, this fictitious gated community where the protagonist Lauren Olamina is living with her family and other families, that they hope will be a sanctuary as the world is falling apart around them. ⁴The drought conversations feel very personal, the fires feel very personal. Why did "Parable of the Sower" speak to you so deeply that you're creating the physical wall from Robledo?

AA

21	This wall was important to me because it feels so Californian and so much of what's described in the novel feels quintessentially Californian, the way wealth distribution becomes so clear within the landscape of Los Angeles. ²I did think about the wall as the symbol of that division. ³In the case of Robledo, every single community has its own wall; there are different scales of walls based on how much money they have, and how much they fear invasion. ⁴And that, to me, felt like taking this thing that was very real about Los Angeles and just kind of escalating it.

TD

22   I find it so fascinating that you're re-creating the Yannis window. ²For readers who don't know what that is, it's a big piece of technology, like a big smart TV, that is basically the sole entertainment for this community. ³You created a short film representing the kind of newsreel that the Robledo community might have been watching. ⁵What's the significance of this in your exhibition?

AA

23   This film seems to be something that Robledo created at a point when they were wealthy and things maybe hadn't hit rock bottom. ²The video supposedly is created by the Robledo Historical Society. ³And, interestingly enough, it's not a tour of Robledo—it's actually a nature tour of the Arroyo Seco Canyon, which is this area that sits between Altadena, Pasadena and La Cañada Flintridge, and so it's pretty close in proximity to where Butler lived and grew up. ⁴It's also where Jet Propulsion Laboratory exists. ⁵It also shares a close border with John Muir High School, where Butler went. ⁶And so, to me that area represents many historical moments and the conflation of different realities. ⁷It appears to be this nature tour of the site, but it's fictional and it's speculative.

TD

24   Octavia did not drive (my husband often drove her places). ²That aspect of her life is also addressed in your exhibition with the representation of the bus stops. ³Why was that important for you to include?

AA

25   I wanted to put these bus stops that
are based on Los Angeles bus stops that Butler
would have sat at, routes she would have taken.
²One of the bus stop signs resembles how they
would have looked in the 1960s and another one
resembles how they would have looked in the
1980s. ³It's a way of not only conflating space—
like the real landscape of Los Angeles with a fictional landscape of Robledo—but also the sense
of time, because you don't really know what time
period you're existing in.

TD

26   I'm thinking about how you named
yourself to pull something out of yourself and
how that really did help remake you. ²It worked
out incredibly well. ³It also worked out incredibly well for Octavia Butler. ⁴It's very fitting that
you have notes from Octavia Butler's journal as
a part of this exhibition. ⁵Some of her quotes
have become memes—"so be it, see to it" comes
to mind—but these pep talks that Octavia gave
herself often were in opposition to the forces that were trying to hold her back. ⁶Listen,
Octavia Butler died in 2006; she finally got on
the New York Times bestseller list with "Parable
of the Sower" in 2020, during the pandemic, so
she's really working against every force against
her, and these forces have been against her since
she was a young Black child growing up in poverty. ⁶I would love to ask you what stands out for
you about the journal excerpts you've chosen for
this exhibition.

AA

27   I wanted to find ways to show Octavia Butler as a descendant of Black people that had migrated to Los Angeles. ²Her mother moved from Louisiana and was working as a cleaner in white people's homes while Octavia Butler was growing up. ³Some of the materials are letters that her mother wrote to her about what it was like to grow up in Louisiana, where there are no schools for Black people, there are only dirt roads. ⁴One letter describes that situation and is juxtaposed with this bus map that Octavia Butler carried. ⁵So, kind of trying to show this progression over time of what Octavia Butler was able to have and achieve relative to her family.

TD

28   I recently taught "Parable of the Sower" in my Afrofuturism class at UCLA and asked my students to create their own Earthseed community—really just a description of a community. ²If you were creating an Earthseed community, what would it look like and who would those members be? ³What are you seeking shelter from?

AA

29   One thing that I think about seeking shelter from, which hasn't really been possible for me, is from institutional obligation. ²From having to align myself with institutions that I feel are compromising my values. ³Being able to create a community that would be autonomous for itself, which seems under capitalism really unrealistic, but it's something to think about. ⁴As far as who I would want to collaborate with, people that are creative and inspiring and nice. [5]People that are interested in creating a world that feels equal.

Octavia E. Butler's connection to the landscapes of Pasadena and Altadena is explored in Section II, which examines her access to Los Angeles through public institutions like local bus routes and library systems. This section highlights how the unique geography of the region shaped Butler's worldview and is reflected in the vivid settings of her fiction.

Section II

**All that you Change
Changes you.**

Conceiving Alternate Worlds for the Present

On the Afterlives of Octavia E. Butler

by Ayana Jamieson

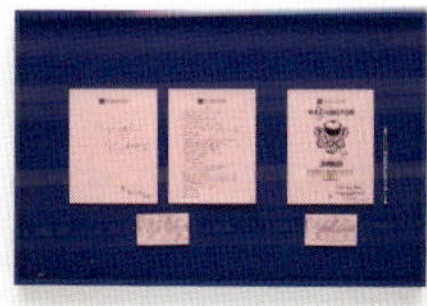

ARTW007a [107]

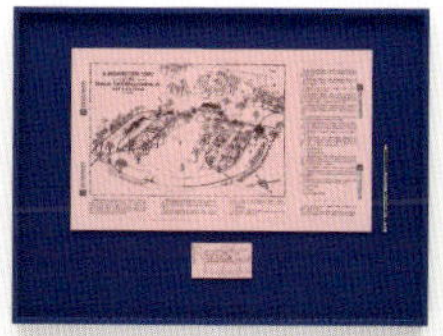

ARTW009 [167]

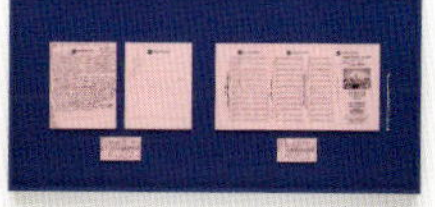

ARTW005a [141]

1   Octavia Estelle Butler passed away in 2006, yet her writing remains in present tense, not only because it anticipates the climate crisis and other political realities, but because it stands as a living testament to her relentless observation and engagement with the world around her. [2]It is active: she is working—drafting new fiction or practicing for public talks, building characters, interacting—in her journals, essays, and published work. [3]Her journals, in particular, offer a glimpse into her real-time engagement with Pasadena and Los Angeles, revealing how deeply these places shaped her narratives. [4]Rooted in themes of youth and coming-of-age, this influence is obvious in Butler's first published works and throughout her career, from her earliest *Patternist* novels* to the *Parables* duology published closer to the end of her life (1993 and 1998).

2   Butler's consideration of geographical and social dynamics extends beyond the obvious textual inclusions in her novels; we glimpse her inner life alongside external realities, evident in her self-curated archives, letters to contemporaries, and private reflections. [2]She might ask herself in a journal, "What if I lived there?"—a prompt that reflects her broader inquiries into cyclical power dynamics, survival, and human resilience in the face of adversity, challenging one-sided narratives of upward mobility and progress. [3]These questions, rooted in her own experiences and observations, continue to offer valuable insights into the complexities of race, class, landscape, and place. [4]Self-curation in the archives also preserved her mother's personal effects, along with everyday family artifacts and narrative histories. [5]Butler asked her repeatedly to recount—in writing—the details of her rural sharecropping sugar plantation childhood.

3   Butler engaged in what American Artist calls "thought experiments," a concept that reflects the Pasadena-born multidisciplinary artists' own praxis. [2]Though born generations apart, both Butler and Artist share a legacy rooted in the Great Migration, and Artist has brought their own life in conversation with Butler's in multiple iterations. [3]Artist's sources of inspiration also include the Pasadena/Altadena geographical landscape, amplified in Butler's archive at The Huntington Library, and brought to fruition as material, visual, and philosophical thought experiments. [4]Their drawing, *Octavia E. Butler Papers: mssOEB 1-9062 II (The L.A. Area)*, traced from notecards Butler created for her speeches, is layered over the compulsory pink archival researcher's stationery mandated by the library. [5]The archive is simultaneously expansive and mediated. [6]This "research" showed up in Butler's antebellum time travel novel *Kindred* and in the interdependent climate refugee enclaves of the *Parables* duology.

4   Born in Pasadena in 1947, into what she termed "Jim Crow California," Octavia E. Butler's life was marked by the contradictions of her environment. [2]While Pasadena and Los Angeles are now eager to embrace the achievements of noteworthy Black folks such as Butler, many living today can attest to the places from which they were barred and opportunities from which they were denied access. [3]A lifelong public school student, Butler attended John Muir High School and Pasadena City College, where she earned her associate's degree and won her first prize for writing. [4]In a 1998 autobiographical

ARTW008 [89]

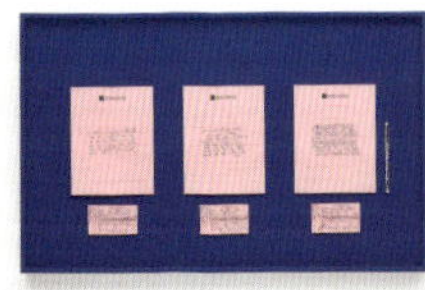

questionnaire, Butler reflected on the schools she attended from kindergarten through seventh grade. [5]She noted that three of the four "no longer exist," while the fourth school—often closed due to low enrollment, white flight, and changing tax laws—was a "fundamental school."[†] [6]Butler described the school formerly known as Washington Junior High as, "the worst junior high school in the city" with a "really terrible reputation." She admitted to being terrified to go there, but it was the only option available to her family, who could only afford to rent a decent house in that area.[‡] [7]This school now bears her name: Octavia E. Butler Magnet. [8]In a 2001 interview, she expressed dismay over the fate of her primary schools, which had all been repurposed (one as a shopping center and another as a post office), rendered defunct, or demolished: "They wiped out my childhood in one swoop." The city and its schools were plagued by inequality and resource disparities, leading to a federal court order in 1970 that forced desegregation after earlier failed litigation in 1963.[§] [9]Perhaps this is why many of her characters are surviving transitions like "second adolescence," as Butler urges humanity to grow out of its self-destructive behavior.[¶]

5   Survival is a prominent theme in *Kindred* (1979), which Butler began writing while she was a student at Pasadena City College. [2]The novel was a response to ignorant comments from a knowledgeable Pan-Africanist peer, who lamented that he would like to kill the older generation "holding us back" with their deferential attitudes and perceived complacency to the established social order. [3]In early drafts, the original protagonist—a contemporary Black man—

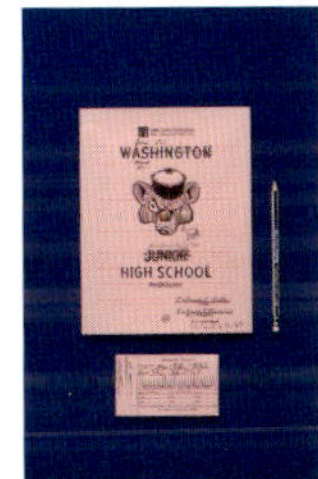

ARTW007b [108]

didn't live long in antebellum Maryland, so Butler adapted, using misogynoir and rape culture to her new female main character's advantage. [4]Edana "Dana" Franklin, a working writer, becomes the central character in *Kindred*, which is set in Altadena and Los Angeles. [5]The story follows Dana's violent, involuntary time travel to the 1800s, where she is forced into complicity to save the life of her previously unknown white slaveholding ancestors. [6]Butler's message in *Kindred*, and much of her work, is clear: none of us have escaped oppression and enslavement unscathed and none of us is above making the best choice out of a host of unsavory options. [7]Similarly, Artist's works present explorations that not only include, but center, marginalized experiences in alternate visions of survival.

6   Butler's stories are deeply rooted in the places she knew—the streets of Pasadena, the city bus lines of Los Angeles, and the California landscape—all of which she used as backdrops for her narratives. [2]My research points to ways Butler grew and developed disparate parts of herself beyond the limitations of her present circumstances and others' expectations. [3]As a child, Artist imagined becoming a mechanical engineer, inspired by the proximity of JPL and Caltech to John Muir High School, where they enrolled 38 years after Butler graduated. [4]Artist's series of works that center Butler started with a research engine mapping landscape and migration. [5]*Shaper of God*, an art installation featuring an original short film, mirrors the separation between public and private spaces, inspired by *Parable of the Sower*. [6]The juxtaposition of the imaginary fictional world with the real landscape of the Pasadena Arroyo creates a

ARTW012 [137]

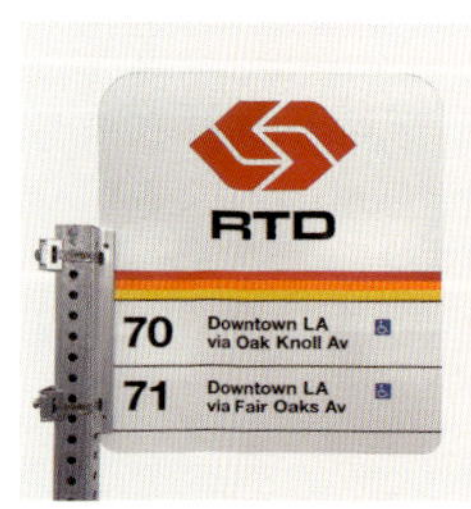

ARTW017a [95]

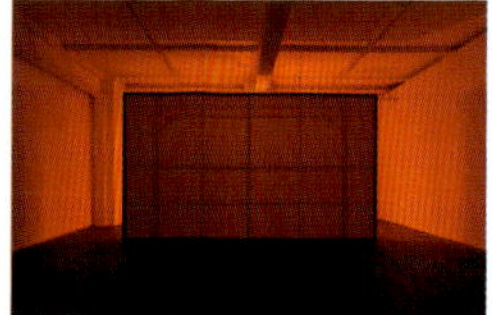

ARTW014a [103]

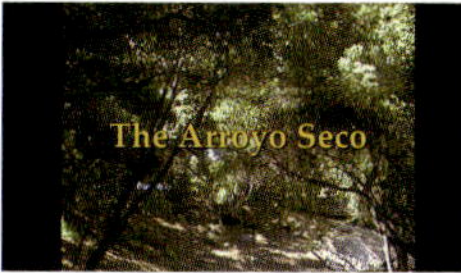

ARTW013 [129]

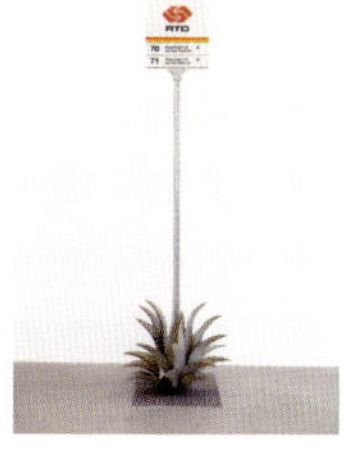

layered engagement with the Butlerian universe.

7   In notes for a 1986 public talk titled "Why I Write," Butler remarked, "Somehow it never occurred to me to accept the universe as a segregated neighborhood or human beings as men only while women were something less than human."** [2]Power dynamics—the interplay between the powerless and the powerful—are a recurring theme of her writing and discussions about it. [3]Indeed, Butler's writing offers reparative alternatives to the status quo, serving as both personal and collective acts. [4]Creatives and culture workers like Artist, along with scholars, activists, scientists, educators, and people from all levels of society, continue to draw inspiration from liberation narratives in her stories. [5]In notes on her first published novel, *Patternmaster* (1976), set in an unspecified future representing the remnants of our current civilization,[††] Butler described it as a love story between two brothers vying for leadership of the psionic order—a concept rooted in character traits explored in "Childfinder." [6]This early piece, also exploring psionic powers, is set in a run-down suburban apartment that could easily have been located on North Madison Avenue in Pasadena.

8   *Patternmaster*—which was published when Butler was nearly thirty but started during Butler's adolescence—established the future home of the first Patternmaster, a multiracial Black girl named Mary with traffic-light-green eyes, introduced in *Mind of My Mind*. [2]Butler drew from her childhood, incorporating prominent landmarks and locations, including sections of the city of Pasadena, bus rides through downtown Los Angeles, and her grandmother's desert ranch. [3]Larkin House, located in the fictional city of Forsyth (a stand-in for Pasadena), is described in *Mind of My Mind* with the following passage: "He drove me over to Palo Verde Avenue, where the rich people lived.... It was a three-story white stucco mansion. [4]Spanish roof, great arched doorway, acres of front lawn, one square block of house and grounds."‡‡ [5]This grand residence starkly contrasts the less affluent part of the city where Butler grew up, highlighting the social and economic divides that often permeate her work.

9   Butler also featured the public bus lines of Pasadena and Los Angeles in the short story "Speech Sounds" (1983), in which a character travels to connect with a relative during a crisis, picking up orphaned children along the way. [2]For Butler, place is also interior and relational, shaped by the intersections of race, class, and power. [3]This is prominently reflected in the town of Robledo (another stand-in for Pasadena) in *Parable of the Sower* (1993) and *Parable of the Talents* (1998). [4]In these novels, a walled-in suburban cul-de-sac serves as the origin story for a group of refugees that must flee when their wall is knocked down by the unhoused walking poor outside. [5]Butler's characters are interdependent, relying on sustainable practices to survive, such as making acorn bread from abundant available supplies when flour is not easily obtainable. [6]In Butler's fictional 2024, the refugees eventually establish a new community called Acorn after walking alongside the San Gabriel Mountains and up the coast to Northern California. [7]Another lesson of Butler's: your teachers are all around you and everyone is a potential ally tied up in mutual liberation or destruction. [8]Through fifteen-year old protagonist Lauren Oya Olam-

ARTW005b [142]

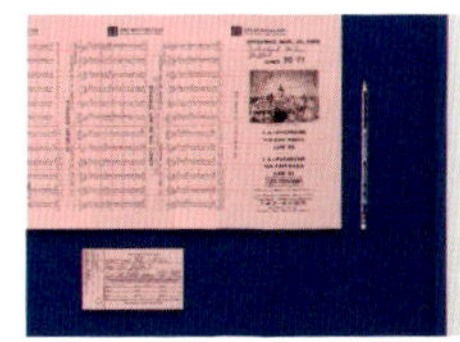

ARTW010a [157]

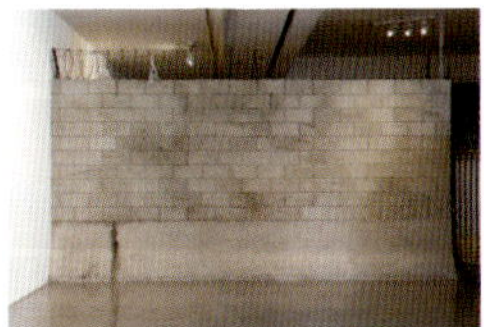

ARTW010b [158]

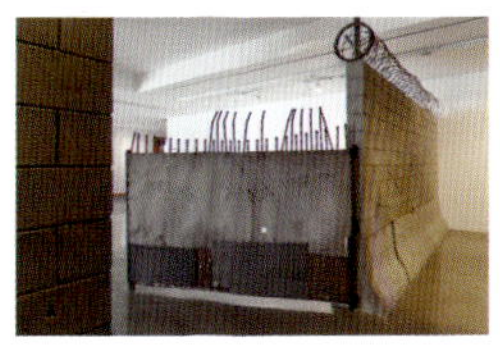

ARTW011a [145]

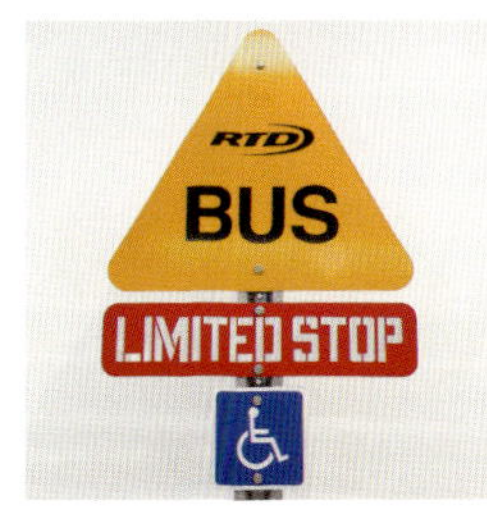

ina, Butler writes, "All struggles are essentially power struggles," symbolizing our universal need for a safe and just place in the world.

10   In the afterword of "Childfinder," Butler writes, "After a few years of watching the human species make things unnecessarily difficult for itself, I have little hope that it will do anything more than survive and continue its cycle of errors."[§§] [2]Yet, through her work, Butler offers us a blueprint for how we might begin to navigate these difficulties—by understanding and engaging with the places we inhabit, psychologically, physically and socially. [3]Her writing challenges us in the present moment to consider how our environments shape us and how, in turn, we might shape them for the better. [4]Butler's work remains not just relevant but urgent—a call to action for those of us who, like her, see the world not just as it is, but as it could be.

ARTW014b [115]

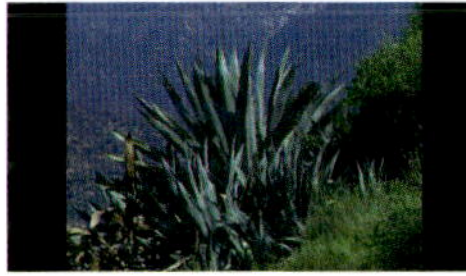

* The original *Patternist* novels consist of *Patternmaster* (1976), *Mind of My Mind* (1977), *Survivor* (1978), *Wild Seed* (1980), and *Clay's Ark* (1984), while the standalone novel *Kindred* was published in 1979.

† OEB 97

‡ Ayana Rehema Abdallah, "Africentric Transgressive Creativity: A Reader's Meditation on Octavia Butler" (PhD. diss., University of Iowa, 2001),http://proxy.library.cpp.edu/login?url=https://www-proquest-com.proxy.library.cpp.edu/dissertations-theses/africentric-transgressive-creativity-readers/docview/276261008/se-2 (accessed July 8, 2024).

§ Jackson v. Pasadena City School District, June 27, 1963; Pasadena City Board of Education et al., Petitioners, v. Nancy and Spangler et al (brought in 1968); and Pasadena City Board of Education v. Spangler, 427 U.S. 424 (1976).

¶ Octavia E. Butler, "Dawn," in *Lilith's Brood*, (Grand Central, 1987), 1–249,and Octavia E. Butler, "The Monophobic Response," in *Dark Matter : A Century of Speculative Fiction from the African Diaspora*, edited by Sheree R. Thomas, (Warner Books, 1994), 415–16.

** OEB 2937

†† Note that the *Patternist* series was published out of chronological order but developed out of stories Butler made up in her childhood and her teens. The chronological series consists of *Wild Seed* (1980), *Mind of My Mind* (1977), *Clay's Ark* (1984), *Survivor* (1978), and *Patternmaster* (1976). *Seed to Harvest* (2007) excluded *Survivor* because the author had denounced it as a book that needed more editing. However, she sold it to fund her research for *Kindred*, her most well-known standalone novel.

‡‡ Octavia E. Butler, *Mind of My Mind in Seed to Harvest* [Compilation] (*Warner Books, 2007*), 278.

§§ Octavia E. Butler, *Unexpected Stories*. (Open Road Media, 2014).

Fred Moten and Stephano Harney, *The Undercommons: Fugitive Planning and Black Study*, 2013.

"After all, the subversive intellectual came under false pretenses, with bad documents, out of love. Her labor is as necessary as it is unwelcome."

"'Can kids come in here?' I asked the woman at the cash register once I was inside. I meant could Black kids come in. My mother, born in rural Louisiana and raised amid strict racial segregation, had warned me that I might not be welcome everywhere, even in California.**"**

GREAT MIGRATION
CELLULAR RESPONSE TO VIOLENCE
PRIMITIVE INTELLIGENCE
ACCOUNTABILITY
UNIVERSAL ACCOUNTABILITY
SLIME MOLD MOVES LIKE POPULATIONS

BLAINE O'NEILL

WHAT DO YOU WANT PEOPLE TO UNDERSTAND
ABOUT BUTLER'S MATERNAL LINEAGE
& SLIME MOLD
A CLASS CAN ONLY BE SO MANY THINGS:
COMMUNITY
LECTURE (INFO DUMP)
TUTORIAL
DEMO
ACCESS TO RARE MATERIALS
COLLABORATIVE CONVERSATION
WITNESS TO Q & A
THE SLIME MOLD DOESN'T CHOOSE TO
"WORK WITH ME EXACTLY, BUT IT IS
A COLLABORATION OF SORTS" HEATHER B.
FRANKENSTEIN, LIGHTNING STRIKE,
DECISION MAKING IN ART VS. RESEARCH

Sketch of the Pasadena library with slime mold by American Artist, 2022.

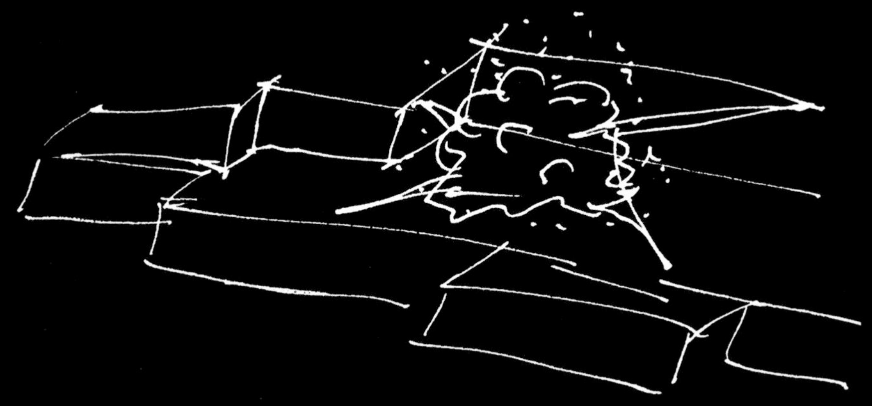

Illustration of item in Box 334. Octavia E. Butler, John Muir High School button pin, ca. 1965.

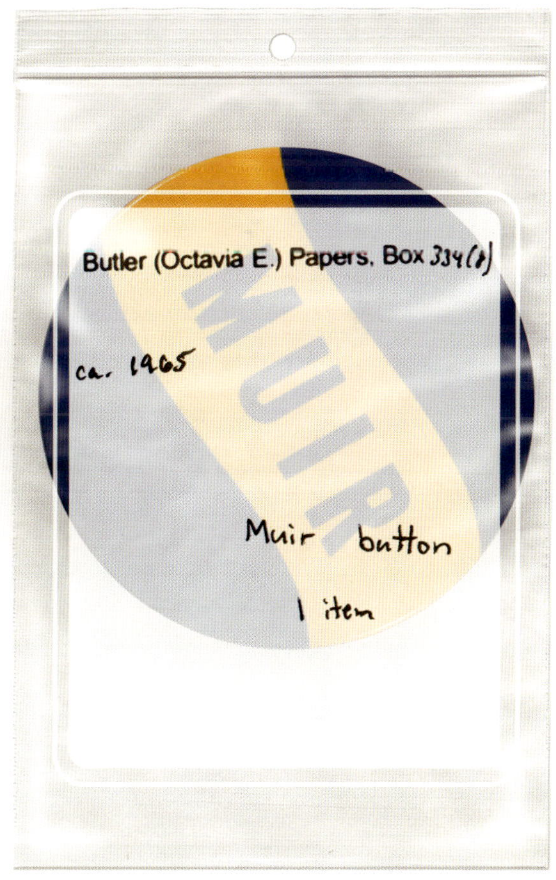

Their drawing, *Octavia E. Butler Papers: mssOEB 1-9062 II (The L.A. Area)*, traced from notecards Butler created for her speeches, is layered over the compulsory pink archival researcher's stationery mandated by the library. The archive is simultaneously expansive and mediated.

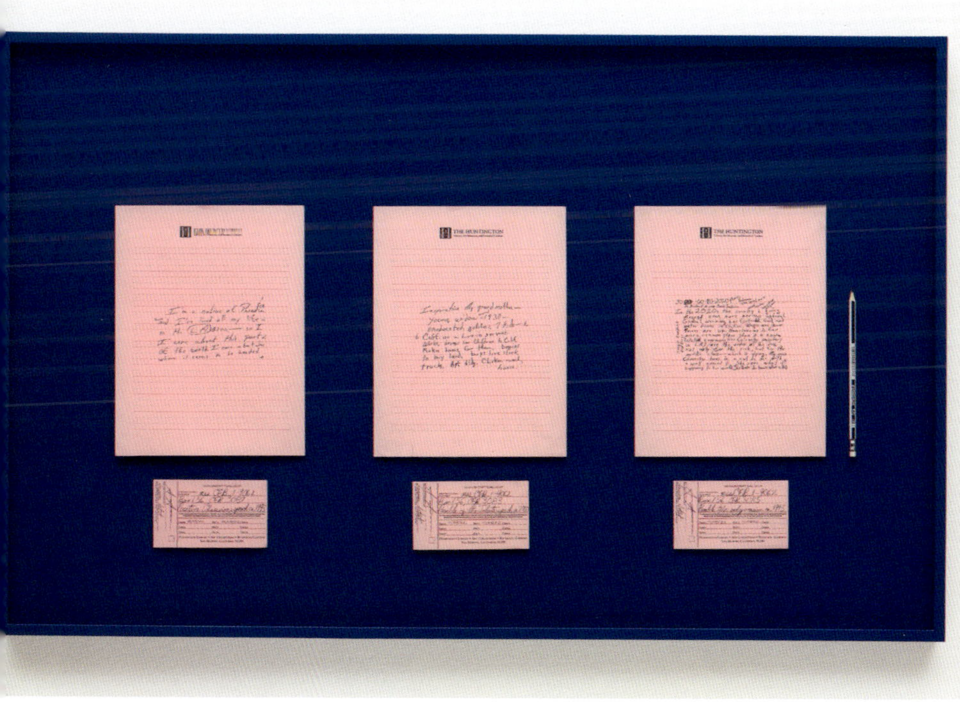

ARTW008
American Artist,
*Octavia E. Butler
Papers: mssOEB 1-9062
II* (*The L.A. Area*), 2022.
the Huntington
stationary, graphite,
pencil, and felt.
26.5 x 42 x 1.5 in.

Sterling Johnson, "The Gamble House - Pasadena, California," 1990. (https://youtu.be/ AUYz0dxiwVk?si=l3-KiVBAMcD3ezAg).

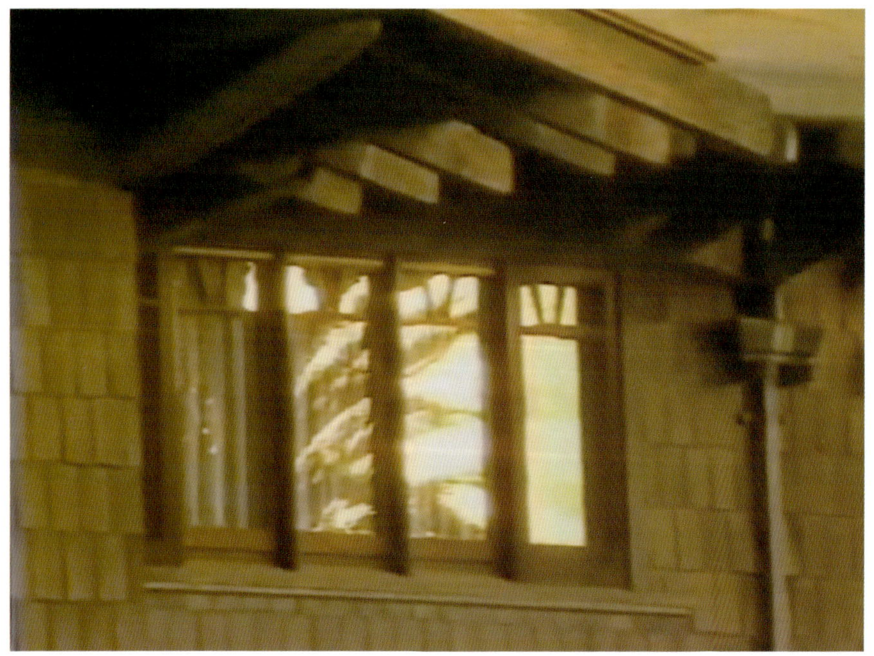

Sterling Johnson, "The Gamble House - Pasadena, California," 1990. (https://youtu.be/AUYz0dxiwVk?si=l3-KiVBAMcD3ezAg).

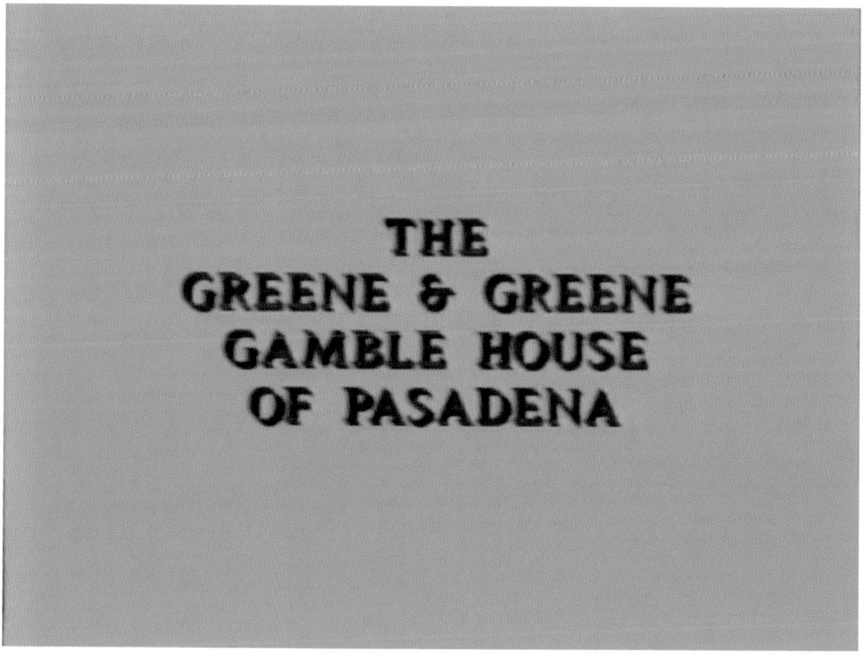

Nikita Gale, from the transcript of A-Team meeting hosted by Jet Propulsion Laboratory, organized by American Artist.

"I have moved to South Pasadena a little over a year ago and was actually thinking about Octavia Butler's relationship to Altadena and Pasadena when I was looking for places to live. And so I remember the day that I got the keys to my place driving up to Altadena to just visit her memorial site and feeling this really profound moment of channeling something."

3D model of *Yannis Window* by American Artist.

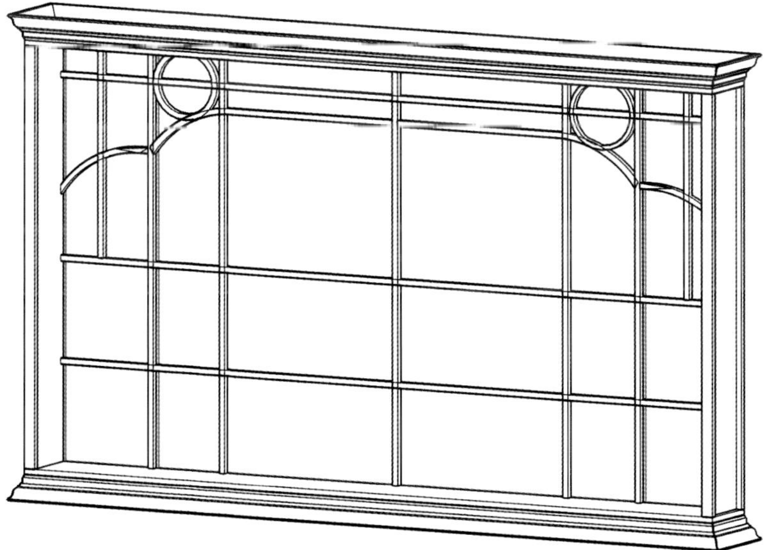

Shaper of God, an art installation featuring an original short film, mirrors the separation between public and private spaces, inspired by *Parable of the Sower*.

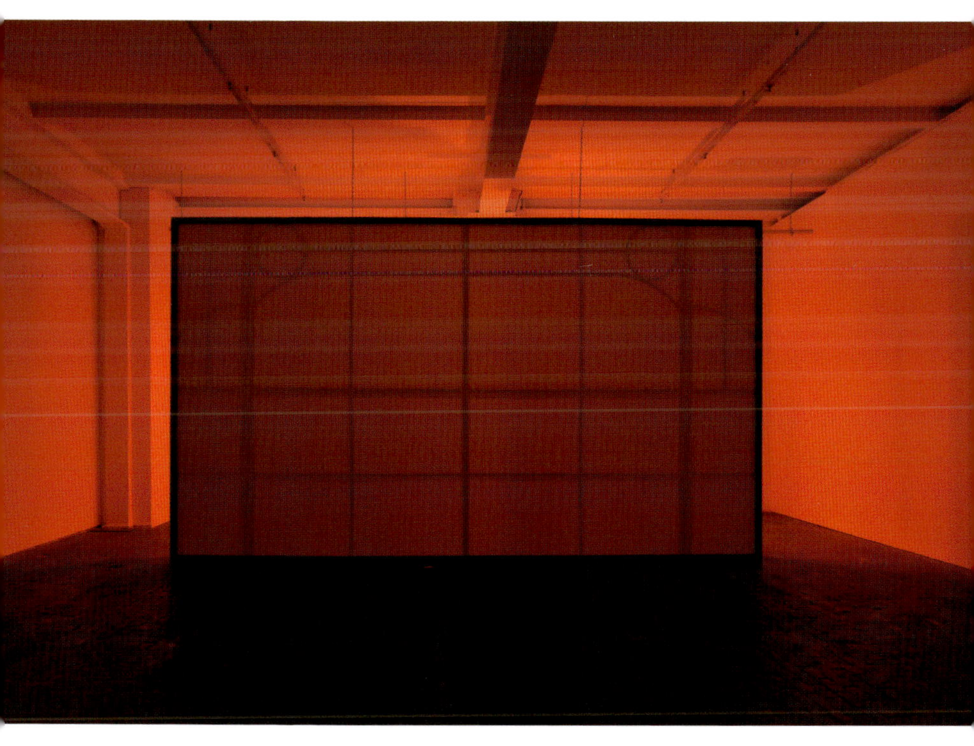

ARTW017a
American Artist, *Yannis Window*, 2022–ongoing. Sculptural projection, single-channel HD video with sound. Dimensions variable.

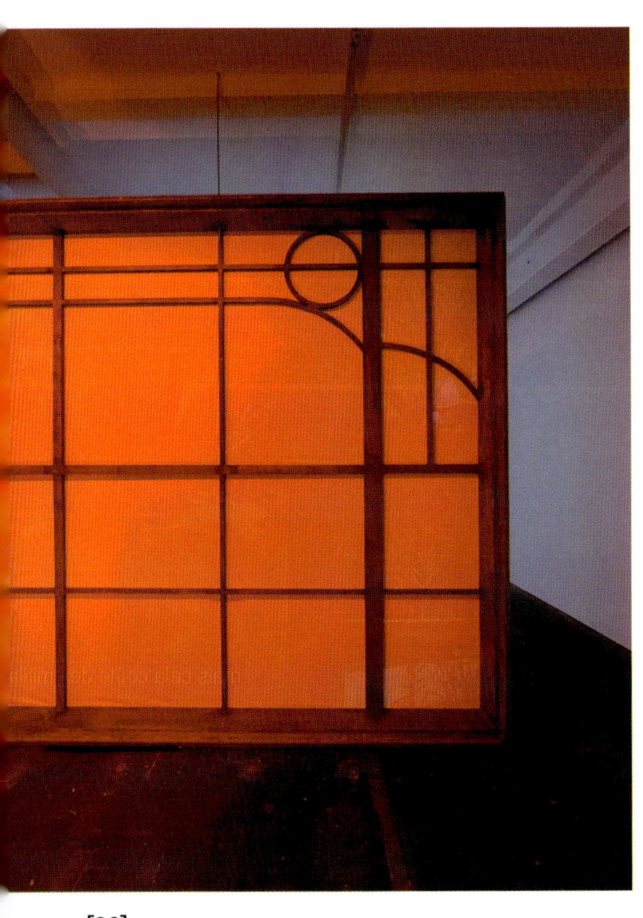

ARTW017b
Detail of American
Artist, *Yannis Window*,
2022–ongoing.

ARTW017c
American Artist, *Yannis Window*, 2022–ongoing. Sculptural projection, single-channel HD video with sound. Dimensions variable.

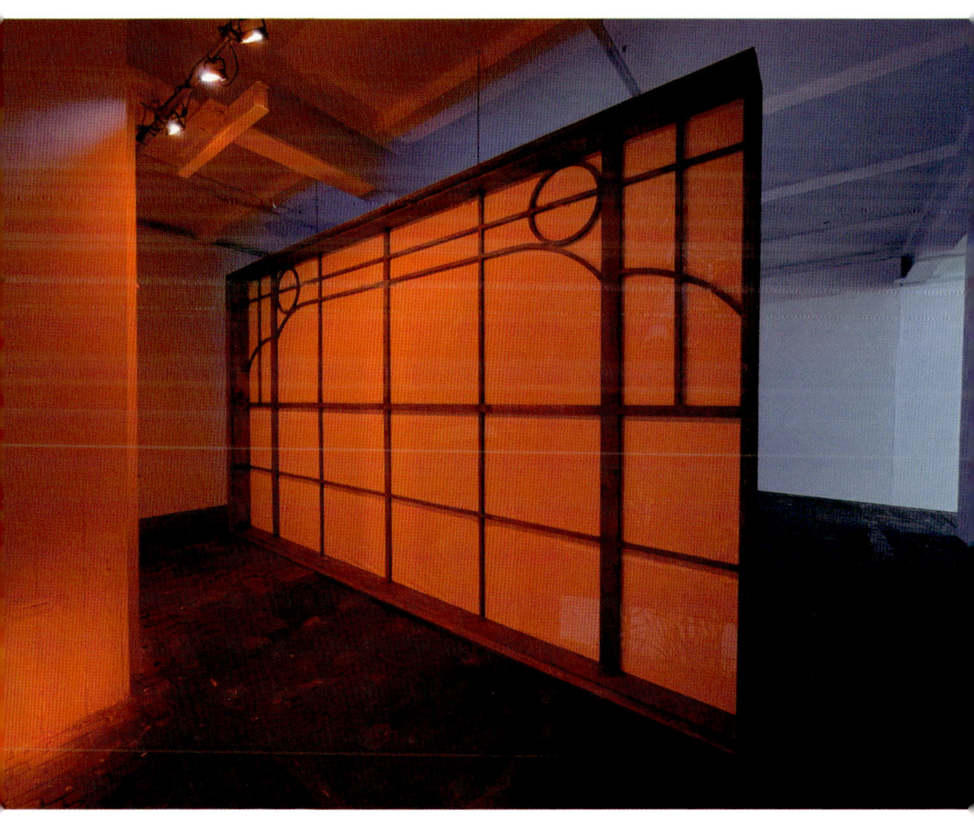

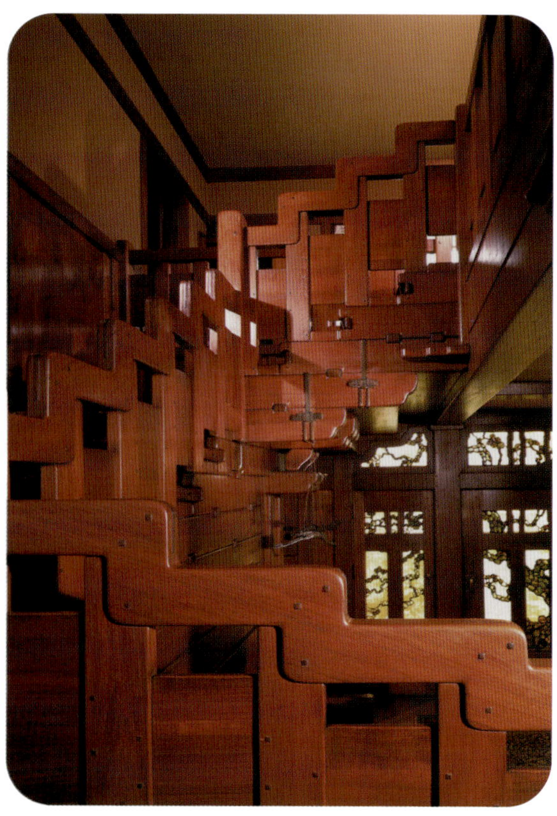

This is cool, have you visited it in person?

I was a docent there in middle school

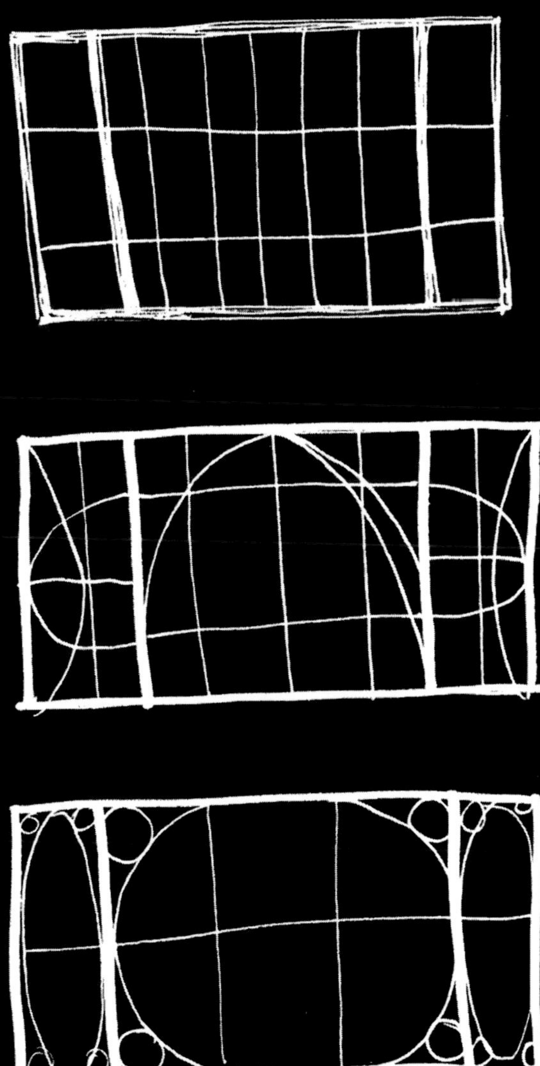

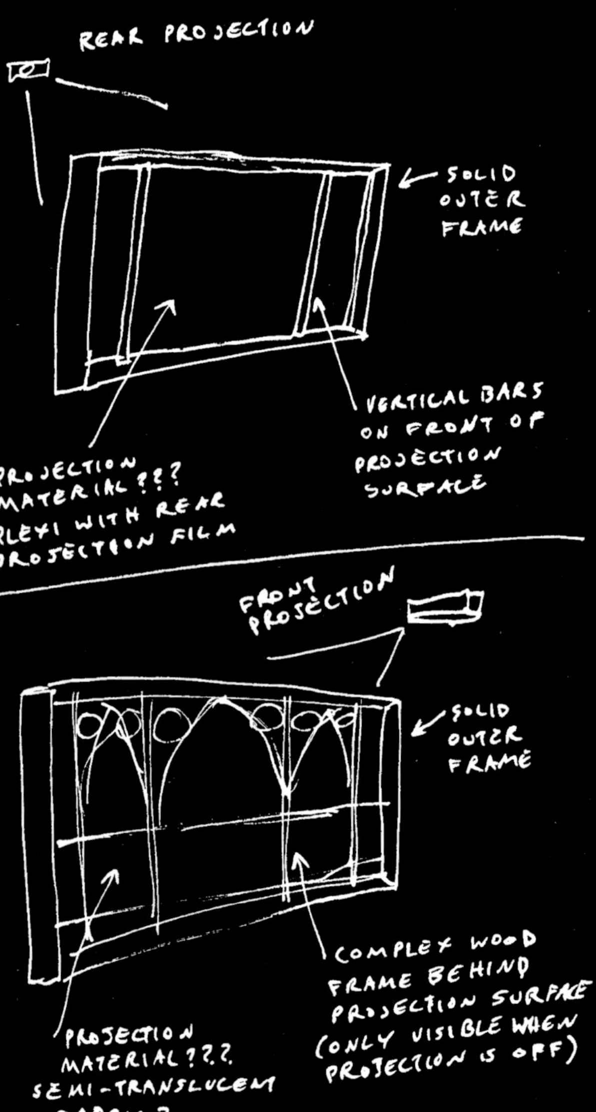
REAR PROJECTION
SOLID OUTER FRAME
VERTICAL BARS ON FRONT OF PROJECTION SURFACE
PROJECTION MATERIAL ??? PLEXI WITH REAR PROJECTION FILM
FRONT PROJECTION
SOLID OUTER FRAME
COMPLEX WOOD FRAME BEHIND PROJECTION SURFACE (ONLY VISIBLE WHEN PROJECTION IS OFF)
PROJECTION MATERIAL ???. SEMI-TRANSLUCENT FABRIC?

Octavia E. Butler, Positive Obsession: speech: notecards, ca. 1993. OEB 3087.

"I'm a native of Pasadena, CA and I've lived all my life in the L.A. area—so I care about this part of the world. I care about where it seems to be headed."

Ayana 6:6

The juxtaposition of the imaginary
fictional world with the real
landscape of the Pasadena Arroyo
creates a layered engagement with
the Butlerian universe.

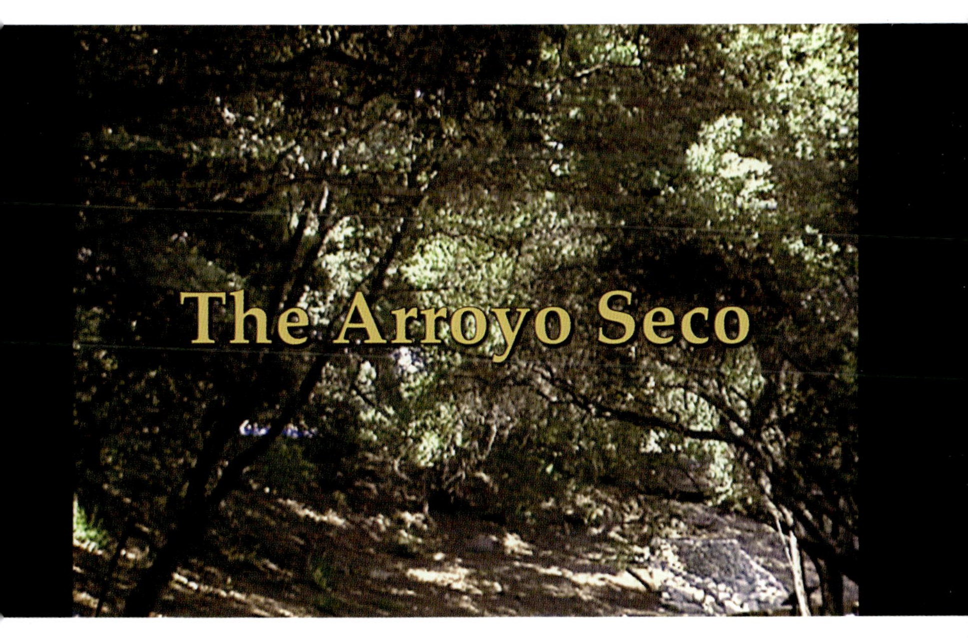

ARTW014a
Film still from American
Artist, *The Arroyo
Seco*, 2022.

Ercoupe Flight Test Crew Date: 1941-08. Courtesy NASA/JPL-Caltech.

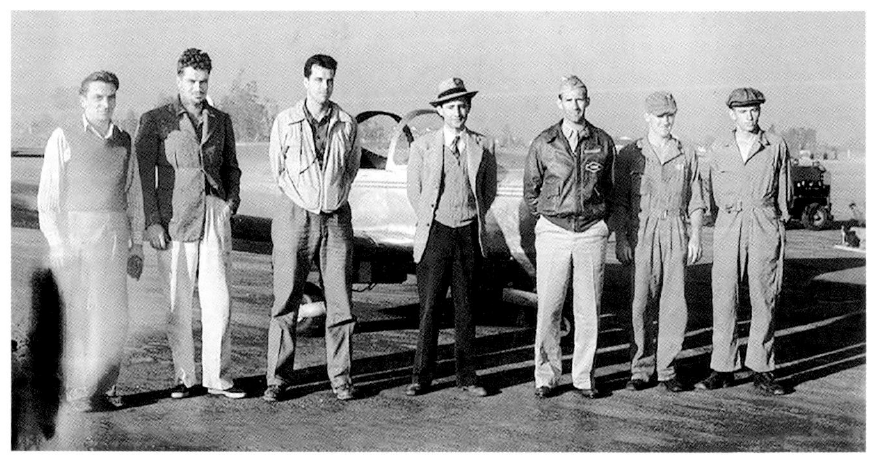

Photo taken at West L.A. Community College during "A Salute to Black Role Models of the Greater Los Angeles Community." Left to right: Betty Myles, Artie Bates, Lady Tyger Trimiar, Octavia E. Butler.

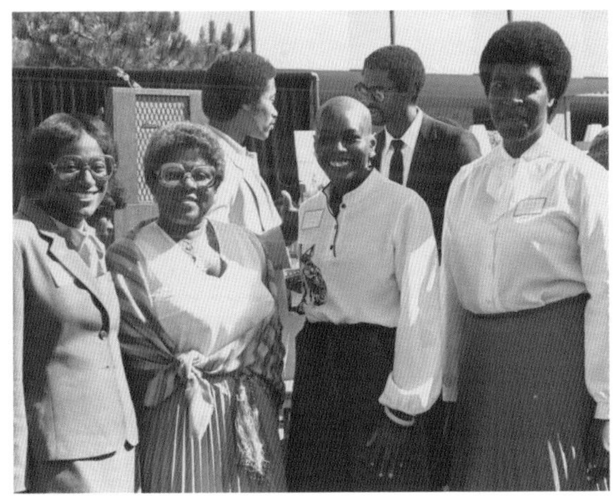

Her journals, in particular, offer a glimpse into her real-time engagement with Pasadena and Los Angeles, revealing how deeply these places shaped her narratives.

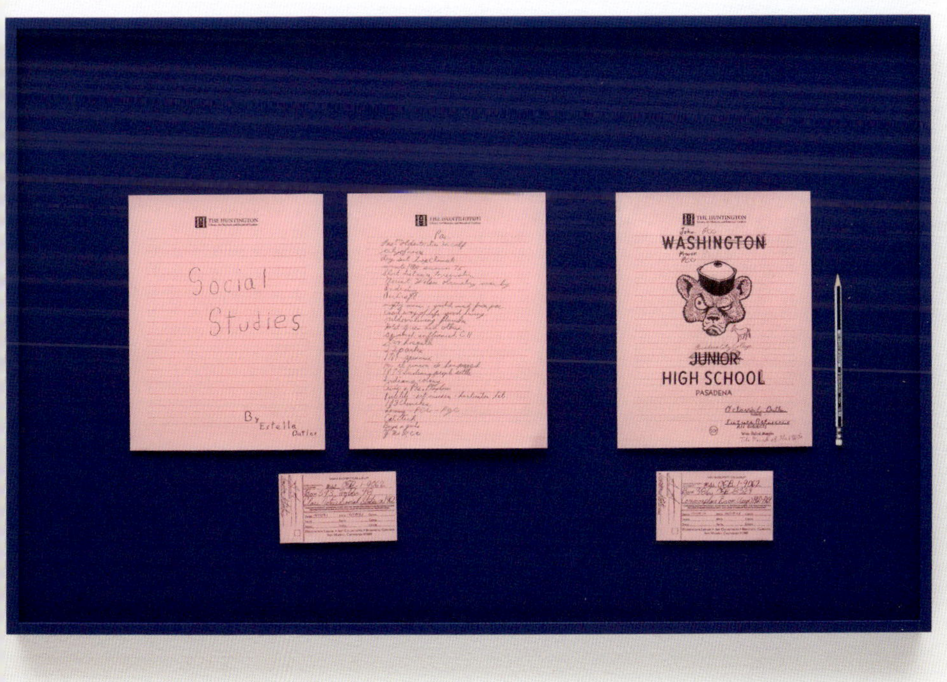

ARTW007a
American Artist,
Octavia E. Butler
Papers: mssOEB 1-9062
I (*Social Studies*), 2022.
the Huntington
stationary, graphite,
pencil, and felt.
26.5 x 38 x 1.5 in.

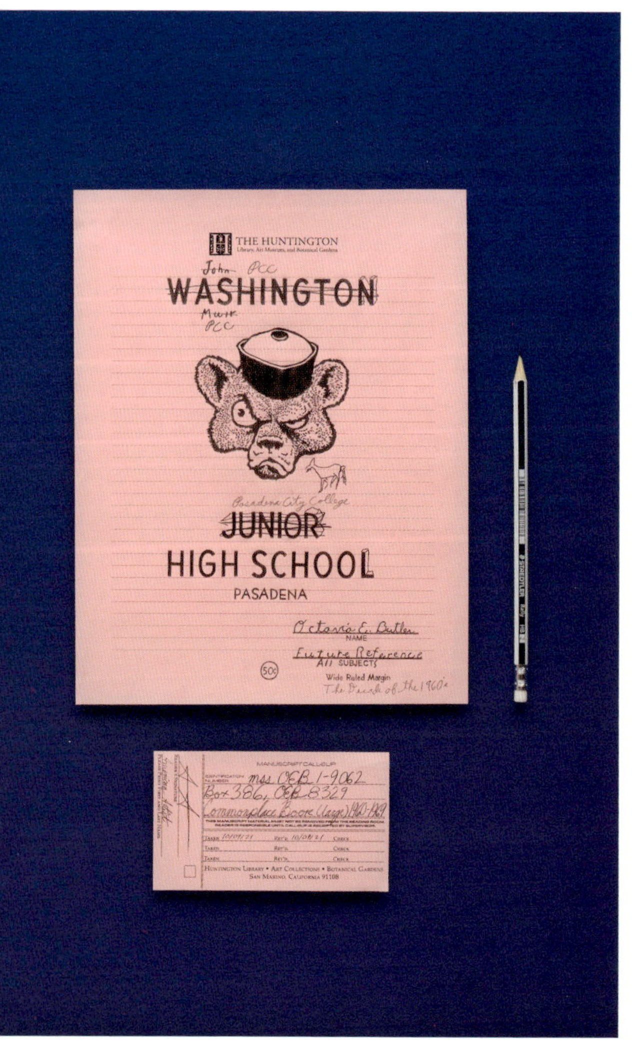

ARTW007b
Detail of American Artist, Octavia E. Butler Papers: mssOEB 1-9062 l (Social Studies), 2022.

Butler described the school formerly known as Washington Junior High as "the worst junior high school in the city" with a "really terrible reputation." She admitted to being terrified to go there, but it was the only option available to her family, who could only afford to rent a decent house in that area.

American Artist photographed by Gioncarlo Valentine, 2022.

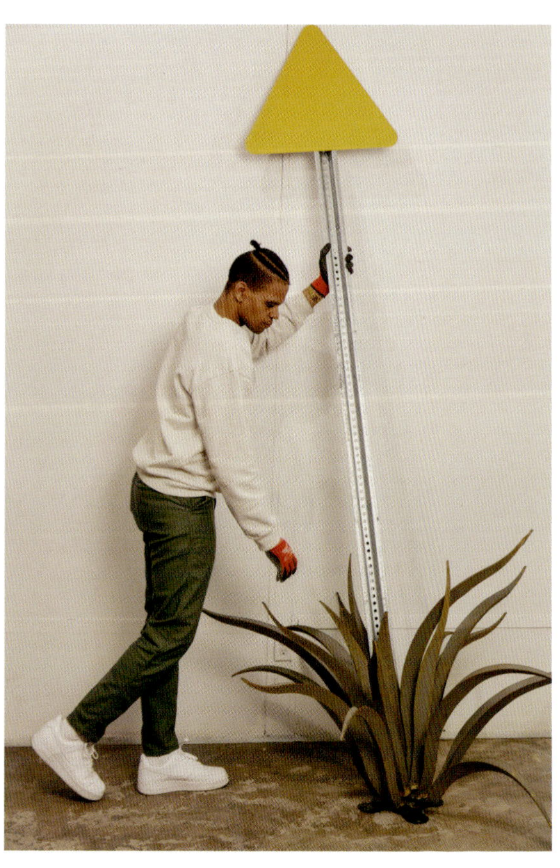

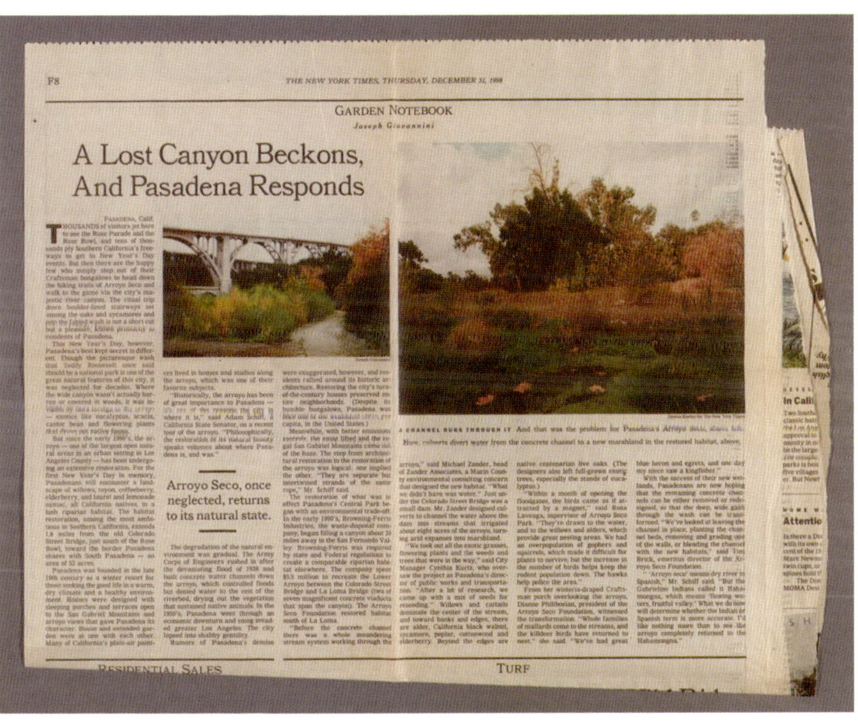

A Lost Canyon Beckons, And Pasadena Responds

PASADENA, Calif.

THOUSANDS of visitors jet here to see the Rose Parade and the Rose Bowl, and tens of thousands ply Southern California's freeways to get to New Year's Day events. But then there are the happy few who simply step out of their Craftsman bungalows to head down the hiking trails of Arroyo Seco and walk to the game via the city's majestic river canyon. The ritual trip down boulder-lined stairways set among the oaks and sycamores and into the fabled wash is not a short cut but a pleasure, known primarily to residents of Pasadena.

This New Year's Day, however, Pasadena's best kept secret is different. Though the picturesque wash that Teddy Roosevelt once said should be a national park is one of the great natural features of this city, it was neglected for decades. Where the wide canyon wasn't actually barren or covered in weeds, it was invaded by lush foreign growth in the arroyo — exotics like eucalyptus, acacia, castor bean and flowering plants that drove out native fauna.

But since the early 1990's, the arroyo — one of the largest open natural areas in an urban setting in Los Angeles County — has been undergoing an extensive restoration. For the first New Year's Day in memory, Pasadenans will encounter a landscape of willows, toyon, coffeeberry, elderberry, and laurel and lemonade sumac, all California natives, in a lush riparian habitat. The habitat restoration, among the most ambitious in Southern California, extends 1.8 miles from the old Colorado Street Bridge, just south of the Rose Bowl, toward the border Pasadena shares with South Pasadena — an area of 52 acres.

Pasadena was founded in the late 19th century as a winter resort for those seeking the good life in a warm, dry climate and a healthy environment. Houses were designed with sleeping porches and terraces open to the San Gabriel Mountains and arroyo views that gave Pasadena its character. House and extended garden were at one with each other. Many of California's plein-air painters lived in homes and studios along the arroyo, which was one of their favorite subjects.

"Historically, the arroyo has been of great importance to Pasadena — it's one of the reasons the city is where it is," said Adam Schiff, a California State Senator, on a recent tour of the arroyo. "Philosophically, the restoration of its natural beauty speaks volumes about where Pasadena is, and was."

Arroyo Seco, once neglected, returns to its natural state.

The degradation of the natural environment was gradual. The Army Corps of Engineers rushed in after the devastating flood of 1938 and built concrete water channels down the arroyo, which controlled floods but denied water to the rest of the riverbed, drying out the vegetation that sustained native animals. In the 1950's, Pasadena went through an economic downturn and smog invaded greater Los Angeles. The city lapsed into shabby gentility.

Rumors of Pasadena's demise were exaggerated, however, and residents rallied around its historic architecture. Restoring the city's turn-of-the-century houses preserved entire neighborhoods. (Despite its humble bungalows, Pasadena was once one of the wealthiest cities, per capita, in the United States.)

Meanwhile, with better emissions controls, the smog lifted and the regal San Gabriel Mountains came out of the haze. The step from architectural restoration to the restoration of the arroyo was logical: one implied the other. "They are separate but intertwined strands of the same rope," Mr. Schiff said.

The restoration of what was in effect Pasadena's Central Park began with an environmental trade-off. In the early 1990's, Browning-Ferris Industries, the waste-disposal company, began filling a canyon about 20 miles away in the San Fernando Valley. Browning-Ferris was required by state and Federal regulations to create a comparable riparian habitat elsewhere. The company spent $5.5 million to recreate the Lower Arroyo between the Colorado Street Bridge and La Loma Bridge (two of seven magnificent concrete viaducts that span the canyon). The Arroyo Seco Foundation restored habitat south of La Loma.

"Before the concrete channel there was a whole meandering stream system working through the arroyo," said Michael Zander, head of Zander Associates, a Marin County environmental consulting concern that designed the new habitat. "What we didn't have was water." Just under the Colorado Street Bridge was a small dam. Mr. Zander designed culverts to channel the water above the dam into streams that irrigated about eight acres of the arroyo, turning arid expanses into marshland.

"We took out all the exotic grasses, flowering plants and the weeds and trees that were in the way," said City Manager Cynthia Kurtz, who oversaw the project as Pasadena's director of public works and transportation. "After a lot of research, we came up with a mix of seeds for reseeding." Willows and cattails dominate the center of the stream, and toward banks and edges, there are alder, California black walnut, sycamore, poplar, cottonwood and elderberry. Beyond the edges are native centenarian live oaks. (The designers also left full-grown exotic trees, especially the stands of eucalyptus.)

"Within a month of opening the floodgates, the birds came as if attracted by a magnet," said Rosa Laveaga, supervisor of Arroyo Seco Park. "They're drawn to the water, and to the willows and alders, which provide great nesting areas. We had an overpopulation of gophers and squirrels, which made it difficult for plants to survive, but the increase in the number of birds helps keep the rodent population down. The hawks help police the area."

From her wisteria-draped Craftsman porch overlooking the arroyo, Dianne Philibosian, president of the Arroyo Seco Foundation, witnessed the transformation. "Whole families of mallards come to the streams, and the killdeer birds have returned to nest," she said. "We've had great blue heron and egrets, and one day my niece saw a kingfisher."

With the success of their new wetlands, Pasadenans are now hoping that the remaining concrete channels can be either removed or redesigned, so that the deep, wide gash through the wash can be transformed. "We've looked at leaving the channel in place, planting the channel beds, removing and grading one of the walls, or blending the channel with the new habitats," said Tim Brick, emeritus director of the Arroyo Seco Foundation.

"'Arroyo seco' means dry river in Spanish," Mr. Schiff said. "But the Gabrielino Indians called it Hahamongna, which means 'flowing waters, fruitful valley.' What we do now will determine whether the Indian or Spanish term is more accurate. I'd like nothing more than to see the arroyo completely returned to the Hahamongna."

Natalie Russell, from the transcript of A-Team meeting hosted by Jet Propulsion Laboratory, organized by American Artist.

"I'm Natalie Russell. I am the assistant curator of the literary collection at The Huntington Library, and I've been here for about fifteen years. Of those fifteen years, I have been working with the Octavia Butler papers for about thirteen of them. I was in the lucky position to catalog and process the papers when they arrived at The Huntington.**"**

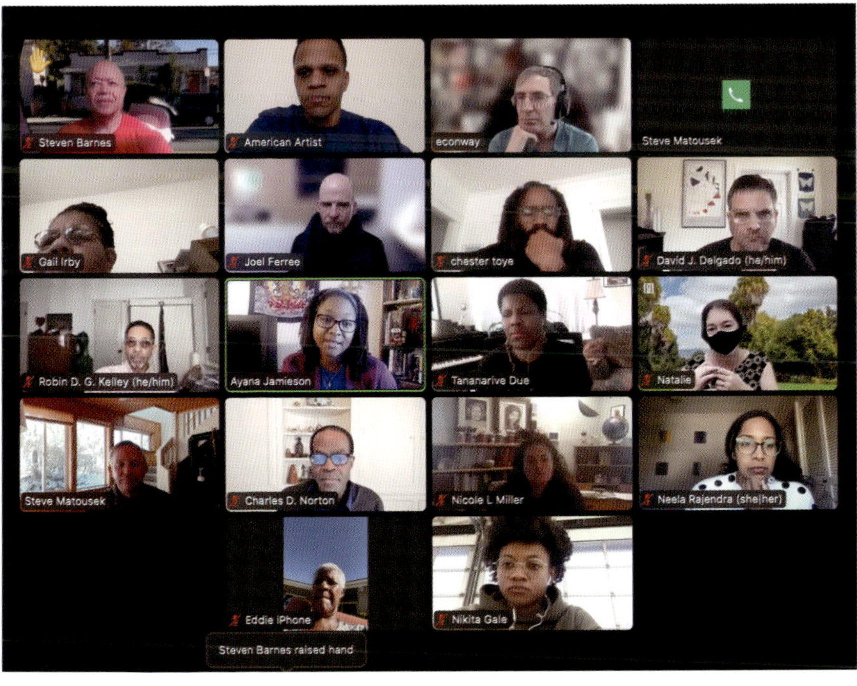
Steven Barnes
American Artist
econway
Steve Matousek
Gail Irby
Joel Ferree
chester toye
David J. Delgado (he/him)
Robin D. G. Kelley (he/him)
Ayana Jamieson
Tananarive Due
Natalie
Steve Matousek
Charles D. Norton
Nicole L Miller
Neela Rajendra (she/her)
Eddie iPhone
Nikita Gale
Steven Barnes raised hand

Her writing challenges us in the present moment to consider how our environments shape us and how, in turn, we might shape them for the better.

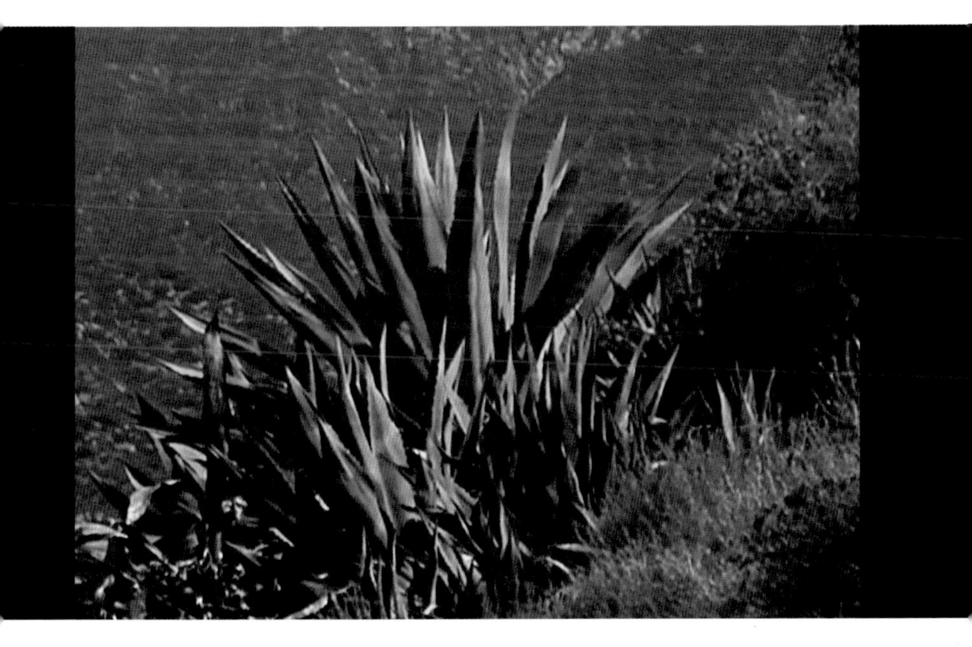

ARTW014b
Film still from American
Artist, *The Arroyo
Seco*, 2022.

Aerial view of Jet Propulsion Labratory, Pasadena, CA, 1964.

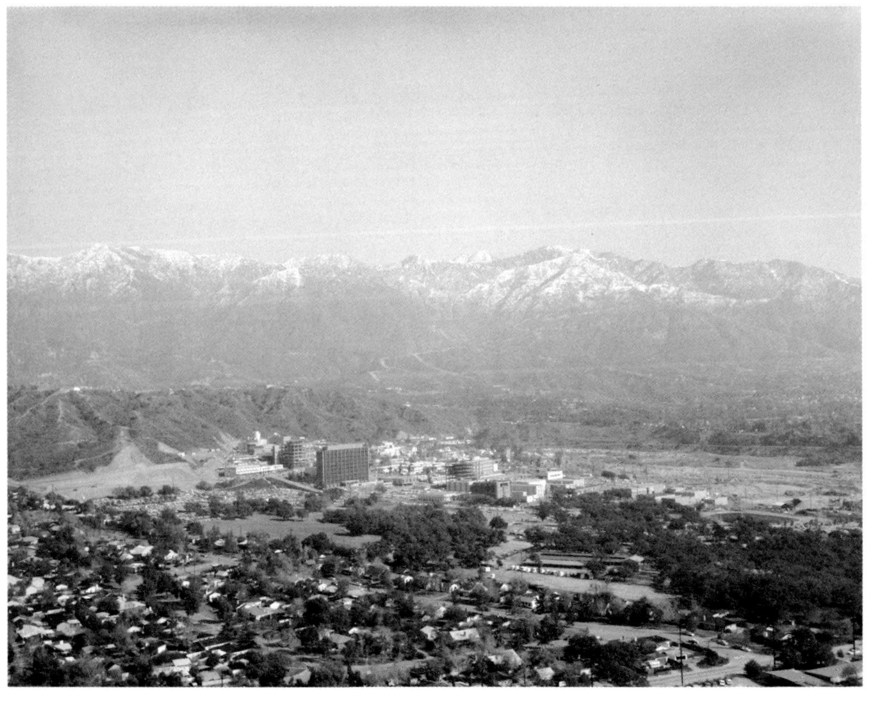

Sketch of *Robledo Community Wall* by American Artist, 2021.

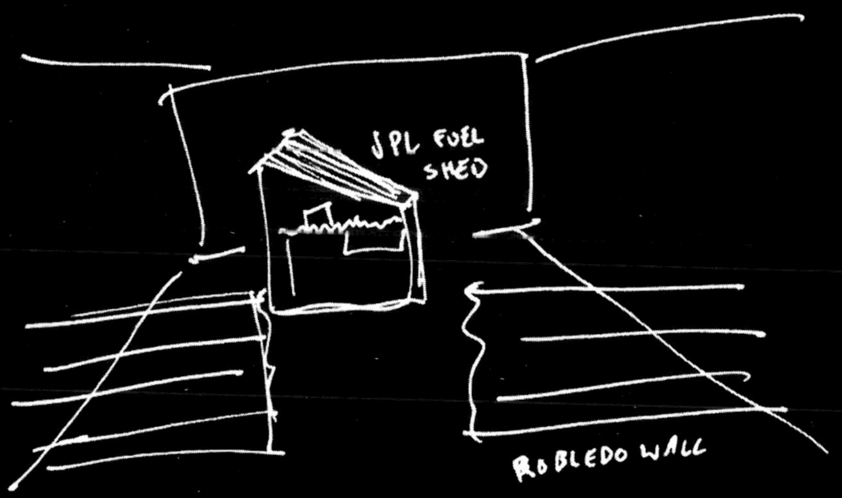

. ITS JUST A MATTER OF CITING ARTIFACTS FROM
ALL REALMS AND PLACING THEM IN THE SAME
SPACE TIME

Sketch of *Robledo Community Wall (Olamina cul-de-sac)* by American Artist, 2021.

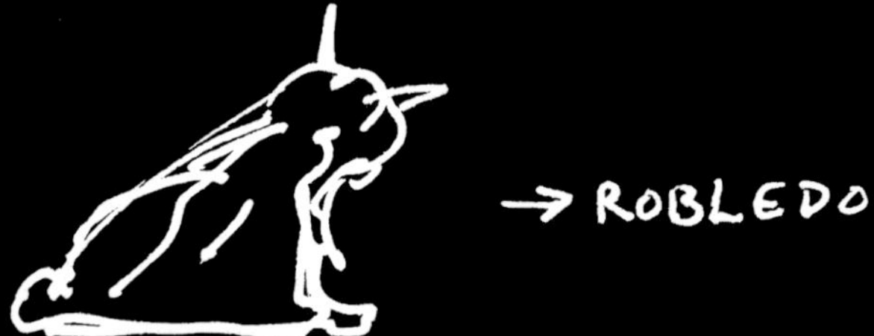

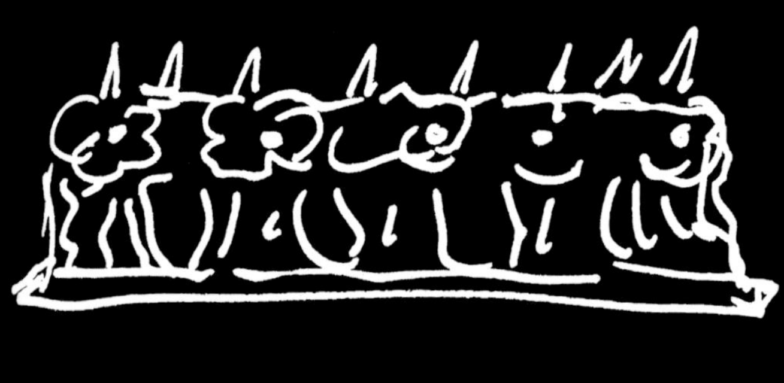

3D model of *Robledo Community Wall (Olamina cul-de-sac)* by American Artist, 2021.

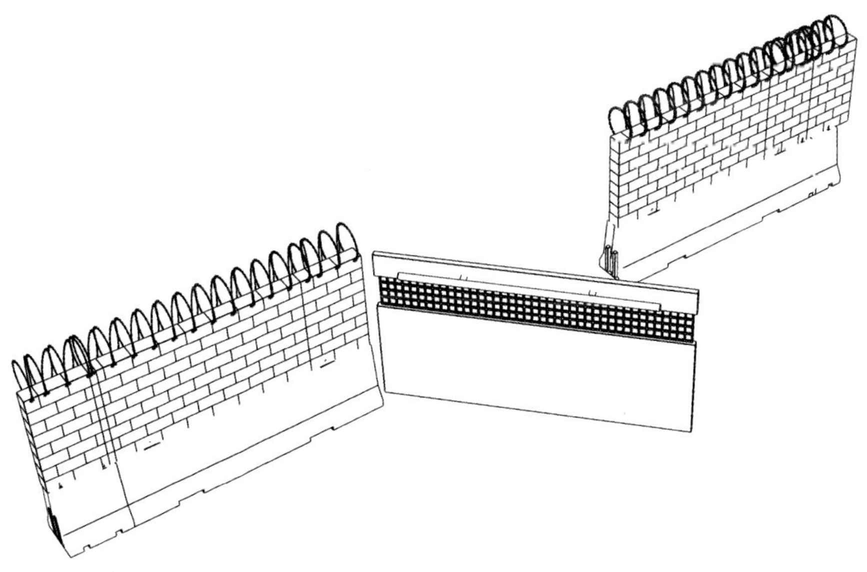

Aerial view of two buildings on fire during Watts Riots, Los Angeles, CA, August 1965.

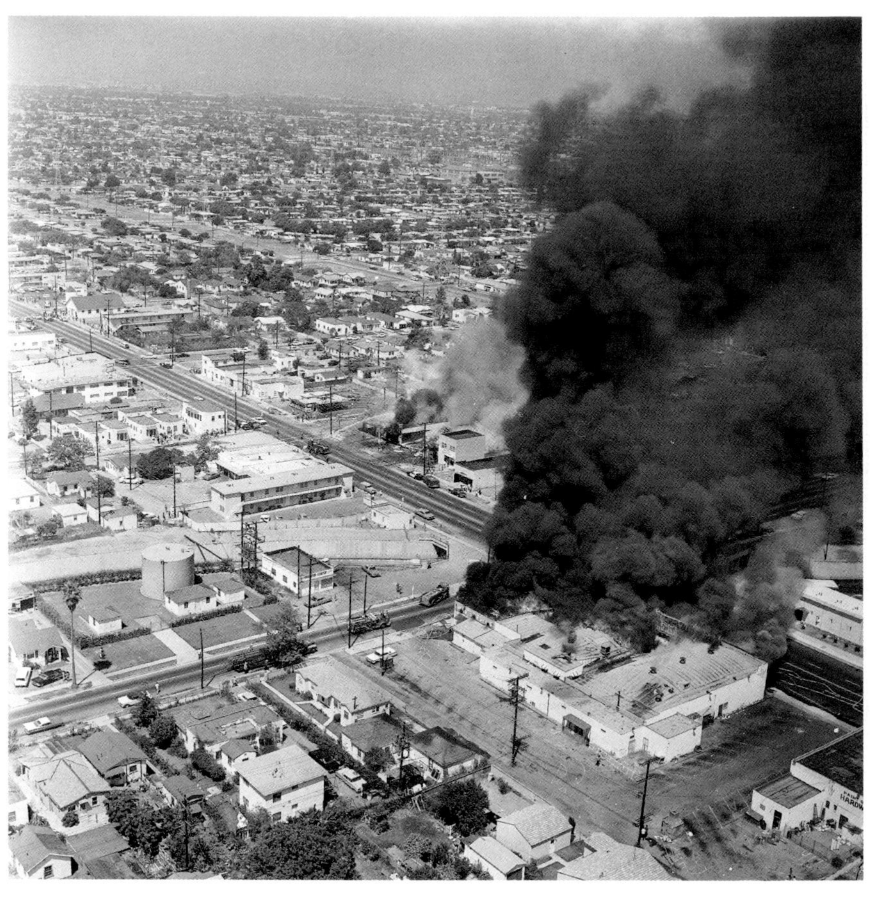

Hey mom, do you remember what year you moved to California?

Yes

June 1965

My sister was graduating from high school and my mother wanted to make sure we had better opportunities to attend college. LACC was low tuition

Why do you ask?

I've been learning about the 40s-70s and Black families moving to Los Angeles during that time

When did our family move from Oklahoma?

I'll have to research that one because my Grandmother had two marriages going back and forth with short stays between Oklahoma and Arizona...This was during the 30's

Text message between American Artist and their
mother Lily Braden, 2020.

Oh ok, that's good to know. I'd love to
know more. And I forget, what was
grandmother doing for work when you
moved to Cali?

She was a practicing nurses aid. She'd
just gotten her certificate

And what about in Arizona?

She was a housekeeper for white families

Ok, I do remember that but I wanted to
be sure

What about your father?

My biological father was a barber. After
he and my mom divorced, she married
my stepfather who worked at the dry
cleaners.

Illustration from Richard L. Morrill, *Spatial Organization of Society*, 1965.

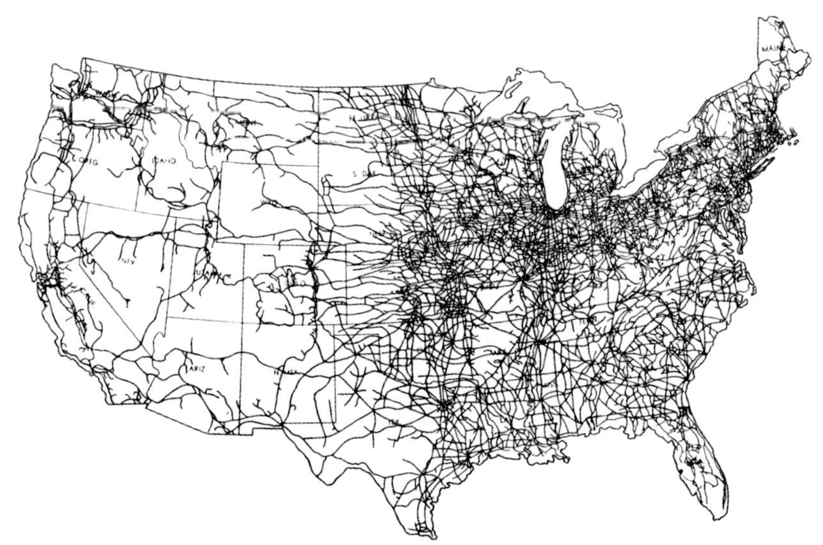

36th Anniversary, first rocket firing at JPL, October 31, 1968. Courtesy NASA/JPL-Caltech.

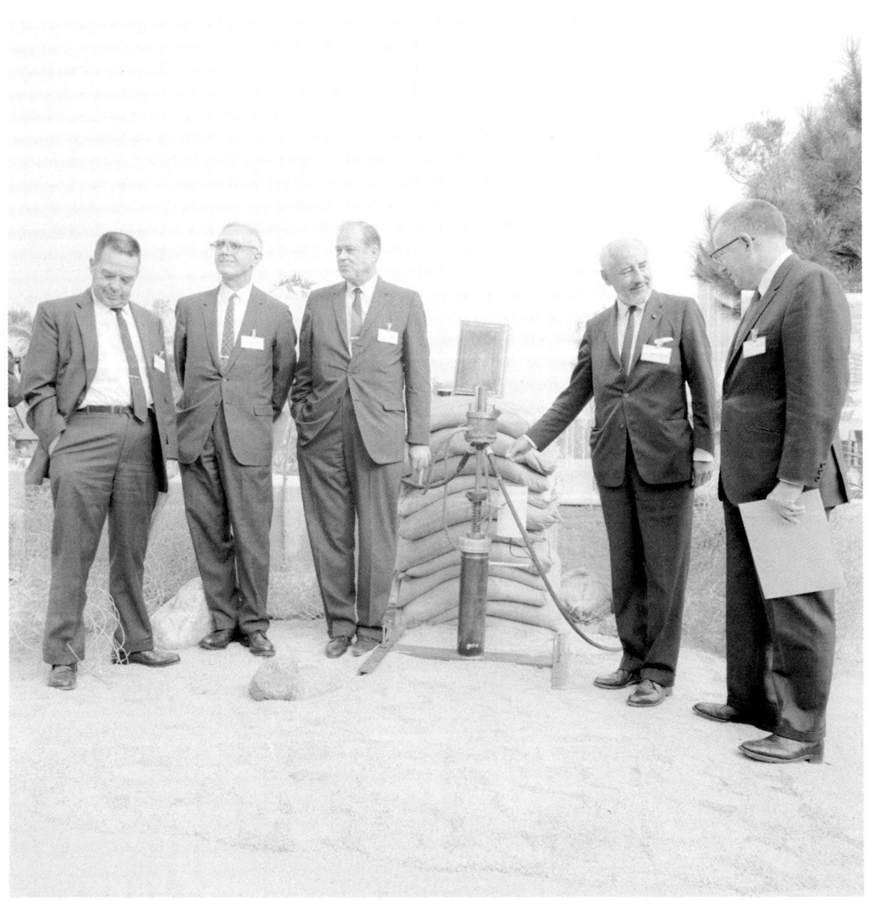

Sketch of *To Acorn* series by American Artist, 2022.

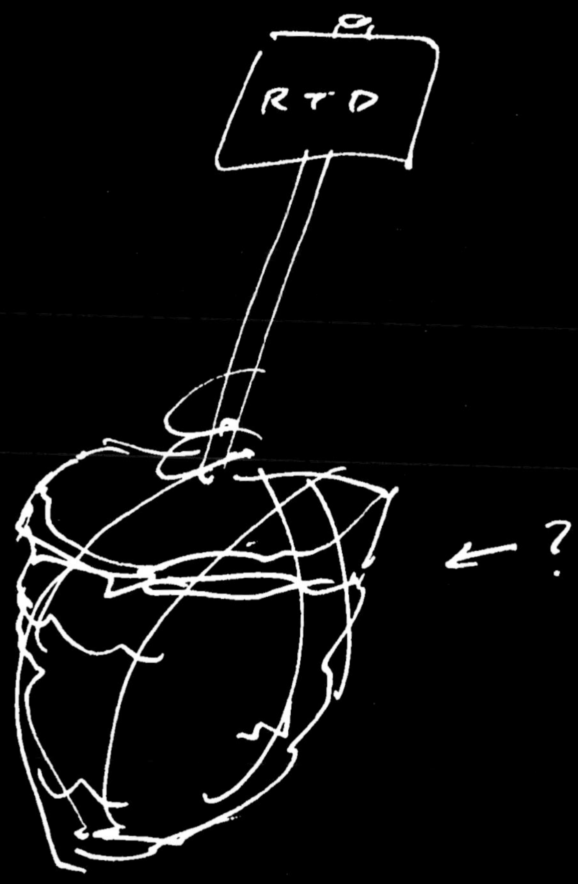

Sketch of *To Acorn* series by American Artist, 2022.

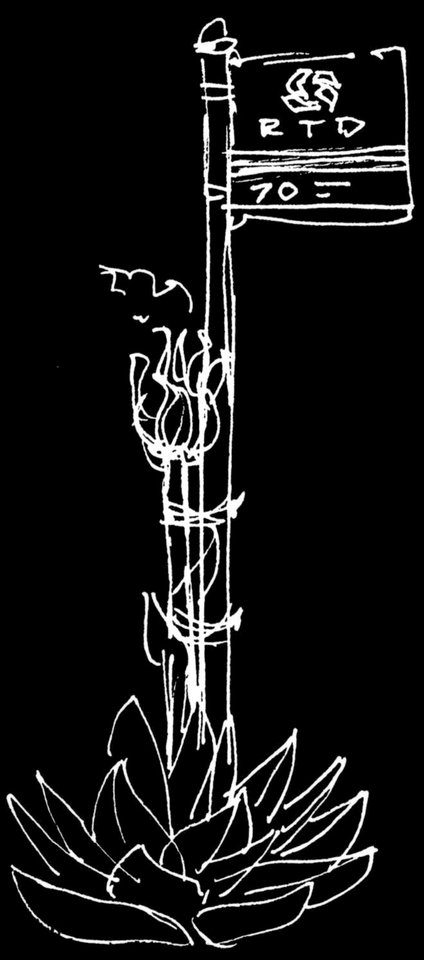

Text message message between American Artist and
Adam Kleinman, 2022.

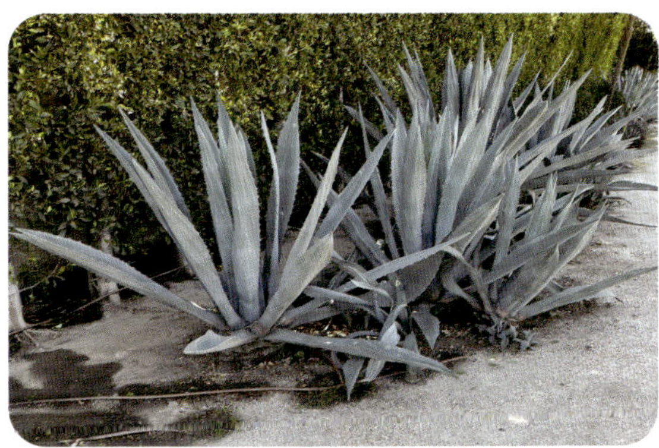

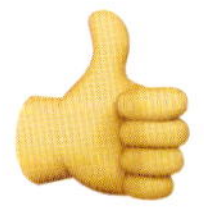

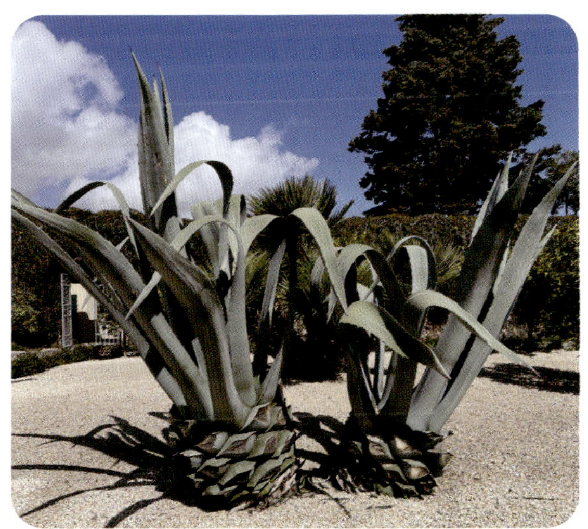

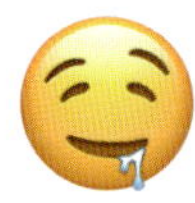

Butler drew from her childhood, incorporating prominent landmarks and locations, including sections of the city of Pasadena, bus rides through downtown Los Angeles, and her grandmother's desert ranch.

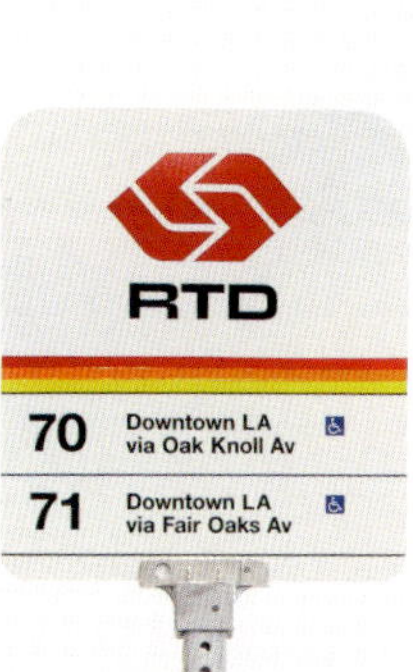

ARTW013
American Artist, *To Acorn (1985)*, 2022.
Steel, acrylic, and hardware.
107 x 33 x 33 in.

The Jet Propulsion Laboratory in the upper Arroyo
Seco and San Gabriel Mountains foothills, of Pasadena
and Altadena, Southern California, 1991. Courtesy
NASA/JPL-Caltech.

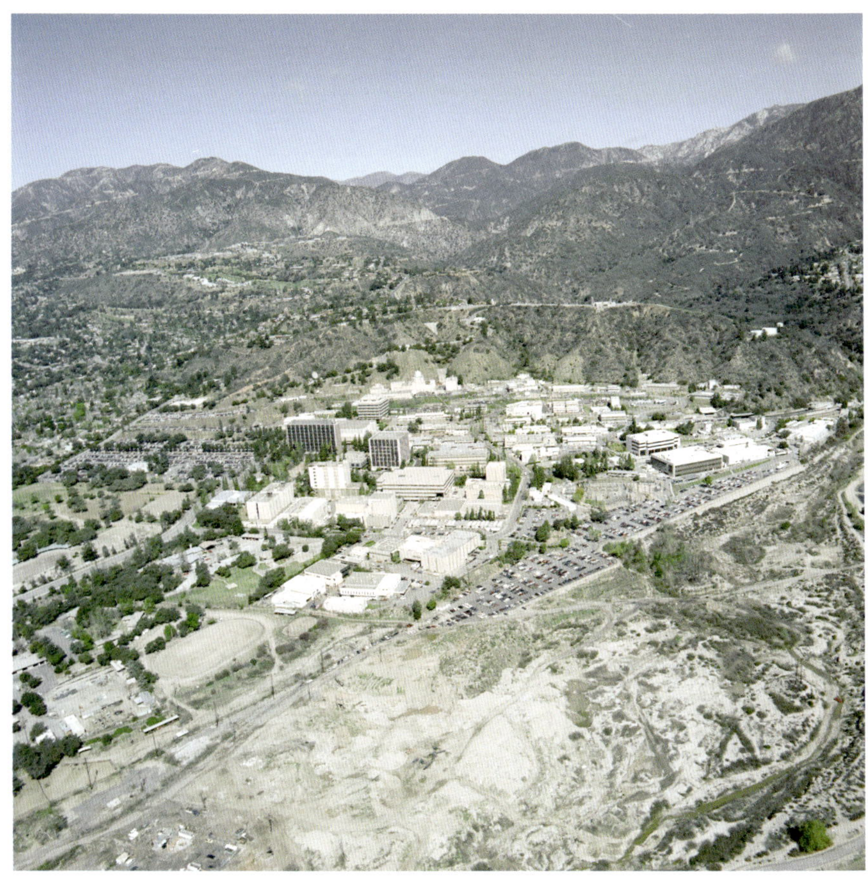

American Artist, from the transcript of A-Team meeting hosted by Jet Propulsion Laboratory, organized by American Artist.

"The first thing that came to mind when you said 'Altadena,' actually, I was just thinking about my dad. Even though as his primary work he was a mechanic on large vehicles for Southern California Edison, he also—as a sort of hobby he was a poet. And I recently remembered that he had written a poem about Altadena for some public event. I don't remember what it was for, but I want to see if I can find this poem that he wrote. So, that came to mind when you said 'Altadena.'"

I found the passage Joel was referring to

"We collect any herb, fruit, vegetable, or nut-producing plant, any plant at all that we know or suppose to be useful. We have, always, a special need for spiny, self-sufficient desert plants that will tolerate our climate. They serve as part of our thorn fence. Cactus by cactus, thornbush by thornbush, we've planted a living wall in the hills around Acorn."

Photograph of The Huntington Library, Art Museum, and Botanical Gardens taken by American Artist. 2022.

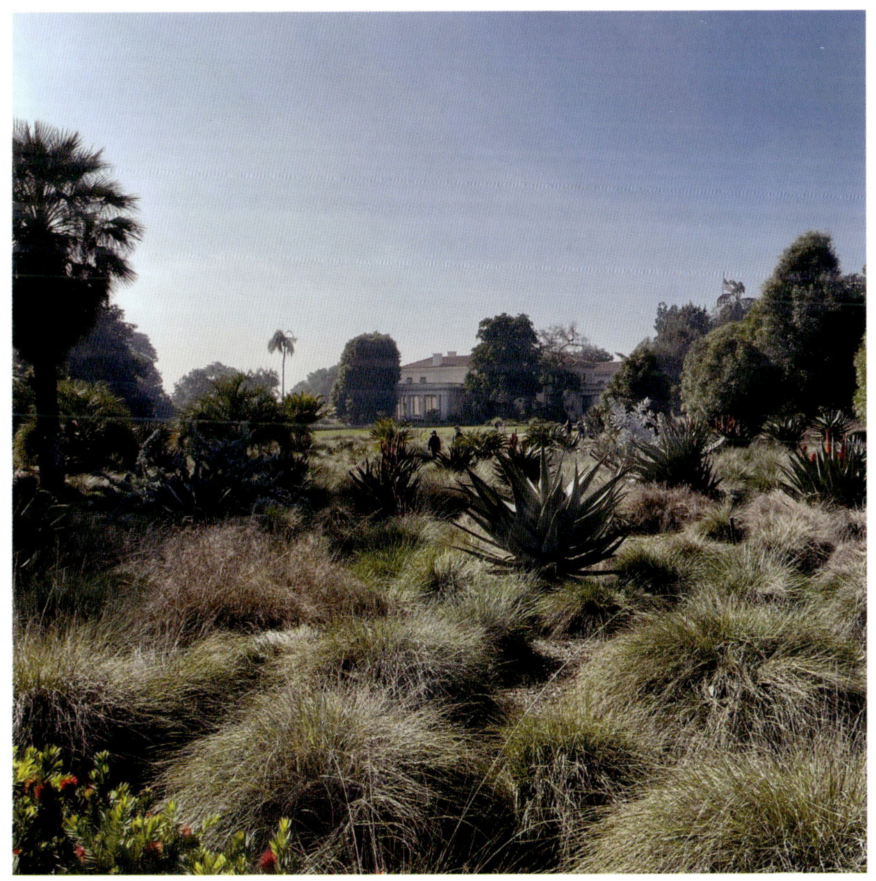

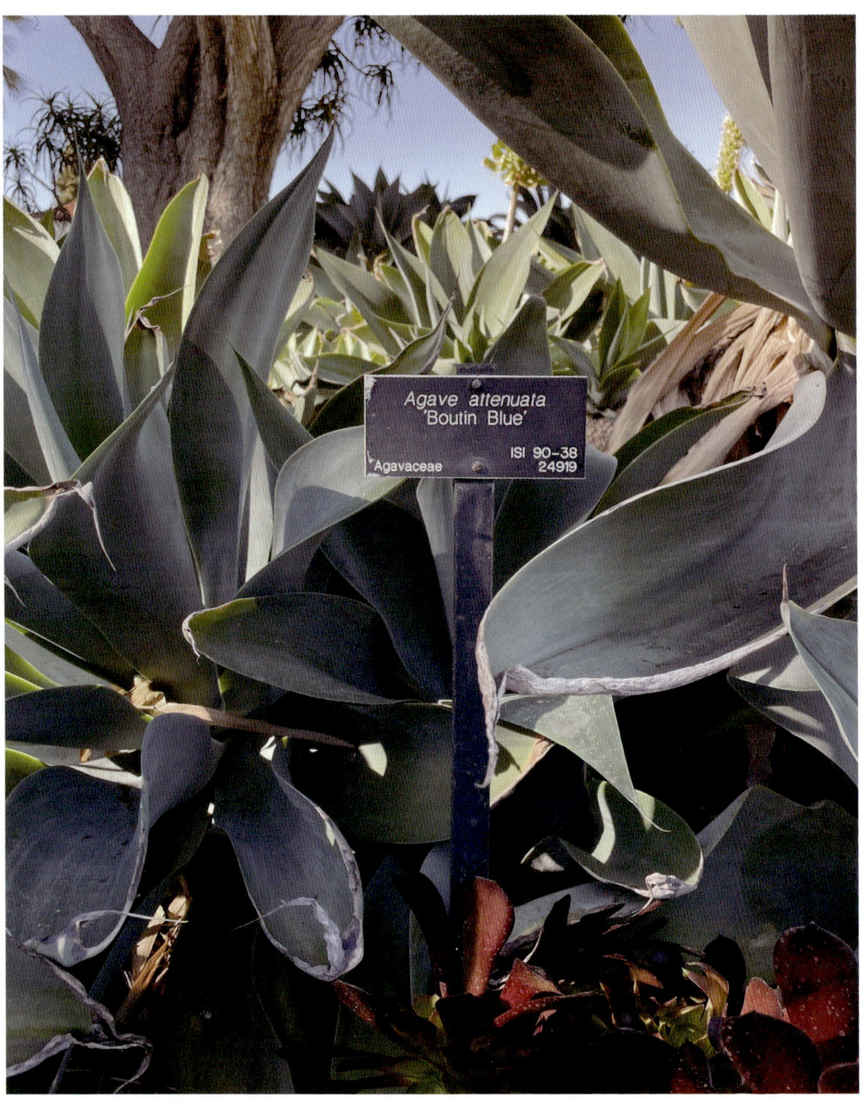
Agave attenuata
'Boutin Blue'
ISI 90-38
Agavaceae   24919

Text message between American Artist and Chester
Toye, 2022.

"Our wall won't keep determined people out, of course. No wall will do that. Cars and trucks will get in if their owners are willing to absorb some damage to their vehicles, but cars and trucks that work are rare and precious in the mountains, and most fuels are expensive. Even intruders on foot can get in if they're willing to work at it. But the fence will hamper and annoy them. It will make them angry, and perhaps noisy. It will, when it's working well, encourage people to approach us by the easiest routes, and those we guard 24 hours a day. It's always best to keep an eye on visitors. So we intended to harvest agave."

Kind of sounds like trying to get into JPL

Butler's stories are deeply rooted in the places she knew—the streets of Pasadena, the city bus lines of Los Angeles, and the California landscape—all of which she used as backdrops for her narratives.

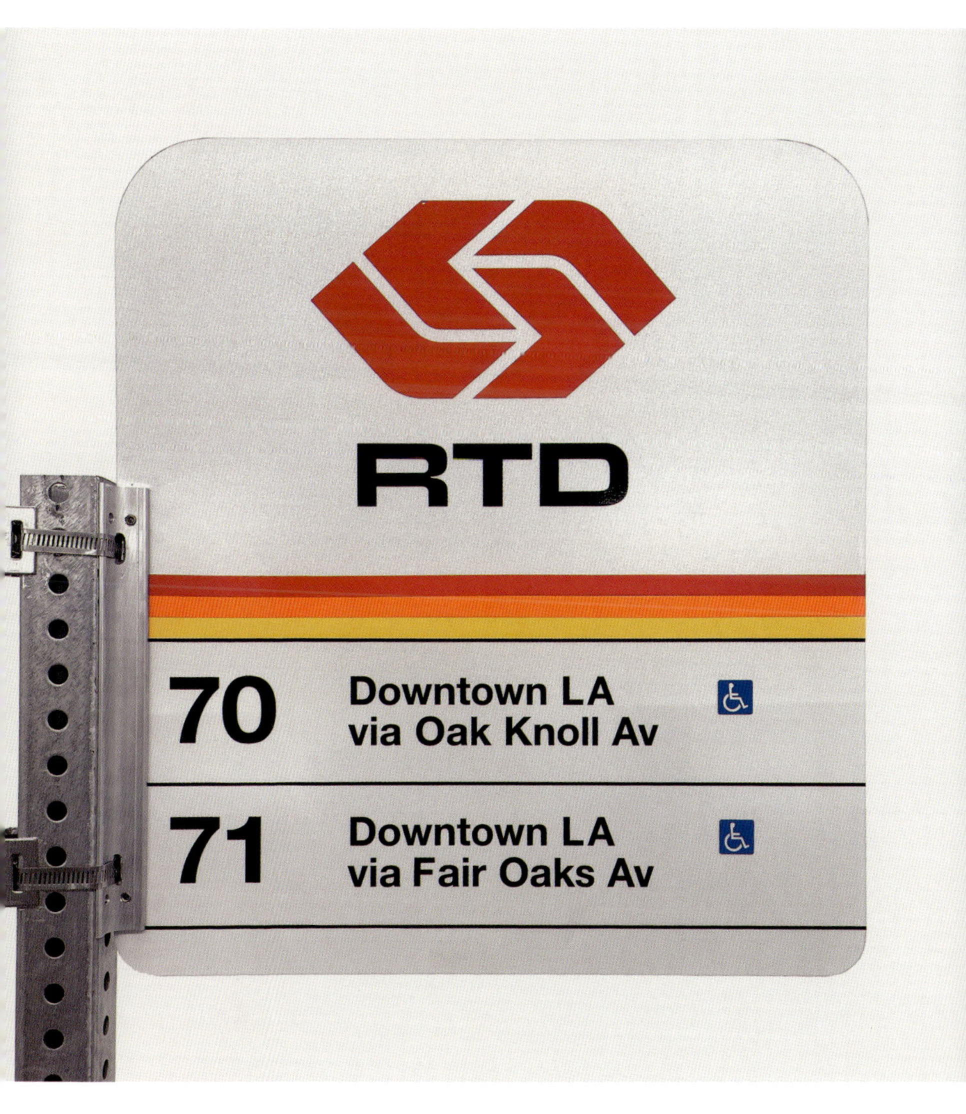

ARTW012
Detail of American
Artist, *To Acorn (1984)*,
2022.

Photograph of Munger Research Center, where the Octavia E. Butler Papers are located at The Huntington, taken by American Artist in 2022.

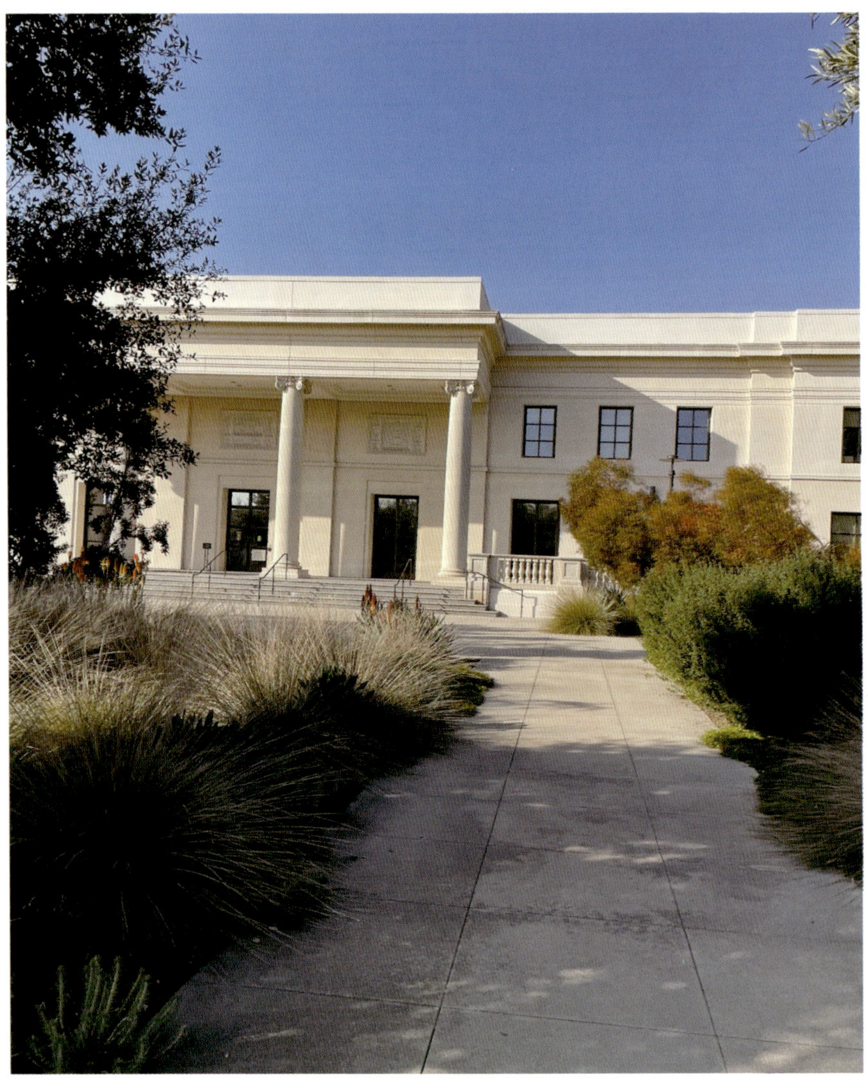

Octavia E. Butler, Ephemera - Travel. Box 342, Folder 5,
Southern California Public Transportation, 1968–1998.

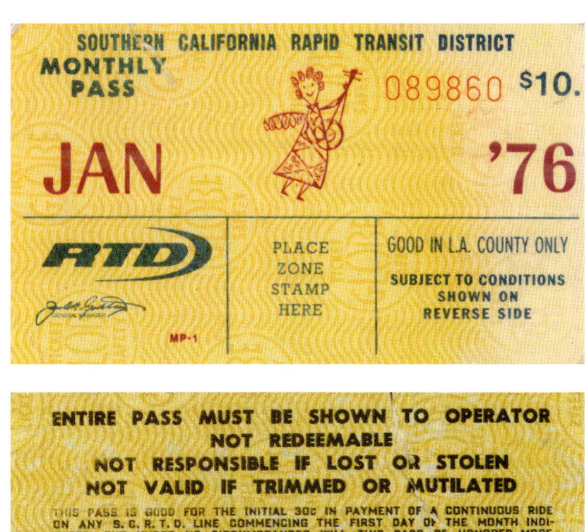

Self-curation in the archives also preserved her mother's personal effects, along with everyday family artifacts and narrative histories.

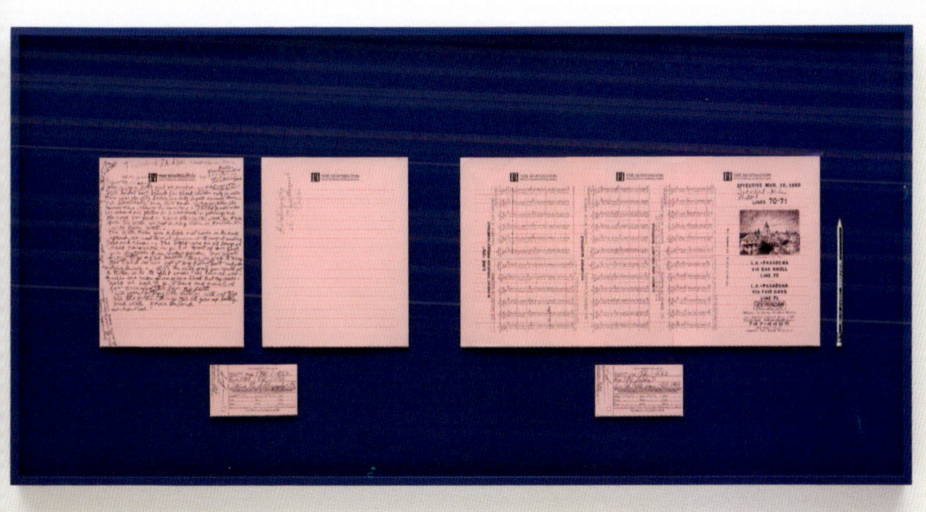

ARTW005a
American Artist, *Octavia E. Butler Papers: mssOEB 1-9062 I (Only Dirt Roads)*, 2022.
The Huntington stationary, graphite, pencil, and felt.
26.5 x 52.5 x 1.5 in.

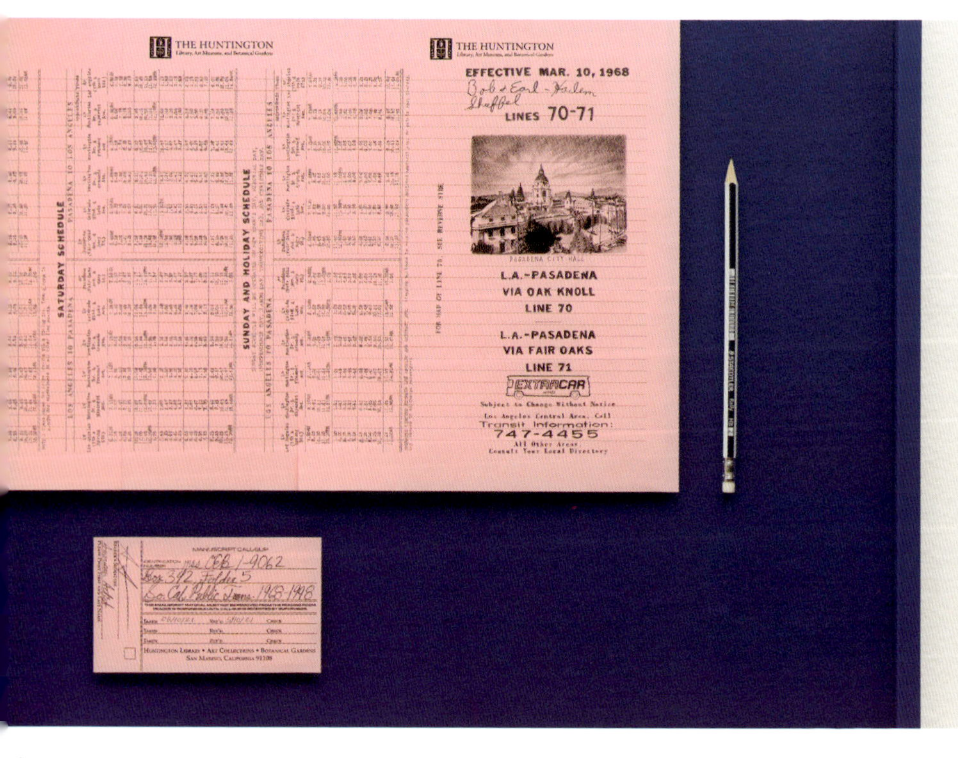

ARTW005b
Detail of American
Artist, *Octavia E.
Butler Papers: mssOEB
1-9062 I (Only Dirt
Roads)*, 2022.

Butler also featured the public bus lines of Pasadena and Los Angeles in the short story "Speech Sounds" (1983), in which a character travels to connect with a relative during a crisis, picking up orphaned children along the way.

In Butler's fictional 2024, the refugees eventually establish a new community called Acorn after walking alongside the San Gabriel Mountains and up the coast to Northern California.

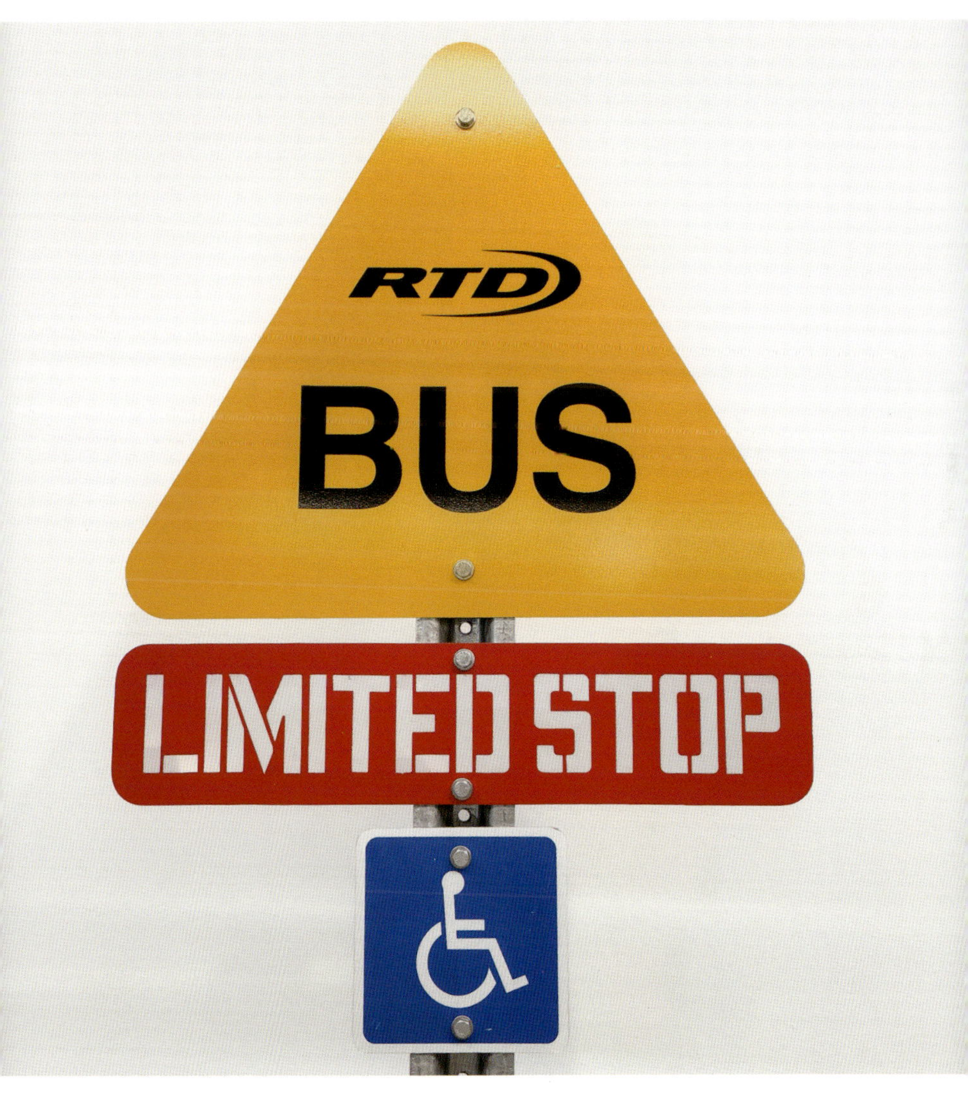

ARTW011a
Detail of American
Artist, *To Acorn* (*1968*),
2022.

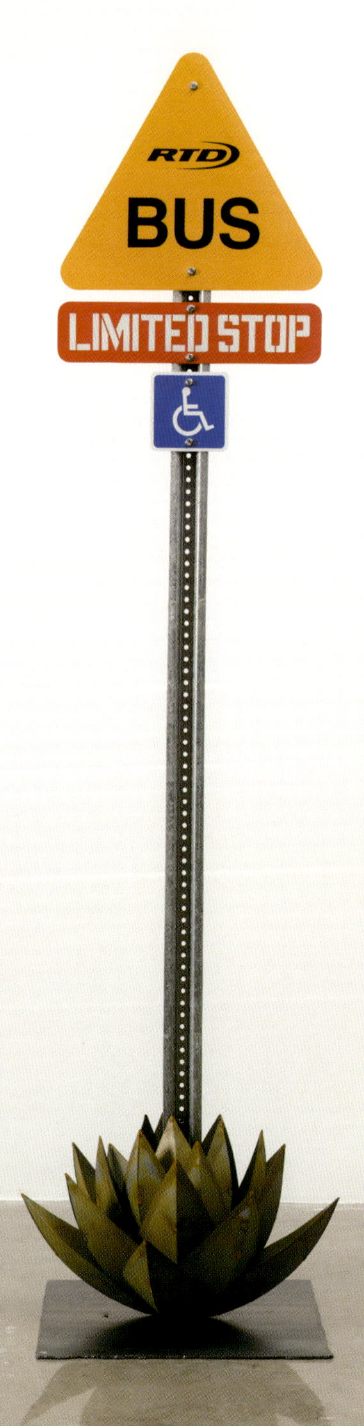

ARTW011b
American Artist, *To Acorn* (*1968*), 2022. Steel, acrylic, and hardware.
108 x 30 x 30 in.

Photograph of Los Angeles bus stop sign, ca. 1960.

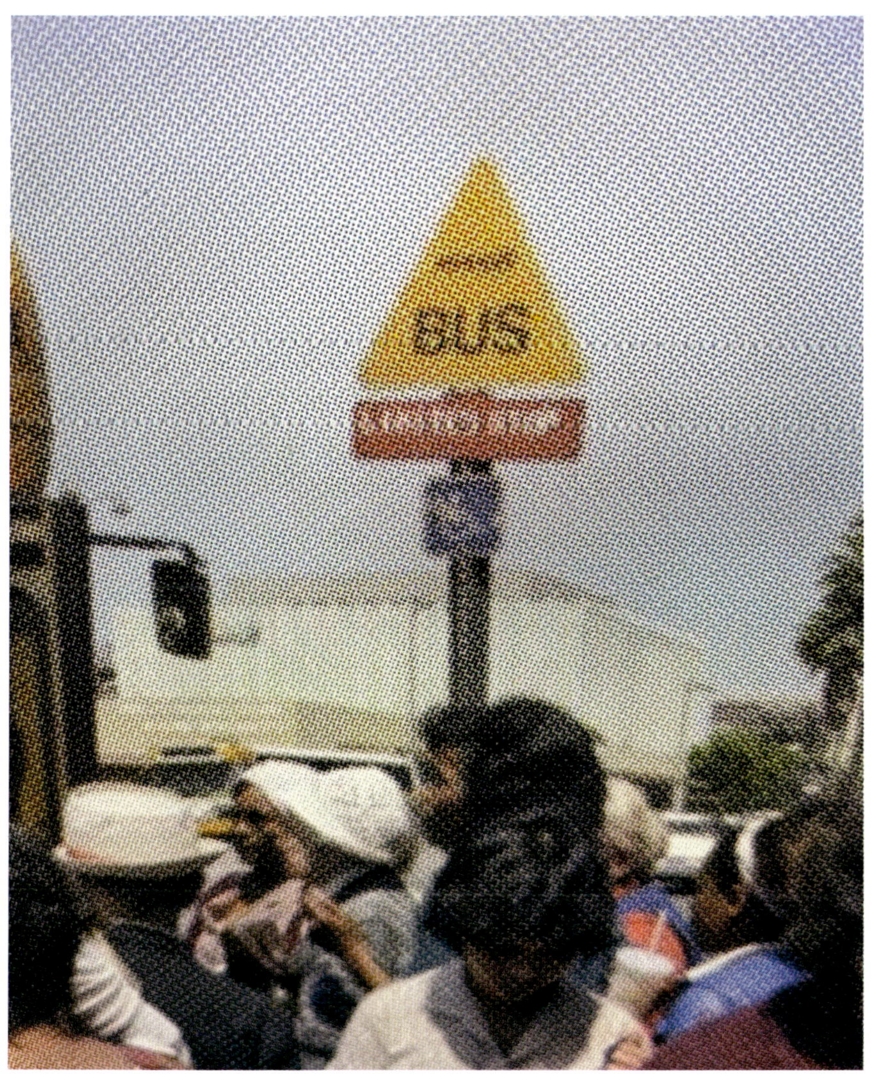

The Los Angeles Public Library burning, on April 29, 1986. Ben Martin/The LIFE Images Collection/Getty Images.

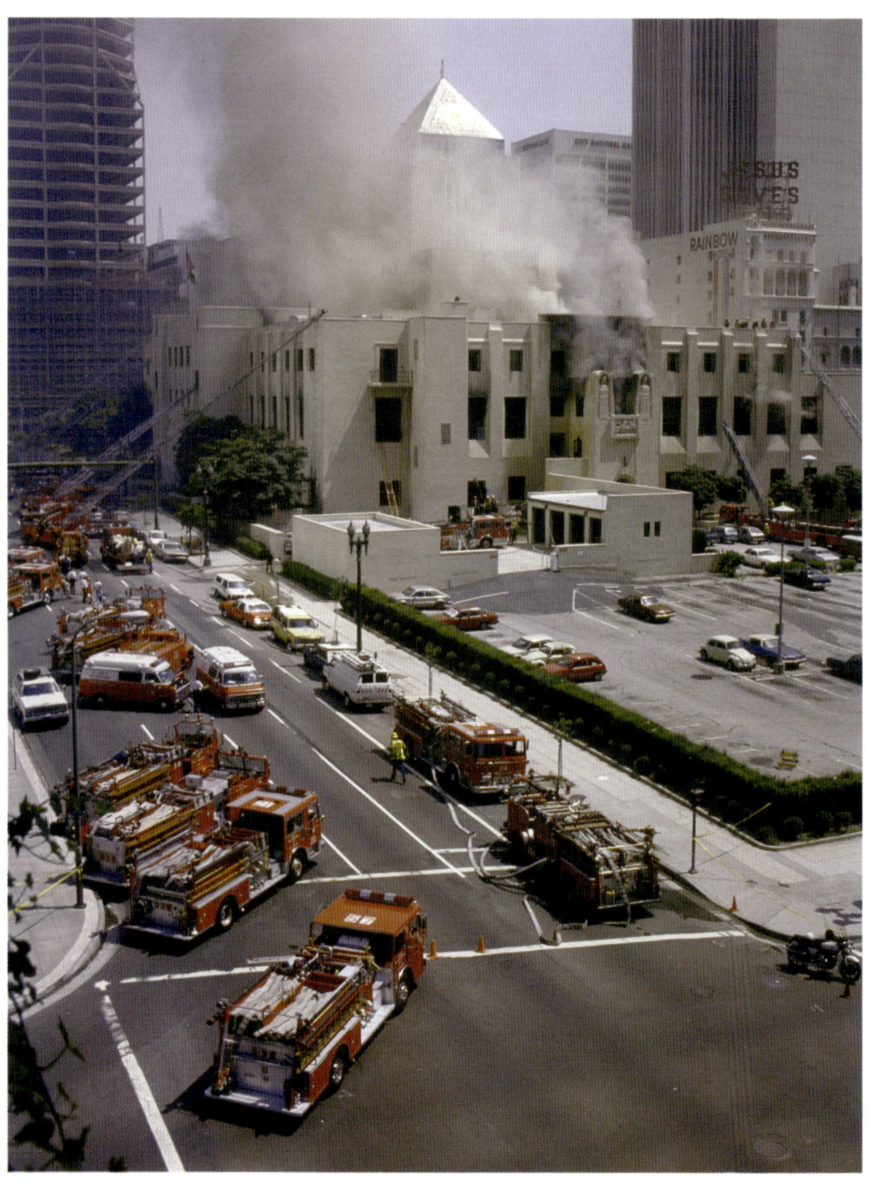

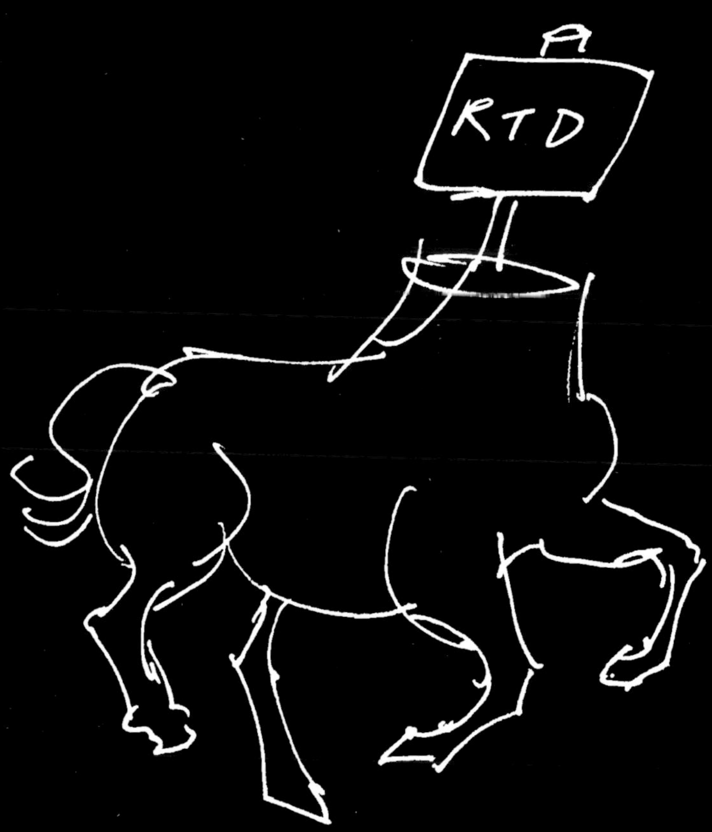
A
RTD

PLACES BUTLER & FAMILY LIVED:
- LOUISIANA
- ALTADENA
- PASADENA
- SEATTLE
- LOS ANGELES
- VICTORVILLE

PLACES BUTLER WORKED & RESEARCHED:
- PASADENA LIBRARY
- LA LIBRARY
- MARYLAND
- MACCHU PICCHU
- CLARION, PENNSYLVANIA

PLACES BUTLER'S CHARACTERS WENT:
- ROBLEDO
- ALTADENA
- ARIZONA
- FORSYTH
- MARYLAND
- ACORN
- ALASKA
- OREGON
- WASHINGTON

LOS ANGELES
PUBLIC LIBRARY
EXP.
49993249 01   01-18-94
OCTAVIA E BUTLER
475 E WASHINGTON BL #6
PASADENA   CALIF 91104
NONRESIDENT

Conversation between Joanne Garfield and Lauren Olamina in Octavia E. Butler, *Parable of the Sower*, 1993.

"'Someone's going to just smash in our wall and come in?' 'More likely blast it down, or blast the gate open. It's going to happen some day. You know that as well as I do.'"

Sketch of *Robledo Community Wall (Olamina cul-de-sac)* by American Artist, 2022.

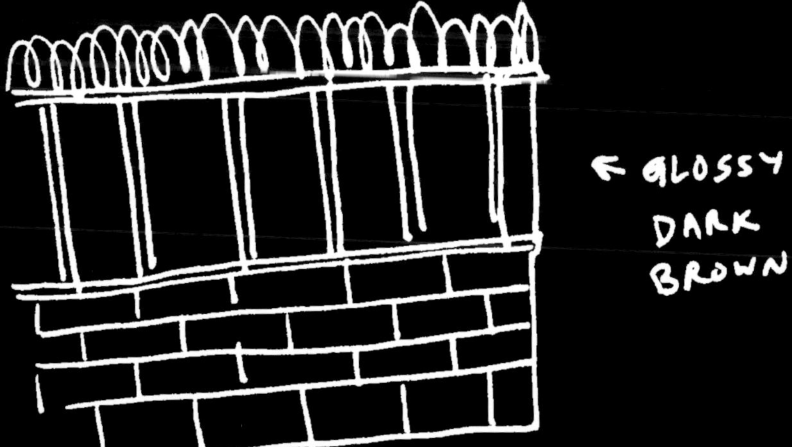

Sketch of *Robledo Community Wall* (*Olamina cul-de-sac*) by American Artist, 2022.

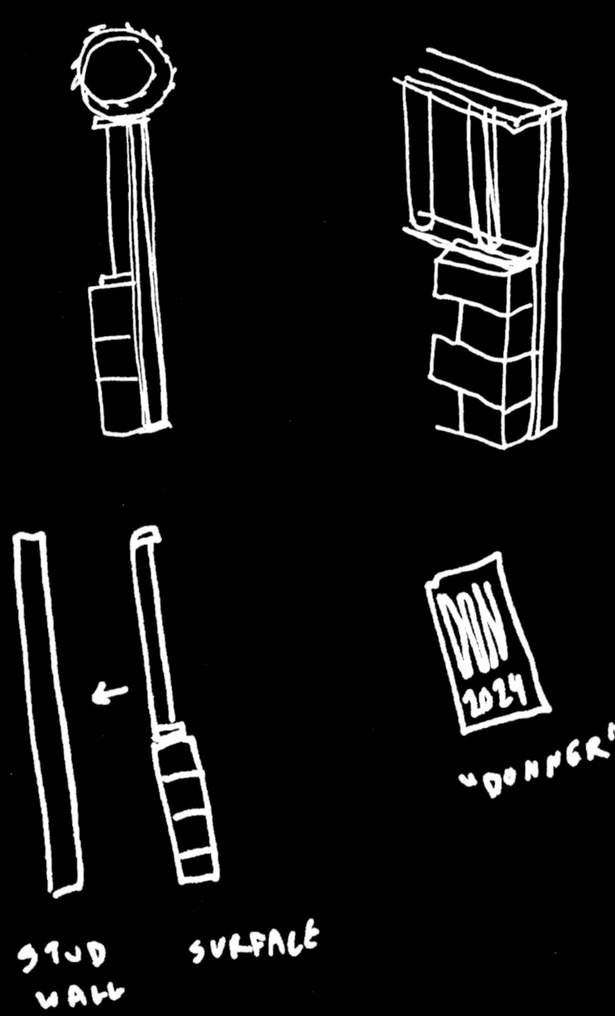

Text message between Chester Toye and American Artist, 2022.

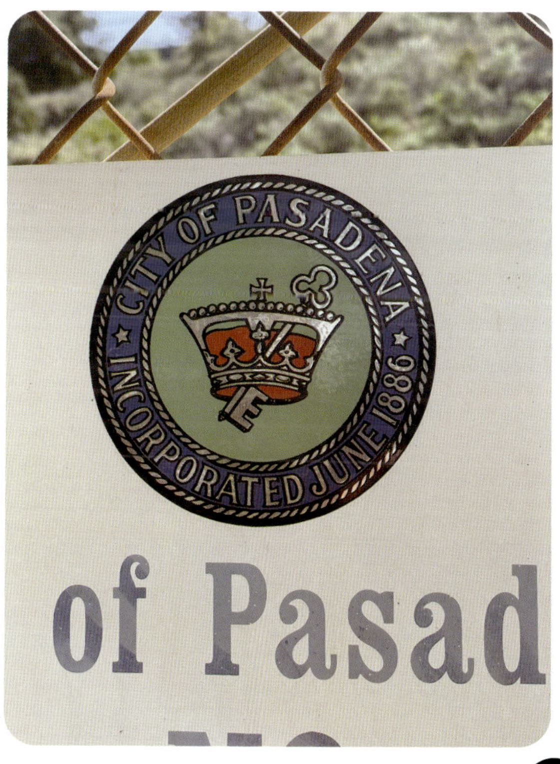

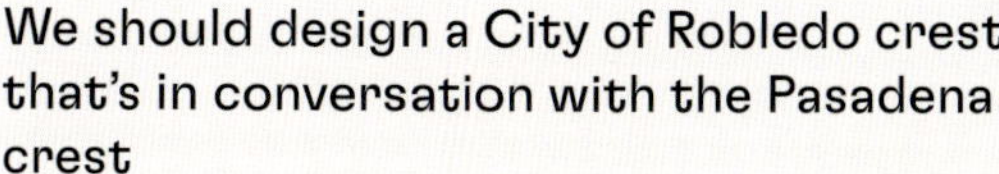

We should design a City of Robledo crest that's in conversation with the Pasadena crest

For Butler, place is also interior and relational, shaped by the intersections of race, class, and power. This is prominently reflected in the town of Robledo (another stand-in for Pasadena) in *Parable of the Sower* (1993) and *Parable of the Talents* (1998).

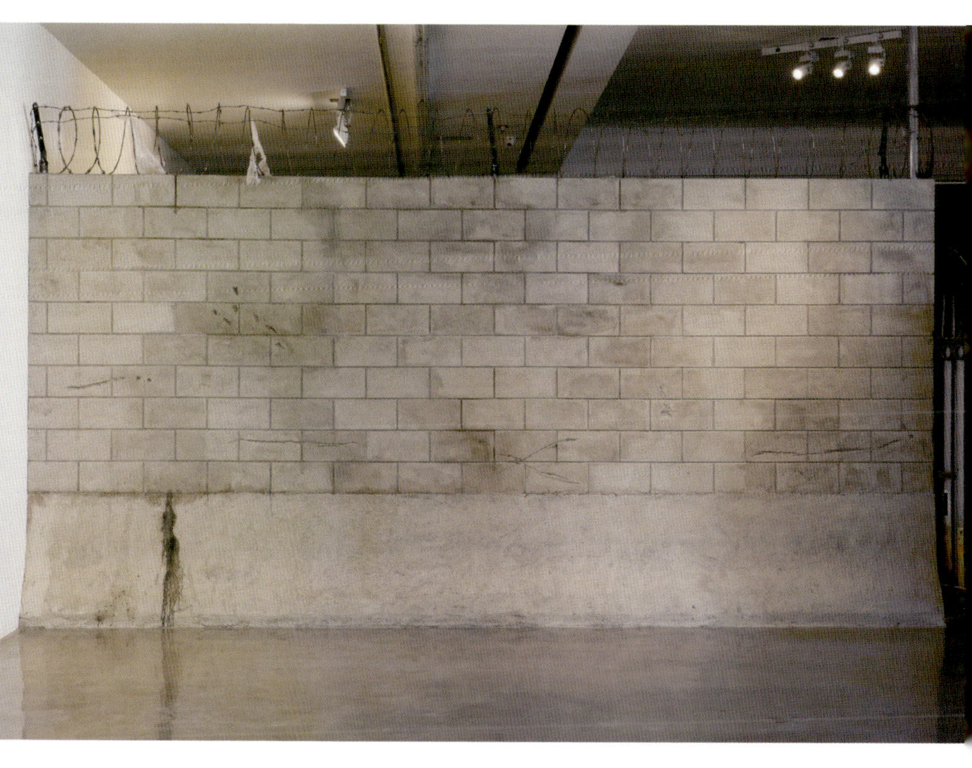

ARTW010a
American Artist,
Robledo Community Wall (*Olamina cul-de-sac*), 2022.
Steel, cement, stucco, wood, razor wire, paint.
Dimensions variable.

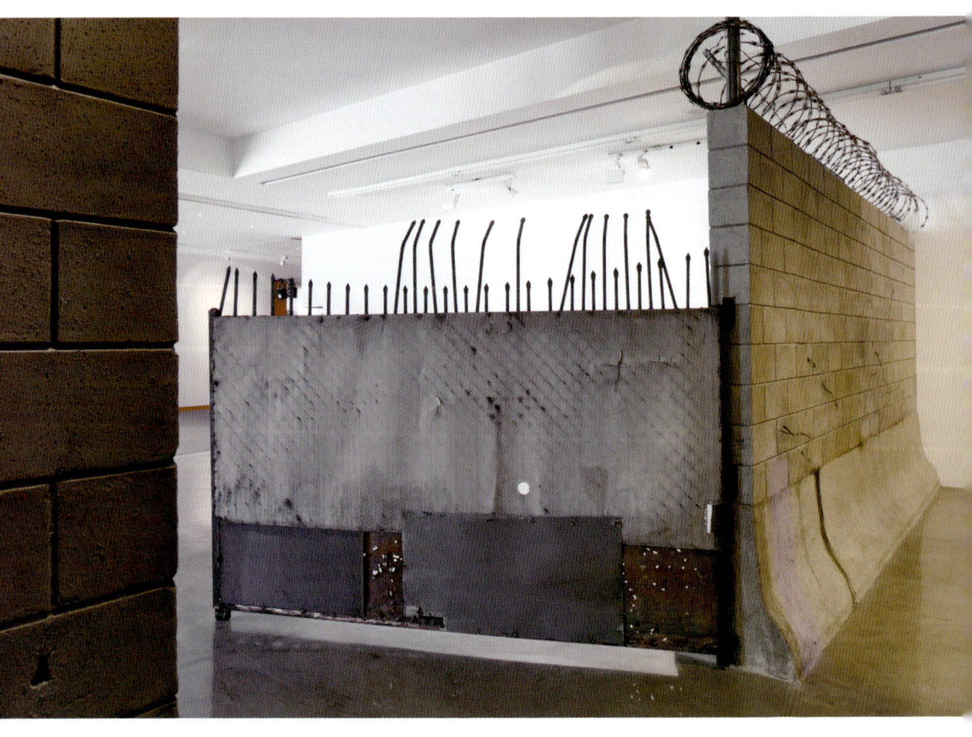

ARTW010b
American Artist,
*Robledo Community
Wall (Olamina
cul-de-sac)*, 2022.
Steel, cement, stucco,
wood, razor wire, paint.
Dimensions variable.

In these novels, a walled-in suburban cul-de-sac serves as the origin story for a group of refugees that must flee when their wall is knocked down by the unhoused walking poor outside.

Fabrication of Robledo Community Wall (Olamina cul-de-sac), 2022.

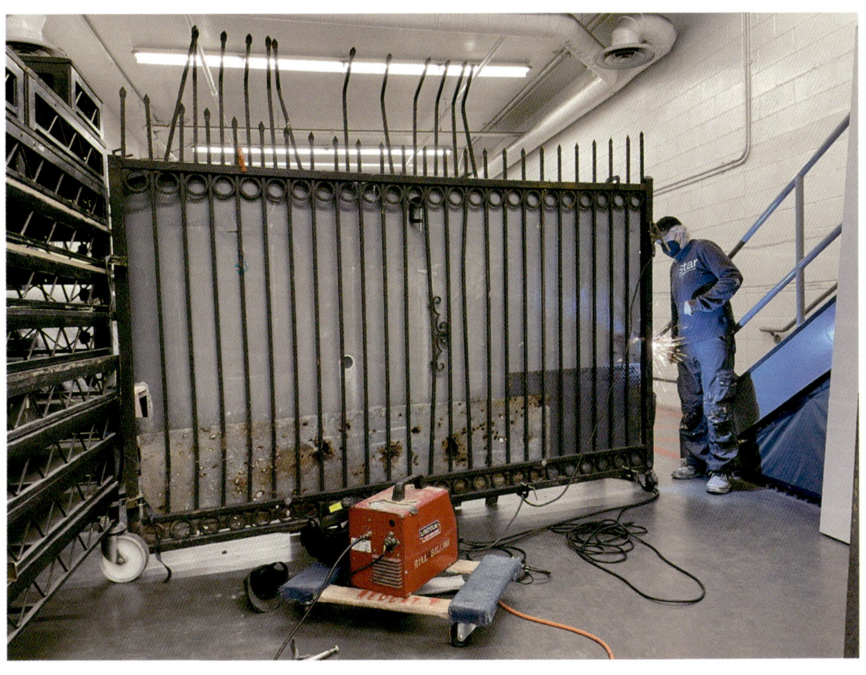

Sketch of Robledo Community Wall (Olamina cul-de-sac) by American Artist, 2022.

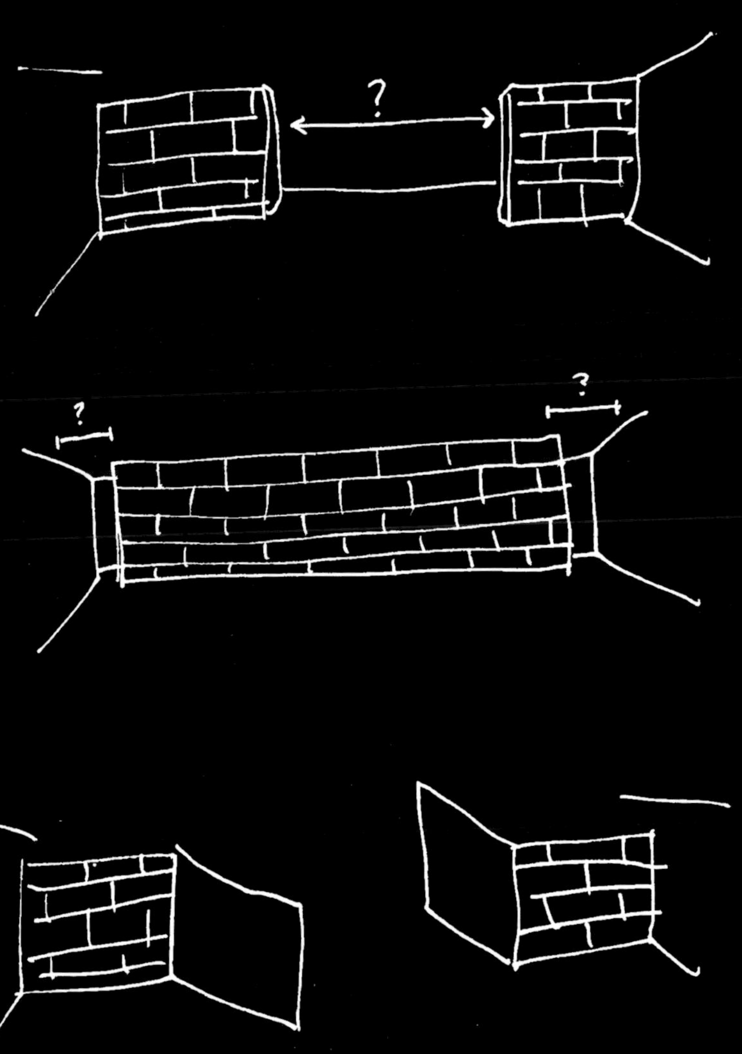

Sketch of *Robledo Community Wall* (*Olamina cul-de-sac*) by American Artist, 2022.

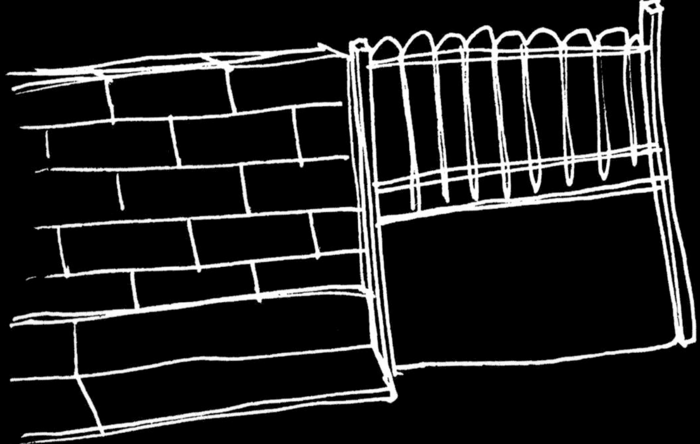

Steven Barnes, from the transcript of A-Team meeting hosted by Jet Propulsion Laboratory, organized by American Artist.

"If you take a look at the background in my picture, that is where Octavia lived most of the time that I knew her off of West Boulevard and Washington in Los Angeles. I didn't know her when she was living in Pasadena. When I think about Pasadena, I probably think of the Rose Parade more than anything else.**"**

Detail of The Huntington, "A Guide to Octavia E. Butler's Pasadena," 2022.

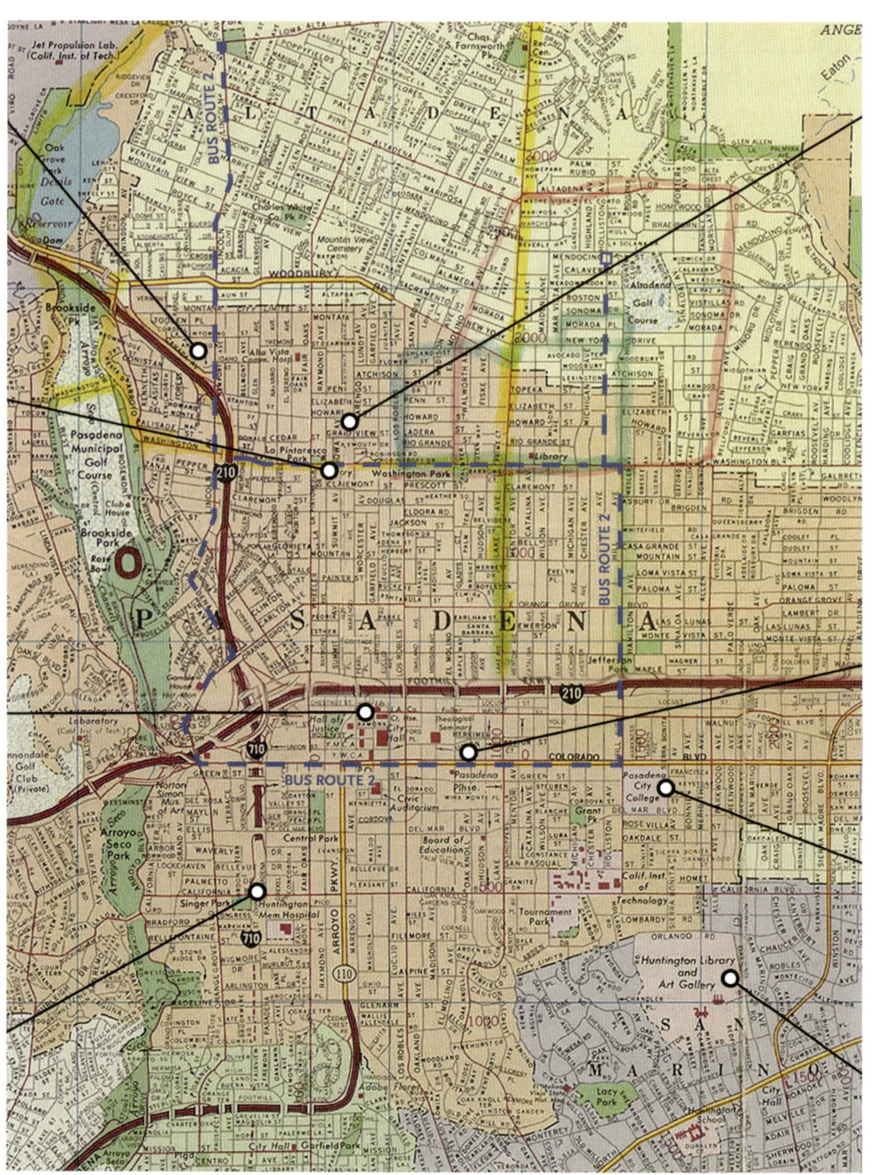

Illustration from Richard L. Morrill and O. Fred Donaldson, "Geographical Perspectives on the History of Black America," 1972.

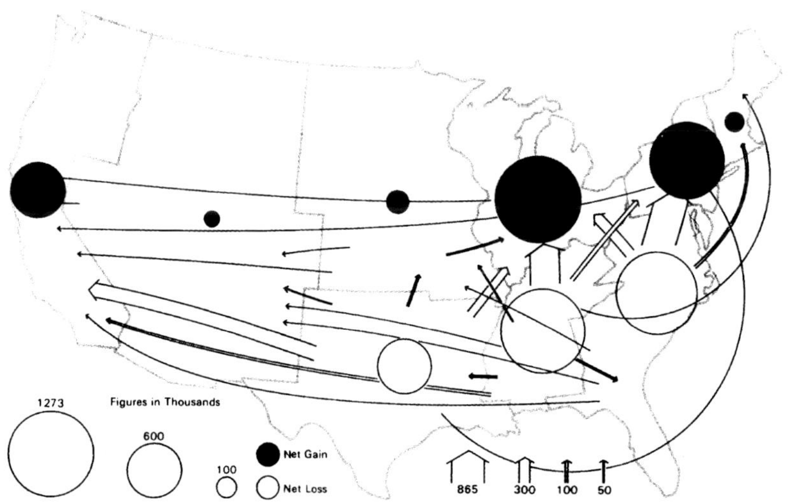

Fig. 11.   Lifetime migration of blacks to 1960.

She might ask herself in a journal, "What if I lived there?"—a prompt that reflects her broader inquiries into cyclical power dynamics, survival, and human resilience in the face of adversity, challenging one-sided narratives of upward mobility and progress.

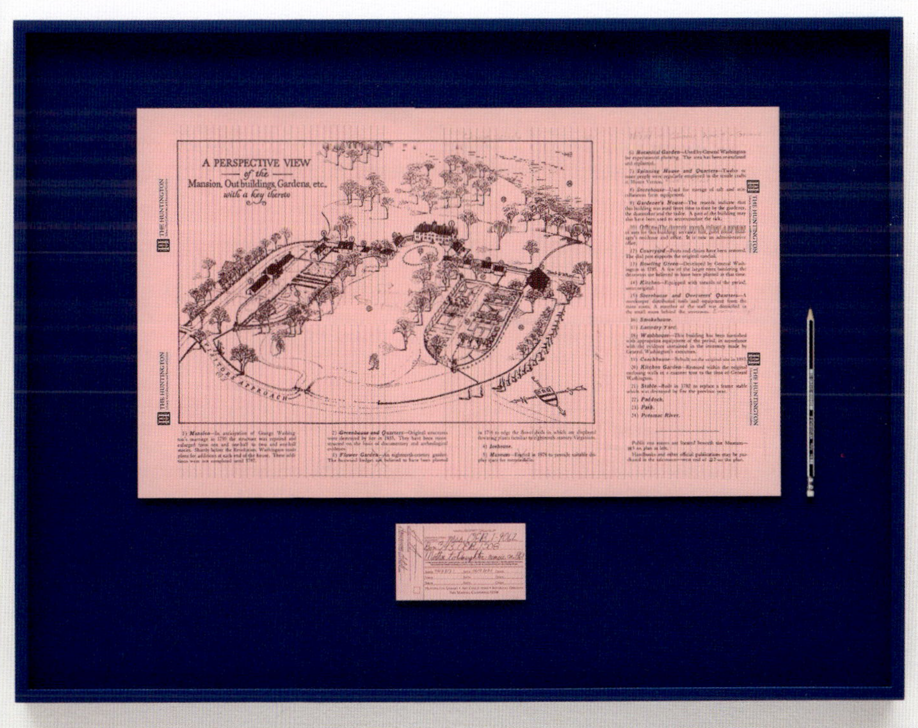

ARTW009
American Artist,
Octavia E. Butler Papers:
mssOEB 1-9062 II (*Waylin*
Plantation), 2022.
The Huntington
stationary, graphite,
pencil, felt.
26.5 x 36 x 1.5 in.

Science Fictions

by Lou Cournum

The following conversation between Lou Cornum and American Artist was originally published in *Art in America* on August 29, 2022.

Copyrighted © 2022. Penske Media Corporation.

1 In their exhibition, "Shaper of God," on view at REDCAT in Los Angeles from May 28 through October 2, 2022, American Artist probes the life of science fiction writer Octavia E. Butler (1947–2006). ²Both Butler and Artist grew up in the nearby town of Pasadena, and the show highlights how the novelist's imagined worlds were shaped by the environment they shared. ³The show includes two sculptures based on bus stops as they would have looked when Butler traveled from Pasadena to LA—the author never drove, she took the bus her whole life—alongside tracings Artist made of documents from her archive, housed at The Huntington Library in San Marino. ⁴One is a ca. 1993 note card on which Butler makes a prediction about Los Angeles in the 2020s, anticipating it will have more walled communities. ⁵Artist, who is based in New York and teaches at Yale, spoke with science fiction scholar Lou Cornum, a post-doctoral fellow at Wesleyan University, about how the imagining of other worlds is so often born of dissatisfaction with present and past ones.

American Artist

2 Octavia Butler and I went to the same high school. ²This got me thinking about what the Pasadena area means—socially, historically. ³My experience of the place came 50 years later, but seeing the same institutions—like Caltech and NASA's Jet Propulsion Laboratory—informed my thinking about what it means to aspire toward something like a scientifically engaged practice.

3 The centerpiece of my show is a wall that divides the space. [2]It's based on a wall that [protagonist] Lauren Olamina describes in Butler's book *Parable of the Sower* [1993]; the wall protects the cul-de-sac she lives in. [3]In the book, [which is set in the United States in 2024, after climate change and wealth inequality render it barely habitable] every neighborhood has its own defensive wall. [4]I wanted to bring that to life in the gallery. [5]Around that wall, there are some sculptures and reproductions of things I found in Butler's archive that speak not only to how she imagined the future, but also to her lived experience.

Lou Cornum

4 I often describe Butler as a theorist of power, because she is so interested in hierarchy. But your work also prompted me to consider her as a geographic theorist as well—she is always reflecting on changing landscapes. [2]The wall is reminiscent not only of the wall in *Parable of the Sower*, but also of the border wall and of prison walls. [3]I've been reading Ruth Wilson Gilmore's *Golden Gulag* [2007], a book about the explosion of mass incarceration and prison building in Southern California. [4]The state's prison population increased more than sevenfold between the 1980s and the mid-aughts. [5]Butler was writing right in the middle of that, and you can sense this in her gated communities, as well as in the other forms of enclosure that she describes.

AA

5　I love that you describe her as a theorist of power. ²Often, she would push against the reductive label of "science fiction," because she was really doing something much bigger—she was capturing and observing how various racial, social, and wealth dynamics play out. ³She described herself as a "news junkie." ⁴Really, she was extrapolating from what she saw going on around her.

6　I was definitely thinking about geography—the show includes a video, *The Arroyo Seco* [2022], about a stream that runs between Altadena, Pasadena, and La Cañada Flintridge. ²The stream has become degraded by parties like the Jet Propulsion Laboratory. ³Both Pasadena and Altadena want to claim the Arroyo Seco, but the video points out that it belonged to the Tongva people first. ⁴I'm showing the film on a window-like wall, referencing the home of a wealthy family in *Parable of the Sower*. ⁵Neighbors would watch the news through a window, from outside the rich peoples' house.

7　Often, natural resources become politicized, and can then be used to leverage power against different communities—usually Black, brown, or native—who are moved into areas that are subject to pollution or that have less proximity to certain resources. ²All these things come up in Butler's writing about walling off communities, which was informed by segregation in the city that she grew up in.

LC

8   This is particular to California, but also reminds me of the landscapes I grew up with in central Arizona; I'm familiar with water scarcity, and with extractive industries, like copper mining. ²California is interesting because it is so central to the American utopic imaginary—LA is the dream machine! There's CalTech and rocket science! You see those tensions in *Parable of the Sower*: Lauren is wandering through this dystopic landscape, yet she has a real utopic hope of humanity taking to the stars. ³She toggles between utopia and dystopia; both emerge from the same place.

AA

9   I struggle with that—so much of Butler's work is about coming together in a time of dystopia. ²I feel this in the communities that I find myself a part of, where Black, brown, queer, and Indigenous people are trying to create spaces that feel viable in the face of all we are dealing with. ³But the utopia her *Parables* imagine involves going to the stars, which I find hard to reconcile.

10   In *Parable of the Talents* [1998], as Lauren watches the first rocket ship leave Earth for the starship, which is named Christopher Columbus, she objects to the name and says the ship is not about a shortcut to riches and empire. ²It is not about snapping up slaves and gold and presenting them to some European monarch. ³You talk about this in your essay *Resurfaced Fragments from the Interplanetary Conference of Colonial Prehistorians on the Millennial of Christopher Columbus's Voyage to the Old New World.*

LC

11 I've thought a lot about the ending of *Parable of the Talents*! It shows that things that bring people together can also be really harmful. ²Butler says as much regarding a separate story, *The Monophobic Response* [1995]: she asks whether humans would unite if we were invaded by aliens. ³Would responding to an outside threat cause people to put aside all their deeply ingrained differences for a common cause?

12 She wrote *Parable of the Sower* 500 years after 1492. ²With that quincentenary in mind, Sylvia Wynter wrote *1492: A New World View*, prompting people to consider New World contact not just as something that occurred between the white explorer and the Indigenous subject, but that prepared the way for enslaved Africans to be brought to the Americas. ³I wrote about Octavia Butler in my dissertation because I was interested in under-considered entanglements between Black and Indigenous people in the US. ⁴I don't think it's a coincidence that the ship involved in what she calls "space colonization" is named Columbus. ⁵Racism and colonialism are always entangled, especially in the US, and Butler doesn't separate them. ⁶Yes, she was prophetic, but it's not like she had some magical power that is inaccessible to everyone else. ⁷She was just a student of history. ⁸When you study history deeply, you're better able to understand the present and extrapolate what might happen next.

13 In 2008, the European Space Agency launched Columbus, which is now the largest science lab on the International Space Station. ²That kind of shameless glorification of colonization looks exactly like what Elon Musk and Jeff Bezos are doing now. ³They imagine life on Mars as being good for all of humanity, but really, it stands to benefit a very small group of people—namely, them.

AA

14 Butler definitely helped start a conversation about how Black and Native people are similarly impacted by colonialism. ²She was always writing about people of many different backgrounds, exploring how their different ethnicities and power dynamics play out in complicated ways. ³In *Kindred* [1979], she describes different classes of Black people who are enslaved on one plantation. ⁴Part of why she is able to write in a nuanced way about all these different identities is, I think, because the neighborhood we both grew up in is very diverse. ⁵It was a Spanish colony, and the way that racism exists there is not just a Black and white issue. ⁶It is Asian, it's Latinx, it's Indigenous. ⁷That's not something that all Black writers address.

15 As I think about what it means to try to imagine a future as an artist, I find myself starting with these really fraught points in history, then trying to invert them. ²It's hard to imagine something completely new. ³Do you think imagination always starts as a response to frustrating moments in history, or is it possible to dream up things that are entirely new?

LC

16   That's exactly what draws me to science fiction. ²Butler said that, with the genre, she felt there was no human relation that she couldn't explore. ³Science fiction presents the challenge to think of something new, but really, it often creates a future that is a strange version of the present, offering a critique of the way things are. ⁴This gets coupled with experiments in world-building. ⁵Sci-fi provides the chance to play things out and explore the domino effects. ⁶There are drafts of *Parable of the Trickster*—maybe you came across them in the archive. ⁷It would have been the third book in the series, but it was never finished. ⁸Butler tried out various scenarios, imagining the different ways things might play out when we actually get to the Moon or Mars. ⁹Many of them end terribly. ¹⁰She'd say she was a pessimist, and if she wasn't careful, she'd keep finding endings that revolve around the destructive tendencies of humans. ¹¹She finds herself asking, what if we did become an interplanetary species, but were still stuck with our hierarchies? I wonder if she felt that *Parable of the Trickster* reached the limits of "what if."

17   The story "Bloodchild" [1995] has plenty of relationships involving domination, but a new kind of interaction between humans and aliens also emerges: they mate, as they do in Butler's *Xenogenesis* trilogy [1987–89]. ²I find this account of the creation of new things to be some of her most hopeful writing. ³Humans need an encounter with radical difference in order to generate new forms of relating to each other. ⁴It's not a happy process, but revolutionary change involves sacrifice. ⁵She takes it to the extreme—the change isn't just social, but biological. ⁶That makes me wonder, how far do we have to go to realize something truly new?

AA

18 I sometimes crave science fiction that might help us imagine a society where people aren't, say, punitive and carceral. ²I don't mean stories that are ignorant of these problems, but ones that ask, what if we didn't have this history? Whereas I think Butler's work sees these power dynamics as intrinsic to humanity.
19 What did you think about NASA recently naming their Mars rover touchdown site the Octavia E. Butler Landing?

LC

20 It's cool to see so many people engaging her work these days, but I worry if that was the tipping point. ²What does it mean for NASA, which is so intertwined with the military-industrial complex, to co-opt her utopic visions? I want her to be a celebrated figure, but at what cost?

AA

21 I'm also excited that she is being celebrated, but it's scary to watch the things she warned against unfold, then get named after her. ²It's odd that they were able to make her seem aligned with something we know she was fundamentally opposed to. ³I also worry that people just get excited about space and aliens, and about this Black woman sci-fi writer, without realizing that her stories are really hard and painful.

LC
22   Her growing popularity is all the more reason why we need guidance in reading her, so I'm glad your exhibition explores where she's coming from and what she is speaking to. ²She wasn't just this once-in-a-lifetime clairvoyant thinker, but someone responding to a specific context.

Section III juxtaposes Octavia E. Butler's exploration of space—particularly through the religious community Earthseed in *Parable of the Sower*—with Pasadena's history of rocket science and a contemporary private space race led by figures like Elon Musk and Jeff Bezos. This section draws parallels between Butler's speculative vision and real-world efforts to leave Earth behind, offering a thought-provoking take on the concept of "destiny" and who gets to shape it.

Section III

The only lasting truth
is Change.

[183]

Prodigal

by Alexis Pauline Gumbs

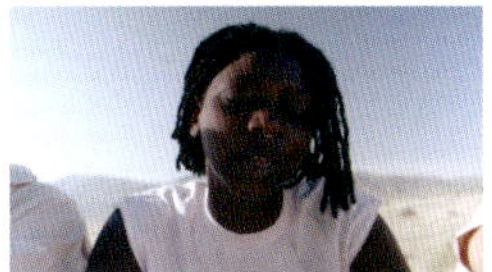

ARTW015d [255]

1   Octavia E. Butler explores multiple contexts of difference through the intimate lives and decisions of her Black female protagonists: the power of dreams, shapeshifting, and apocalyptic response. [2]In the short story "The Book of Martha," a Black woman writer has a meeting with God—who eventually appears to her as a Black woman—where she is given the opportunity to change the world for all humanity in one small way: by giving people richer, more satisfying dreams. [3]In the *Patternist* series, Anyanwu, an African shapeshifter with healing powers, becomes entangled with Doro, a body-jumper who breeds her family members and exploits their powers. [4]In the *Parable* series, a teenage prophet named Lauren Oya Olamina creates a religion and a movement amid apocalyptic crises, centered on a proactive relationship to change.

2   In the story that follows, I add another layer to Butler's exploration of otherness—another possibility for dreaming, new variations on the human, and different ways of relating to change: *sisterhood from a distance*. [2]This story weaves together three timelines and imagines: What if Lauren Oya Olamina had a sister unknown to her through her father, who lived through the same apocalyptic times? [3]A sister who was also the daughter of Martha, in a universe where Martha is of Anyanwu's lineage. [4]Through the lens of sistering obstructed by patriarchy and the lens of fierce daughtering, I ask: What if another powerful being traveled parallel to Lauren, influenced by Anyanwu and raised by Martha? [5]What might her perspective teach us about the rigorous healing possibilities of another world?

3   He didn't have a choice. ²Mama says that's why Baba came back. ³We were his last resort. ³And then she laughed. ⁴Because resort used to mean something else.

4   I knew about my father from my mother's derisive laughter, the photos I found under her bed. ²The letters I taught myself to read on. ³The sweet words I carried forward in one cheek, like a secret. ⁴Mama didn't believe in sweet anymore. ⁵At least, that's what I thought.

5   Until he came home.

✻

6   I didn't hear about my brothers until my father came back, but I always knew about my sister. ³I would name my dolls Lauren. ⁴Talk to Lauren where my mom wouldn't hear. ⁵When she caught me, she would lecture me about how I shouldn't treasure the name of someone who didn't know me. ⁶Who would never know me. Who could never know me because my father kept us a secret. ⁷*And wasn't it humiliating*, she would ask me, *that it doesn't matter what we know?* ⁸That nobody protects us. ⁹That we have to pretend not to exist, all so he can be Reverend Olamina.

7   *Yes.* ²I would say. ³*Of course, Mama.* ⁴I would say. ⁵*I understand Mama.* ⁶I would say it every time.

8   But I never believed it. ²We do exist. ³And in the world I was born into, it's always better to be the one who knows. ⁴The one who knows more.

✻

9 It was an ordinary day. ²But I guess it usually is when everything changes. ³No one had bothered us or stopped too long outside our barricaded apartment door. ⁴I was falling asleep over my journal when we heard the banging. ⁵As usual, I rushed to the back bedroom, grabbed the knife and ducked into the bathtub. ⁶As usual, Mama crouched below the window with the gun.

10 Over the loud sound of our stillness, I heard something I had never heard anyone say: the name from the letters. ²My mother's true name.

11 *Martha.*

*

12 *Baby.* ²My mother called. ³Come help. ⁴She had started moving boards and broken furniture away from the door. ⁵Help me move this stuff, she said again. ⁶I hadn't realized I was standing still. ⁷Dizzy with six letters. ⁸My mother's name. ⁹The secret code.

*

13 We pushed everything aside and opened the front door for the first time in so long. ²We usually left through windows, in case someone was watching to see if anyone was home. ³He staggered in—the man everyone else called Reverend Olamina. ⁴Mama called him his name from before all that. ⁵*Jesus*, she said. ⁶*Mark.*

14 He was mumbling. ¹*I'm sorry.* ²*I know I said I wouldn't ever.* ³*I just...* ⁴He was holding his side. ⁵When he moved his hand, we saw the blood. ⁶Mama pointed and I grabbed the salve, the cloths, the boiled rainwater. ⁷She led him to what had been my pallet on the floor and cleaned his wound. ⁸Tied rags around it. ¹⁵*Put your hands right here*, she said. ⁹*I can't.*

15   She went in the other room, but I knew what she was saying as she paced back and forth.

16   *Motherfucker.* ²*Look who he's still protecting.* ³*He couldn't risk whoever did this following him home.* ⁴*But who cares if they trace his blood tracks here.*

17   I put her pain out of mind. ²It only works if you access love. ³"This is Lauren's father." ⁴I repeated to myself over and over again. ⁵It only works if you access love—that's what my mother told me because that's what her mother told her. ⁶But when I taught my daughter I would say it more simply: "Think about something you want."

*

18   I slept in my mother's bed that night, wading through her thick-ass dreams. ²Waking up listening for the strange man's breathing. ³Healing is consensual. ⁴After my healing, he could definitely live on, but only if he wanted to. ⁵"Live," I whispered. ⁶"Live, live, live, live."

19   I was sitting beside him at first light as he opened his eyes. ²I said the words before he blinked once. ³"Tell me everything about Lauren."

20   It took him a while. It took him a while to heal. ²Was that my fault? ³Because I wanted him to stay around? ⁴It took him a while to open up to me about Lauren. ⁵At first, he only told me boring facts—how she taught the kids, how great she was at making acorn bread, how she was learning to shoot. ⁶And I savored them, because it was more than my mother let slip. ⁷At the time, I couldn't compare what he said then—when he still thought he had a real home to go to—with the depth he'd reveal after he gave up. ⁸He only told me the good stuff after the fire.

✳

21   When it became clear that he would never be going back to that burnt down cul-de-sac, he walked back and forth in our small living room in a daze. ²*Lauren was right*, he said to himself—or so he thought. ³I was sitting there with my journal. ⁴That's when I learned about her hyper-empathy, that she shared feelings but she couldn't control it. ⁵They thought hers was a drug side effect from his first wife—my mother's college roommate.

22   So my mother was right. ²My powers came through her and Grandma Ann. ³No, he wasn't magical. ⁴My mother had told me years ago. ⁵*No.* ⁶*He wasn't magical.* ⁷*Only beautiful.*

23   The last thing he finally admitted was that Lauren didn't believe the way he did. ²She had another idea about God. ³He was mourning, so he rambled out everything. ⁴Her secret notebook. ⁵Her cache of supplies. ⁶He thought he had left her there to die, but I had a sense—a sense worth trusting—that she was out there somewhere alive.

24   Eventually he wandered off. ²We lost track of him again. ³But this time, I had what I needed.

✳

25   For days, my mother looked towards the window. ²As if he would ever come back. ³I curled up to her. ⁴"I just feel so grateful," I said.

26   She turned. ²*For what?* ³She said into the top of my head.

27   "To have the mother I have," I whispered. ²She held me tightly like she could pull the sweetness of my words into her. ³I knew she believed me. ⁴Even though she knew what sweet could do.

✳

28   I named my daughter Marvelline because I loved that core sound of my mother's name. ²But I kept myself looking young, so in just a few years, everyone started to believe she was my sister. ³Being a mother out here? ⁴They see it as a weakness. ⁵But no one really wants to fight with sisters.

29   *What should we name her?* ²Marvelline asked me when I handed her her first baby daughter. ³My grand. ⁴By this time, we had left the apartment. ⁵We lived in a vault at the bottom of what used to be the library. ⁶I thought about it for less than a minute. ⁷"Imara."

30   Marvelline was probably too sweet for her own good, but she could get a man to do anything just by blinking twice. ²And so I always had reports on where Lauren was. ³What she and her people were doing. ⁴Marvelline would send her help in little ways. ⁵Small enough that Lauren wouldn't notice.

31 But Imara. ²Imara was my little researcher. ³The connections she made between the scraps of books that had survived the many fires? ⁴Brilliant. ⁵I told her everything I told her mother about Sister Lauren. ⁶But she did more with it than Marvelline had. ⁷I think she could sense her in the way that I could.

32 *Sister Lauren's famous, Grandma,* she told me one day when she was just a kid. ²*She created a cult called Earthseed.* ³*Remember you said she had another God?*

33 "Yes baby," I said. ²"Keep digging."

34 I still remember the day Imara, as a teenager, came to me almost shaking. ²*Grandma, Sister Lauren has a daughter.* ³She knew what to do, but she waited for me to say.

35 "Good job sweetheart." ²I smiled. ³"Find her."

36 *Grandma,* Imara said finally, when she was a grown woman and I was almost ready to stop living. ²*Sister Lauren's people are going up to space.*

37 "My sugar. ²Go. ³And remember what I told you."

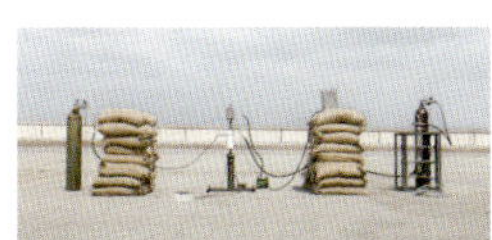

ARTW016a [245]

38 *Yes Grandma, I remember: They may have their God, but we have our hands.*

[193]

The Meaning of Everything

by Alexis Pauline Gumbs

1 First, she bought her mother a house. ²So be it. ³See to it! ⁴Now, she has a claim on Mars in her mother's name, which is also her own name. ⁵Mostly. ⁶Octavia Estelle Butler has shaped how generations of visionaries think about outer space, alien possibility, and the future. ⁷Her experience as an outsider—too poor, too Black, too tall, too feminist, too smart—led her to theorize how the society she was born into relates to otherness. ⁸She called it "the monophobic response." ⁹In her fiction, Butler offered us all ample evidence of how characters relate to difference: alien species, humans transformed by pharmaceuticals and viruses, alternate timelines, shapeshifters, genetic outliers, changing climates, other worlds.

2 And here is where we meet back up with the literal. ²Octavia Butler, the consummate "other," now stands as a representative of the United States space program's early efforts to colonize Mars. ³This does not resolve the contradictions of colonialism, nor the desperation of a species that has failed so deeply to maintain right relationships with all other life on earth that its billionaires now seek to escape it. ⁴But it does invite us to bring the questions of Octavia's work—and the critiques of BIPOC visionaries who resonate most with her work—into the conversation about space travel and planetary claims.

3 This story imagines Octavia Butler meeting Edwin Hubble—a white male astronomer whose name lives on due to the US space program naming the first space telescope after him—at the archives of The Huntington in San Marino, California, where both their papers now reside. ²It is one part of my ongoing process

ARTW015a [67]

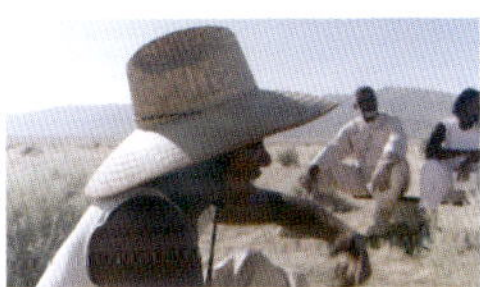

ARTW002b [67]

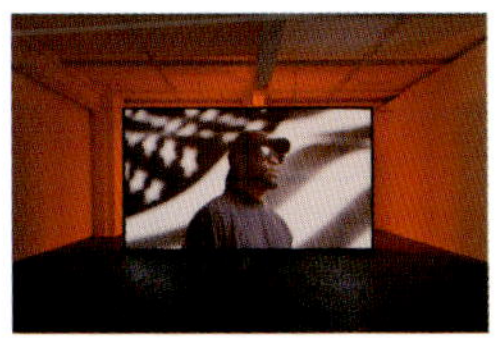

ARTW002a [67]

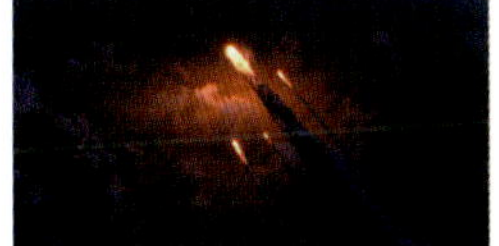

of listening to the dead, who still remain. ³May it provoke conversations among the living.

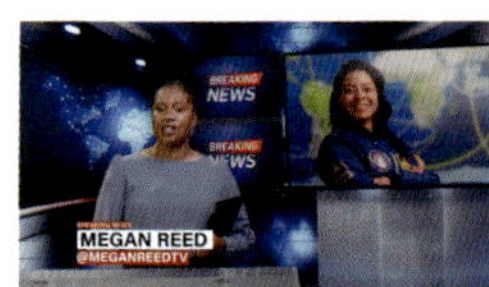

ARTW001a [239]

*

4   *Scene: Octavia E. Butler and Edwin Hubble meet in the hall of The Huntington's archives.*
5   "Habit."
6   That's the first word she actually heard him say the thousandth time they passed each other in The Huntington halls before dawn.
7   "What?" She asked, finally baited by one of her key words. ²Habit over inspiration was her warning, her advice to the aspiring writers she chose to haunt. ³Don't wait to be inspired. ⁴Develop a habit.
8   "Habit," he repeated. ²"I guess it's those all-night sessions with the telescope up the hill that keep me roaming these hallways until dawn. ³What's your excuse?"
9   The presumption. ²The familiarity. ³No one tells you how when you live in the archives your sense of smell heightens. ⁴You become attuned to the nuances of dust. ⁵Octavia could smell the remnants of his slaveholding, "Indian War"-fighting ancestors from one hundred linear feet away. ⁵That's why she had pretended not to see him every early morning until now.

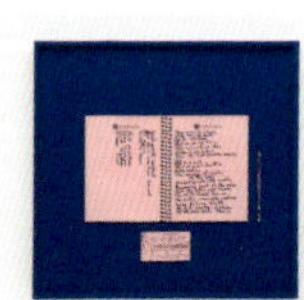

ARTW006 [67]

10   He kept talking. ²Maybe to ease his own spectral nerves. ³"Hale, the guy who built the telescope, used to call it 'the monastery.' ⁴No nuns though. ⁵It was all men back then, so I can't claim a double entendre." ⁶He chuckles. ⁷"You're a writer. Right?"
11   Octavia cleared her throat. ²She could have listed her awards. ³She could have asked if he hadn't seen the pictures sent back from

that orbiting telescope named after him. ⁴The ones of the landing on Mars named after *her*. ⁵Not because she cared, but because that's how you have to deal with these entitled pricks who know exactly which of their ancestors fought in the American Revolution.

12 She surprised herself. ²Maybe it was because she knew families like his. ³Pasadena intellectuals—her mother had worked in their homes. ⁴She had grown up here, too. ⁵Close enough to L.A. to recognize a fake.

13 "I thought you would have a British accent," she sneered. ²²"They say the Rhodes Scholarship never relinquished your throat."

14 He coughed. She could see embarrassment on his face, but just underneath it, pride. ³As unflattering as it was in retrospect, he was pleased that she knew this detail about his life.

15 "Yes. ³Well. ⁴It expired. ⁵That anglophile thing only impressed people for a season. ⁶I'm one of those people who catches accents more than I catch feelings. ⁷Now I'm afraid I sound like the millennials who sort the papers here." ⁸Was he smiling?

16 So then she knew. ²He wasn't like some of the other ghosts here—the scientists who orbited the dry samples from their lab notebooks, happy enough to stay close to the work. ³He moved throughout the entire space, like she did. ⁴Staying current. ⁵And therefore he must have known exactly who she was—The Huntington's Black beacon of relevance, beaming the smug endowment into further fundability in the twenty-first century. ⁶That was her short afro on the banners on the garden paths leading to the entrance. ⁷Her open journals color-copied and blown up on the walls. ⁸The panels and art exhibits and eager stream of researchers—it was because death had not stopped her from achieving her goal of becoming a *New York Times* bestselling author right when the world needed her apocalyptic novels most. ⁹Was she smiling? ¹⁰They were both tall but she felt taller. ¹¹With the launch of the newer, better James Webb satellite telescope last year was anyone even ever saying "Hubble"?

17　　Secretly she had compared herself with the noted astronomer more than with the naturalists or even the other literary figures in the vault. ²Most days, in her own estimation, she won. ³Not only because she was more famous now, but because of the details. ⁴She had bought her mother a house. ⁵He had abandoned his family of origin completely, leaving a younger brother to provide for his many sisters and his mother after their father died. ⁶She was buried in nearby Mountain View Cemetery, with her mother Octavia the first. ⁷He never even had a funeral, just a swift cremation and there was no burial monument to him anywhere at all. ⁸His biographers said he cut his family off as soon as he moved out west so that no one could refute the lies he told about practicing law before giving it all up for astronomy. ⁹Fighting on the frontlines in World War I when in truth he had never seen battle. ¹⁰And far too many stories of jumping into far too many bodies of water to save a ridiculous amount of drowning women while their far too grateful husbands were far too often right there. ¹¹It was no wonder that he trained his telescope not at the stars but at the vague nebulae beyond them. ¹²It was no wonder that even his tribute telescope was floating nearly obsolete in space.

18　　But sometimes she wondered what it would have been like to sit all night inside the

ARTW001b [67]

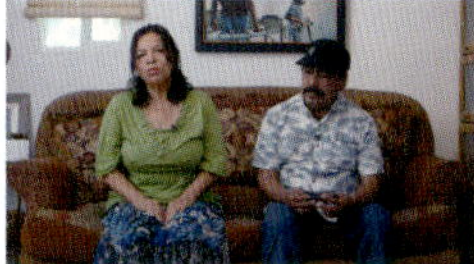

biggest telescope on Earth traveling further and further back in time, charting star after star trying to reach the beginning of the universe. [2]What if someone had paid *her* to stargaze? [3]Her habit for early mornings came from what poverty required—writing in the dark before her factory shift.

19 Did he compare himself to her too? [2]Rifle through her audacious manuscripts of telepathy and shapeshifting, time travel and interplanetary life and think back on his tentative science papers, in which he was careful to emphasize that he was only reporting what his pictures showed. [3]He wasn't even making the claims that other scientists used his work to argue. [4]He never admitted whether or not he believed in an expanding universe with infinite galaxies. [5]He was just documenting what he saw. [6]Justifying his own need to keep looking. [7]Was he jealous of how people all over the world started their days with her guidance, held her books like Bibles, spoke her name like an incantation, while even the physicists who used "Hubble's constant" associated his name more with the rubble of outdated twentieth-century technology.

20 "One question," they both said at the same time, surprising the silence of the marble floors. [2]The exit lights blinked.

21 "What did you want?" [2]"What were you afraid of?"

22 They said it at the same time. [2]Sure like thick file folders landing in unison on a reading room desk.

23 "Everything."

24 Each morning after that, when they passed each other in the time of deep purple sky, under the vaulted ceilings of the old library, they nodded, almost imperceptibly. [2]And kept on.

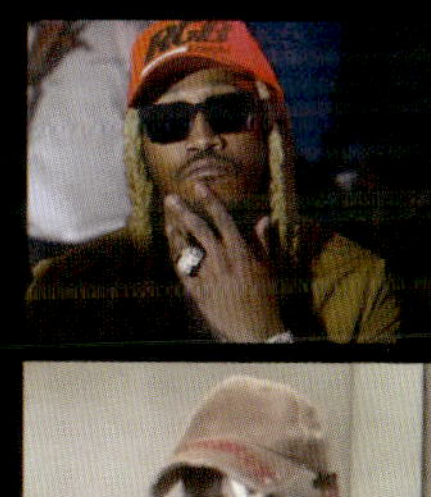
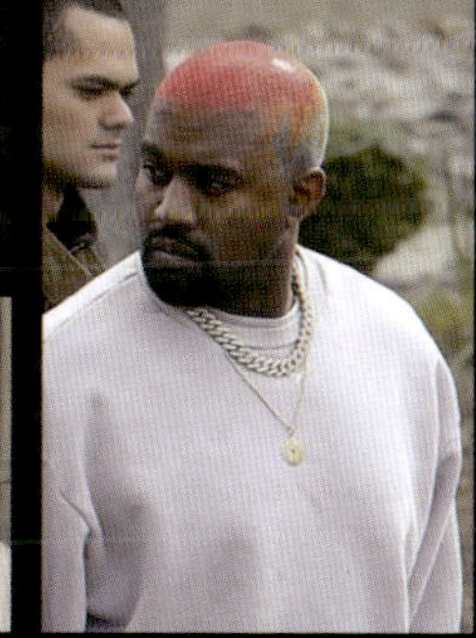
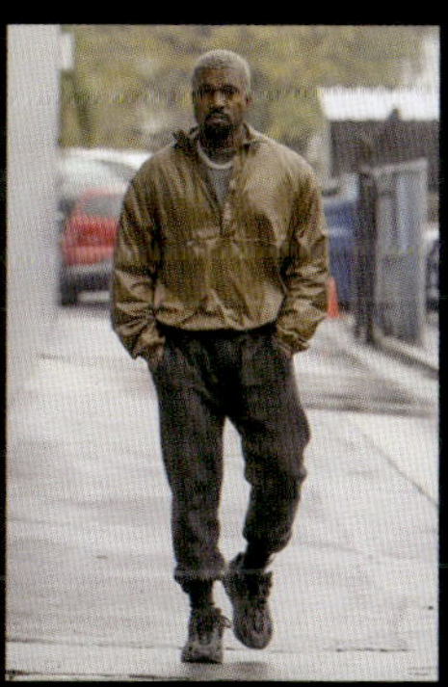

Casting Call-Shaper of God Film:
President Donner

(Black, mid 40s): rapper/entrepreneur/free thinker,
stylish, and esoteric enough to run
for president. Based on fictional character
Christopher Donner in Octavia Butler's novel
Parable of the Sower

Project shoots 1 day during weekend of August 25th (PAID)

shaperofgod2024@gmail.com

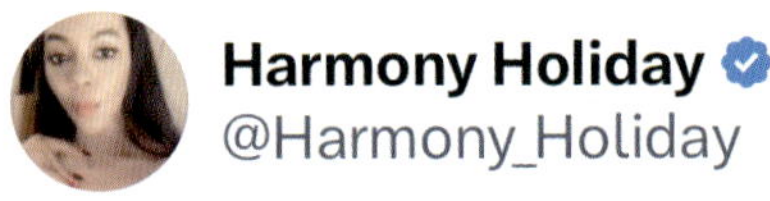

Harmony Holiday ✓
@Harmony_Holiday

The best question in the world was asked by Sun Ra when he asked: What are the black purposes of space travel?

3:46 PM · 7/16/23 · **3.7K** Views

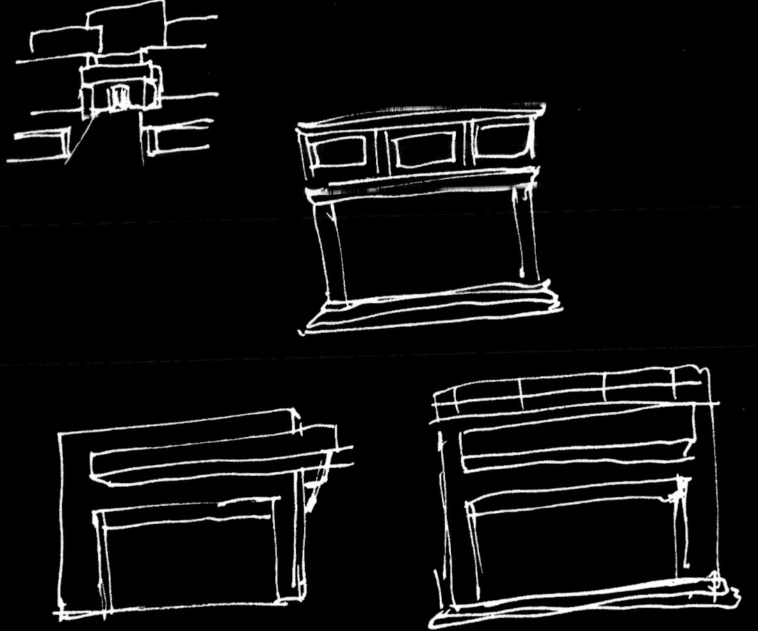

Sketch of California-style windows by American Artist, 2023.

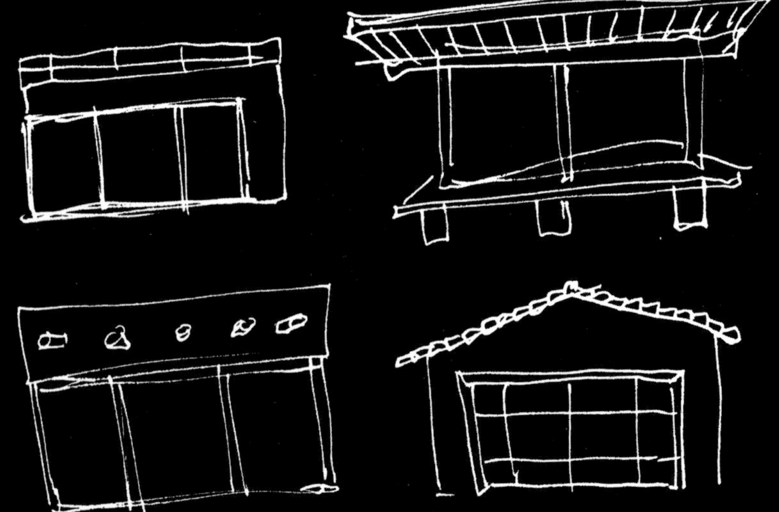

"The space program that drove so many pioneers to explore outerspace, is something we cannot afford to do any longer, while so many of our people, living, breathing, working and building on earth are in need of saving."

This does not resolve the
contradictions of colonialism,
nor the desperation of a species
that has failed so deeply to
maintain right relationships with
all other life on earth that its
billionaires now seek to escape it.

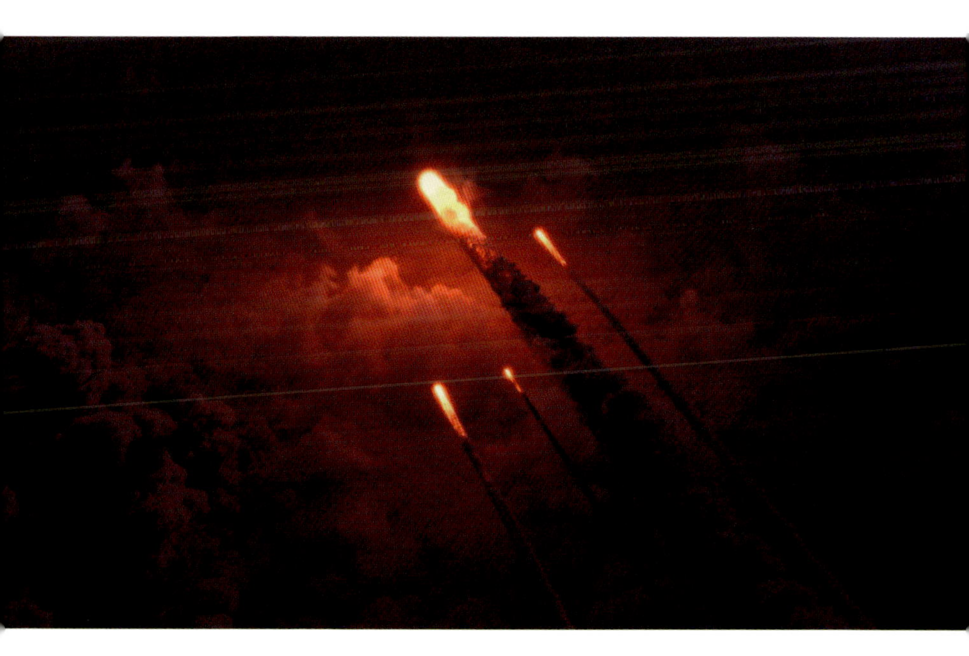

ARTW002a
Film still from American
Artist, *Christopher
Donner*, 2024.

"Kanye West releases presidential campaign ad, invokes God, prayer, family," 2020. (https://www.youtube.com/watch?v=-U-6nA2E26o).

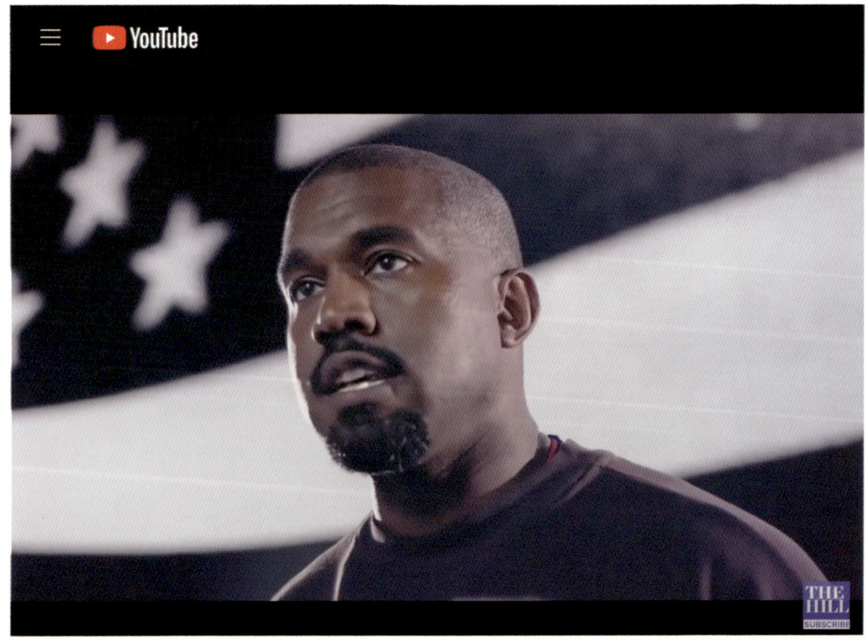

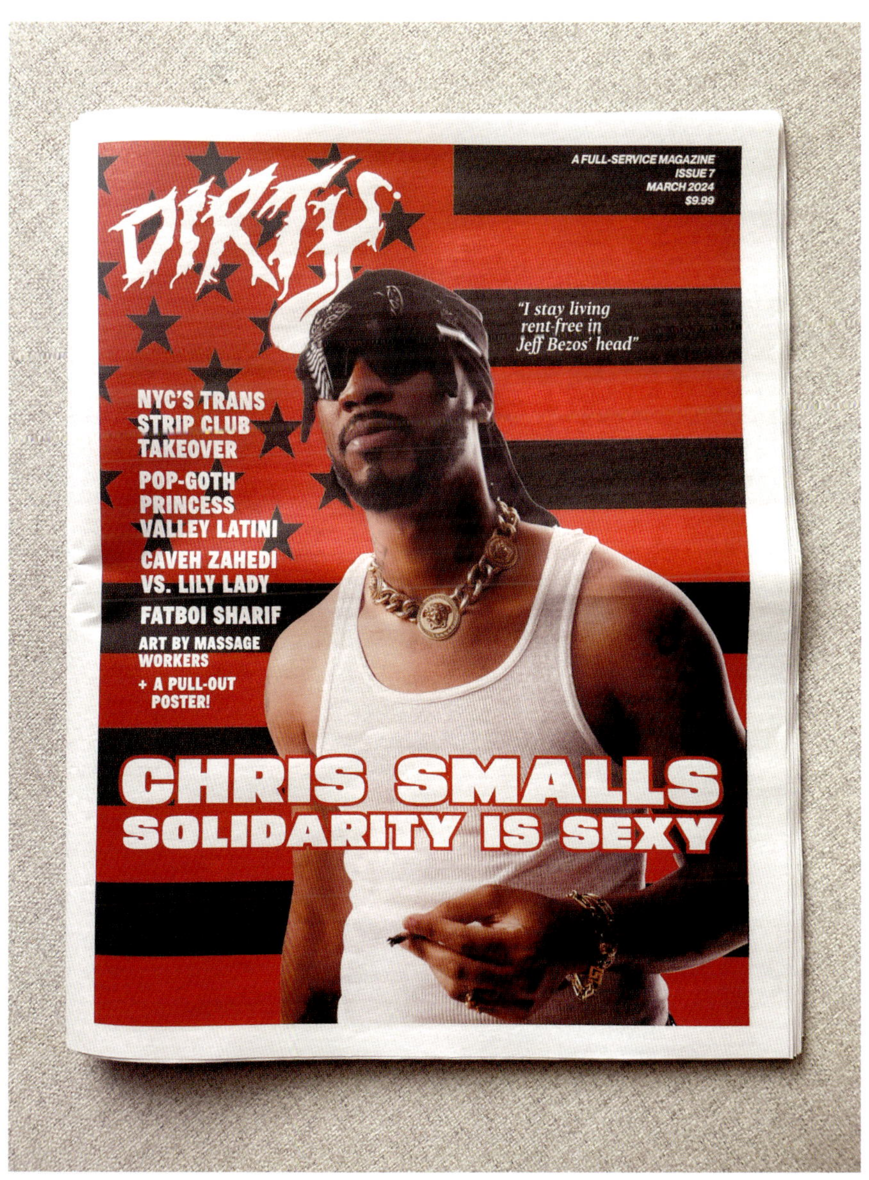
DIRTY
A FULL-SERVICE MAGAZINE
ISSUE 7
MARCH 2024
$9.99
"I stay living rent-free in Jeff Bezos' head"
NYC'S TRANS STRIP CLUB TAKEOVER
POP-GOTH PRINCESS VALLEY LATINI
CAVEH ZAHEDI VS. LILY LADY
FATBOI SHARIF
ART BY MASSAGE WORKERS
+ A PULL-OUT POSTER!
CHRIS SMALLS
SOLIDARITY IS SEXY

Text message between American Artist and Chester Toye.

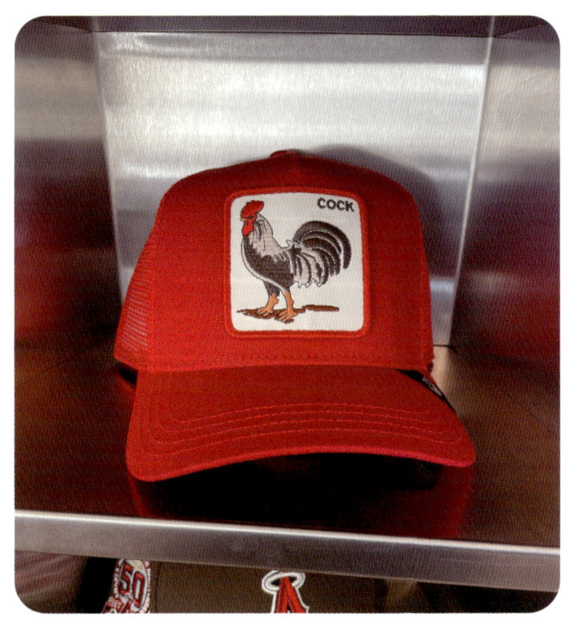

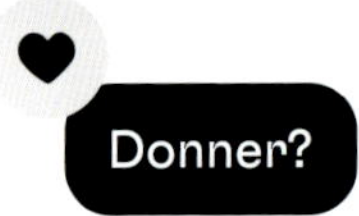

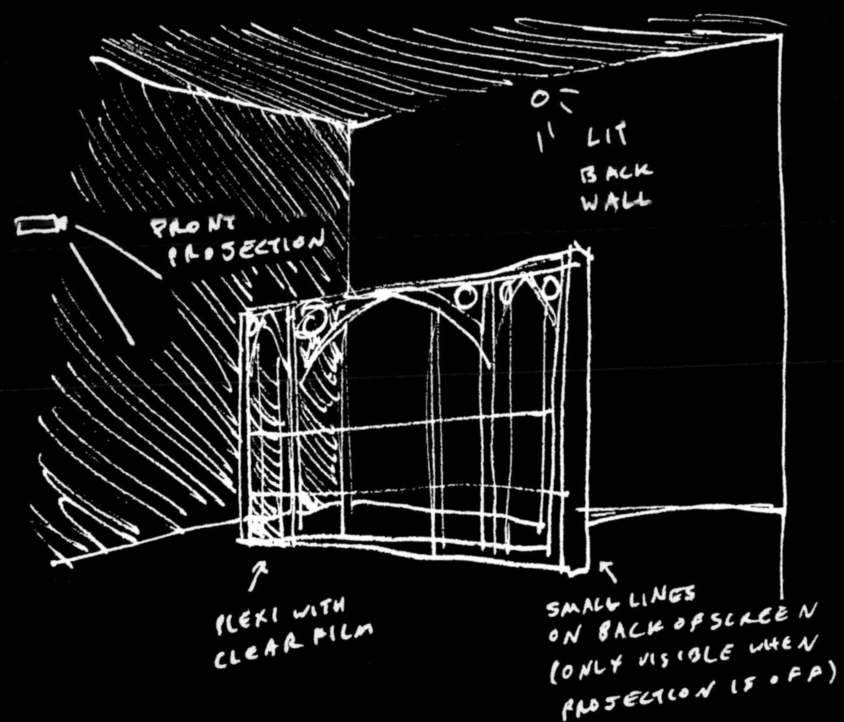
LIT
BACK
WALL
FRONT
PROJECTION
PLEXI WITH
CLEAR FILM
SMALL LINES
ON BACK OF SCREEN
(ONLY VISIBLE WHEN
PROJECTION IS OFF)

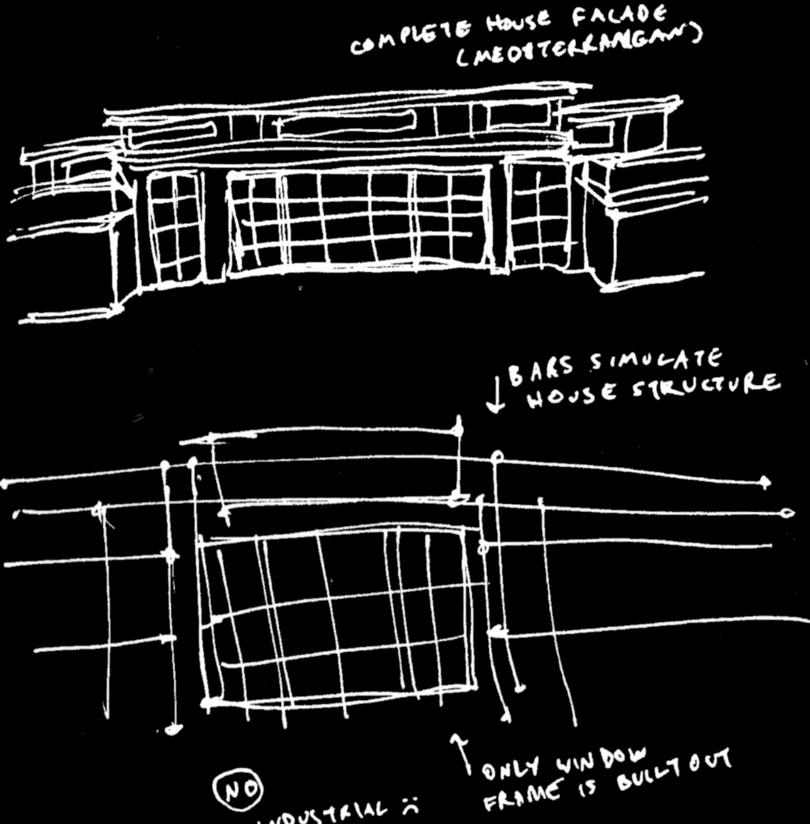
COMPLETE HOUSE FACADE
(MEDITERRANEAN)
BARS SIMULATE
HOUSE STRUCTURE
NO
TOO INDUSTRIAL :(
ONLY WINDOW
FRAME IS BUILT OUT

Christopher Donner 2024 presidential campaign poster by Aldo Arillo.

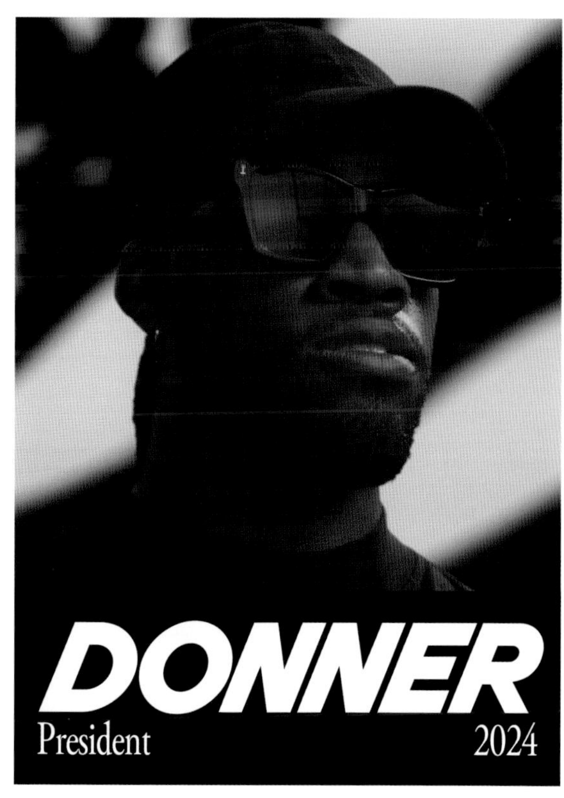

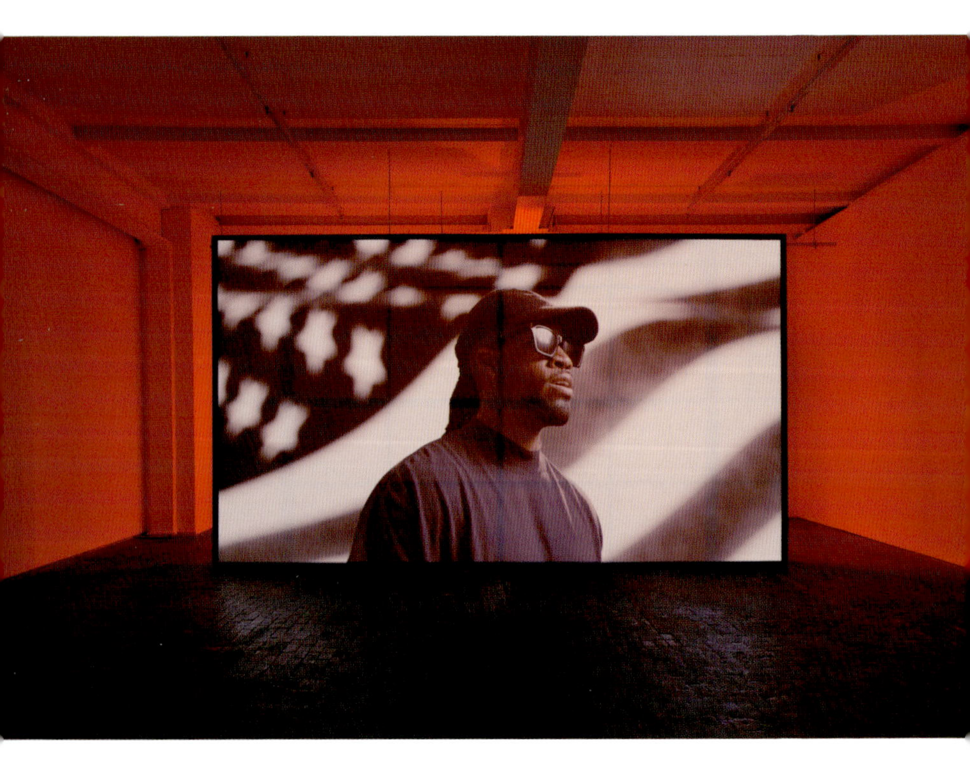

ARTW002b
Film still of American
Artist, *Christopher
Donner*, 2024.

Octavia Butler, the consummate "other," now stands as a representative of the United States space program's early efforts to colonize Mars.

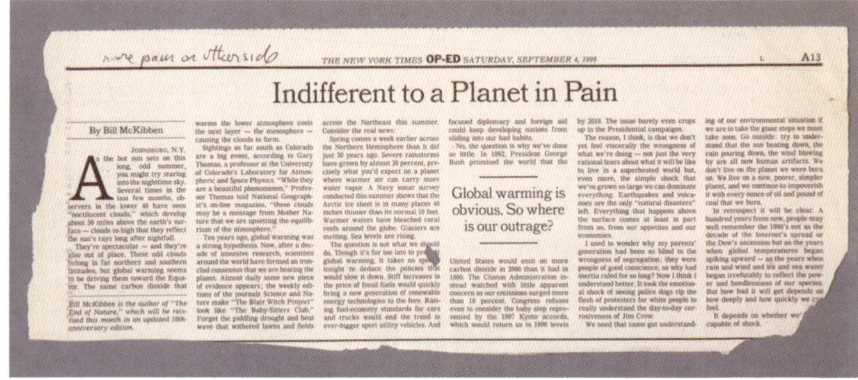

THE NEW YORK TIMES **OP-ED** SATURDAY, SEPTEMBER 4, 1999   L   A13

Indifferent to a Planet in Pain

By Bill McKibben

JOHNSBURG, N.Y.

As the hot sun sets on this long, odd summer, you might try staring into the nighttime sky. Several times in the last few months, observers in the lower 48 have seen "noctilucent clouds," which develop about 30 miles above the earth's surface — clouds so high that they reflect the sun's rays long after nightfall.

They're spectacular — and they're also out of place. These odd clouds belong in far northern and southern latitudes, but global warming seems to be driving them toward the Equator. The same carbon dioxide that warms the lower atmosphere cools the next layer — the mesosphere — causing the clouds to form.

Sightings as far south as Colorado are a big event, according to Gary Thomas, a professor at the University of Colorado's Laboratory for Atmospheric and Space Physics. "While they are a beautiful phenomenon," Professor Thomas told National Geographic's on-line magazine, "these clouds may be a message from Mother Nature that we are upsetting the equilibrium of the atmosphere."

Ten years ago, global warming was a strong hypothesis. Now, after a decade of intensive research, scientists around the world have formed an iron-clad consensus that we are heating the planet. Almost daily some new piece of evidence appears; the weekly editions of the journals Science and Nature make "The Blair Witch Project" look like "The Baby-Sitters Club." Forget the piddling drought and heat wave that withered lawns and fields across the Northeast this summer. Consider the real news:

Spring comes a week earlier across the Northern Hemisphere than it did just 30 years ago. Severe rainstorms have grown by almost 20 percent, precisely what you'd expect on a planet where warmer air can carry more water vapor. A Navy sonar survey conducted this summer shows that the Arctic ice sheet is in many places 40 inches thinner than its normal 10 feet. Warmer waters have bleached coral reefs around the globe. Glaciers are melting. Sea levels are rising.

The question is not what we should do. Though it's far too late to prevent global warming, it takes no special insight to deduce the policies that would slow it down. Stiff increases in the price of fossil fuels would quickly bring a new generation of renewable energy technologies to the fore. Raising fuel-economy standards for cars and trucks would end the trend to ever-bigger sport utility vehicles. And focused diplomacy and foreign aid could keep developing nations from sliding into our bad habits.

- No, the question is why we've done so little. In 1992, President George Bush promised the world that the

> ## Global warming is obvious. So where is our outrage?

United States would emit no more carbon dioxide in 2000 than it had in 1990. The Clinton Administration instead watched with little apparent concern as our emissions surged more than 10 percent. Congress refuses even to consider the baby step represented by the 1997 Kyoto accords, which would return us to 1990 levels by 2010. The issue barely even crops up in the Presidential campaigns.

The reason, I think, is that we don't yet feel viscerally the wrongness of what we're doing — not just the very rational fears about what it will be like to live in a superheated world but, even more, the simple shock that we've grown so large we can dominate everything. Earthquakes and volcanoes are the only "natural disasters" left. Everything that happens above the surface comes at least in part from us, from our appetites and our economies.

I used to wonder why my parents' generation had been so blind to the wrongness of segregation; they were people of good conscience, so why had inertia ruled for so long? Now I think I understand better. It took the emotional shock of seeing police dogs rip the flesh of protesters for white people to really understand the day-to-day corrosiveness of Jim Crow.

We need that same gut understanding of our environmental situation if we are to take the giant steps we must take soon. Go outside: try to understand that the sun beating down, the rain pouring down, the wind blowing by are all now human artifacts. We don't live on the planet we were born on. We live on a new, poorer, simpler planet, and we continue to impoverish it with every ounce of oil and pound of coal that we burn.

In retrospect it will be clear. A hundred years from now, people may well remember the 1990's not as the decade of the Internet's spread or the Dow's ascension but as the years when global temperatures began spiking upward — as the years when rain and wind and ice and sea water began irrefutably to reflect the power and heedlessness of our species. But how bad it will get depends on how deeply and how quickly we can feel.

It depends on whether we're capable of shock.

Bill McKibben is the author of "The End of Nature," which will be reissued this month in an updated 10th-anniversary edition.

Sketch of OEB 2076. Octavia E. Butler, Parable of the Trickster: novel: yellow binder: notes, 1999.

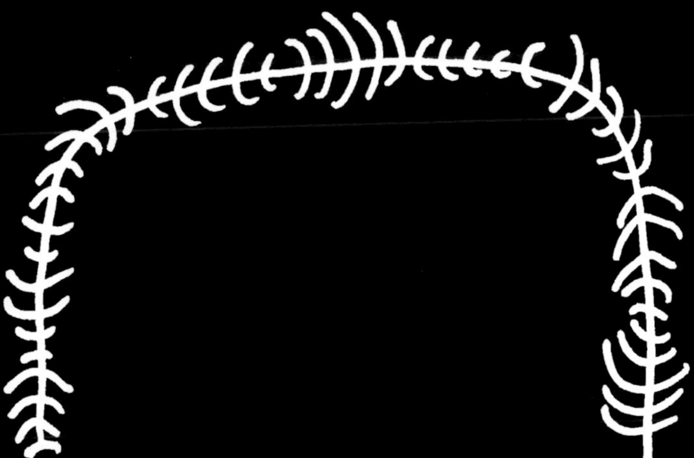

- OEB 2076
  - EACH ARC EQUALS DWELLINGS FOR 100 PEOPLE
  - EACH GROUP OF FIVE ARCS EQUALS DWELLINGS FOR 500 PEOPLE
  - OPEN ARC ALLOWS FOR EXPANSION OF HOUSING GROUP
  - EARTHSEED ROAD ARCS THROUGH EACH COMMUNITY
  - INSIDE THE ARC IS PASTURE & FARMLAND
  - THE COMMUNITY MUST WORK TOGETHER
  - IN UNITY THERE IS SURVIVAL

Sketch of sculpture for Exposition Park, Los Angeles, CA, by American Artist, 2022.

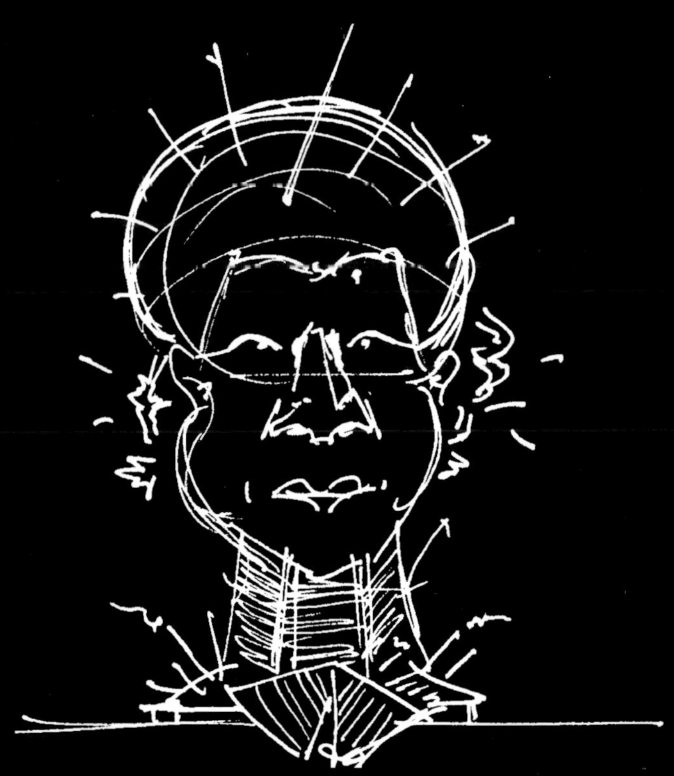

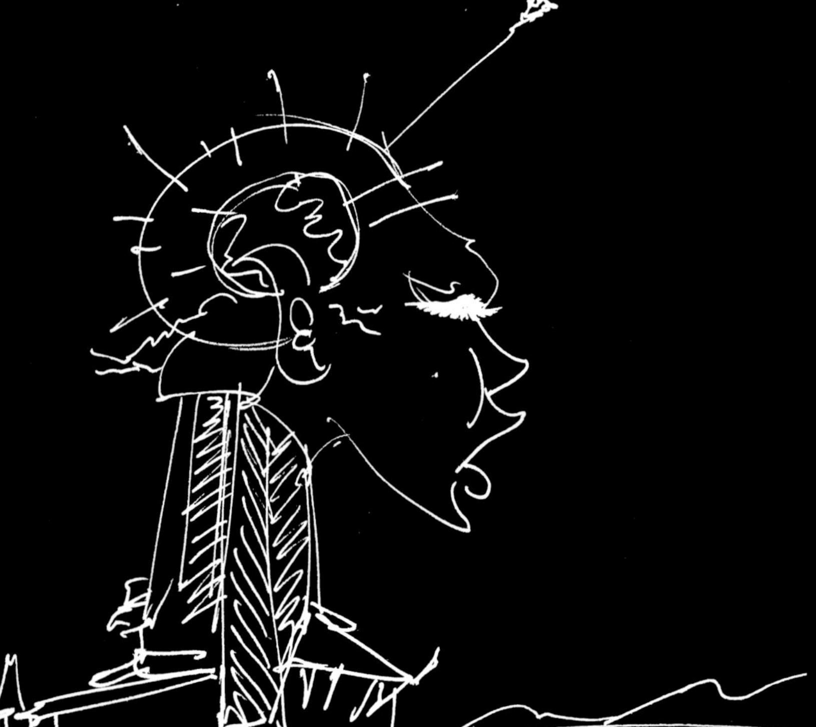

Cover of Octavia E. Butler's *Mind of Mind*, 1980.

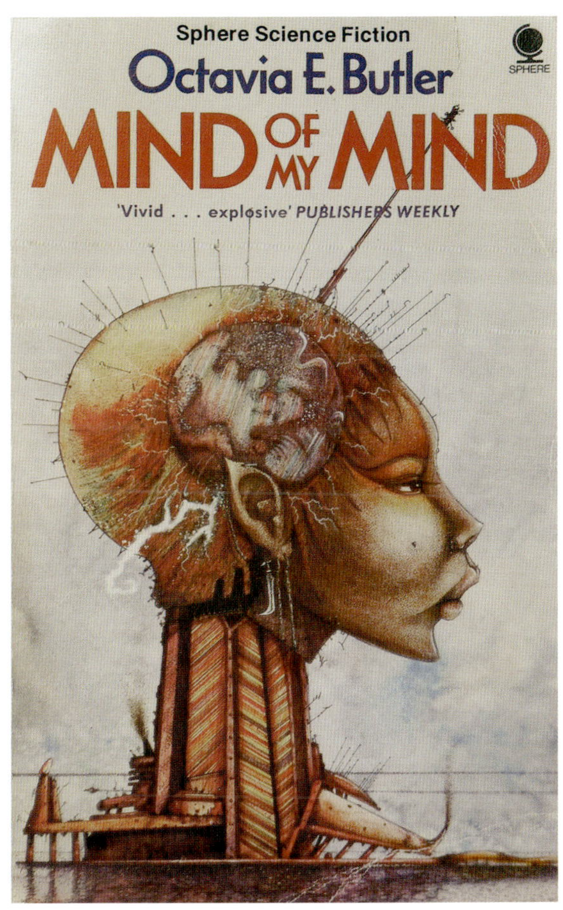

Screenshot of *The Monophobic Response* wardrobe planning document by Tessa Matthias, 2024.

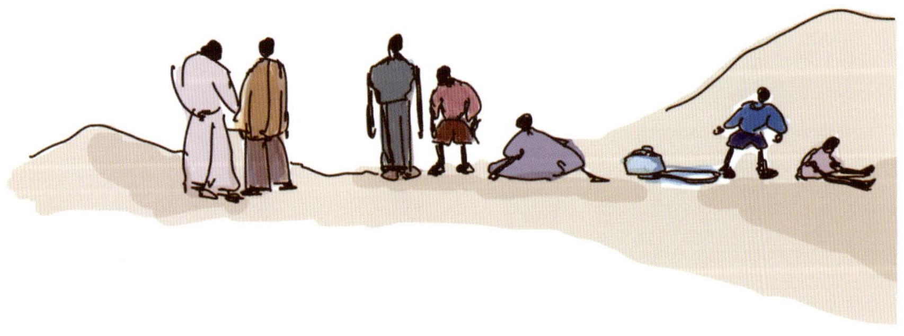

Screenshot of *The Monophobic Response* wardrobe planning document by Tessa Matthias, 2024.

YOUR COLOR PAGE

i LOVE THE WHITE SHADES iN HERE TOO — iF YOU WANT ME TO ADD COLORS iNSTEAD OF EDiT DOWN — NOW iS THE TiME TO DECIDE

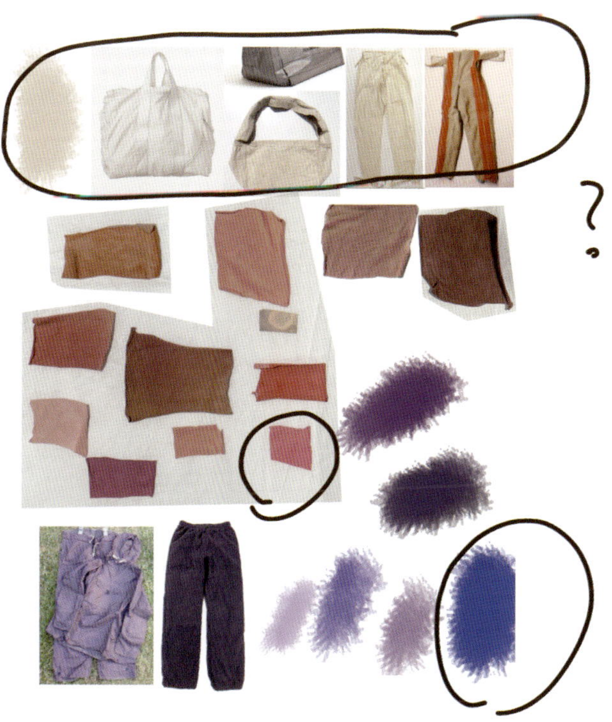

Earthseeders on the set of *The Monophobic Response,* 2024.

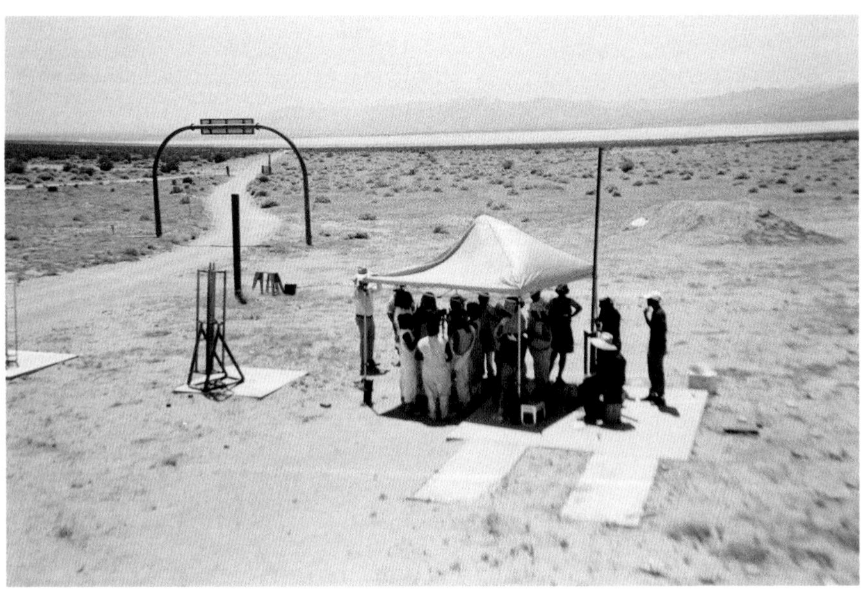

Lauren Oya Olamina in Octavia E. Butler, *Parable of the Talents*, 1998.

"'We call our system Earthseed,' I said. 'My actual title is "Shaper."'"

2 Alexis 1:7

Her experience as an outsider—too poor, too Black, too tall, too feminist, too smart—led her to theorize how the society she was born into relates to otherness. She called it "the monophobic response."

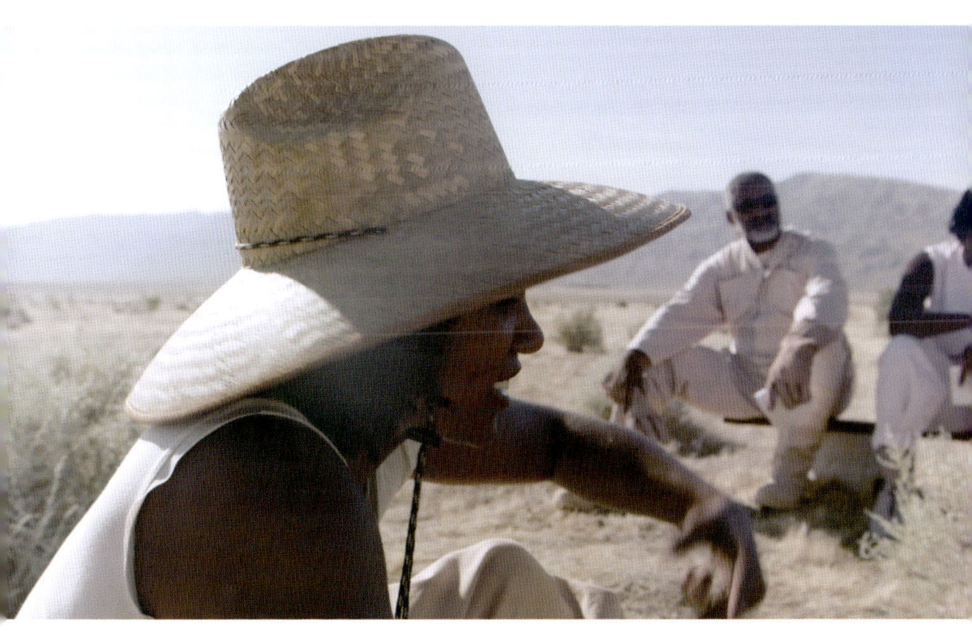

ARTW015a
**Film still from American
Artist,** *The Monophobic
Response,* **2024.**

[227]

ARTW015b
Film still from American
Artist, *The Monophobic
Response*, 2024.

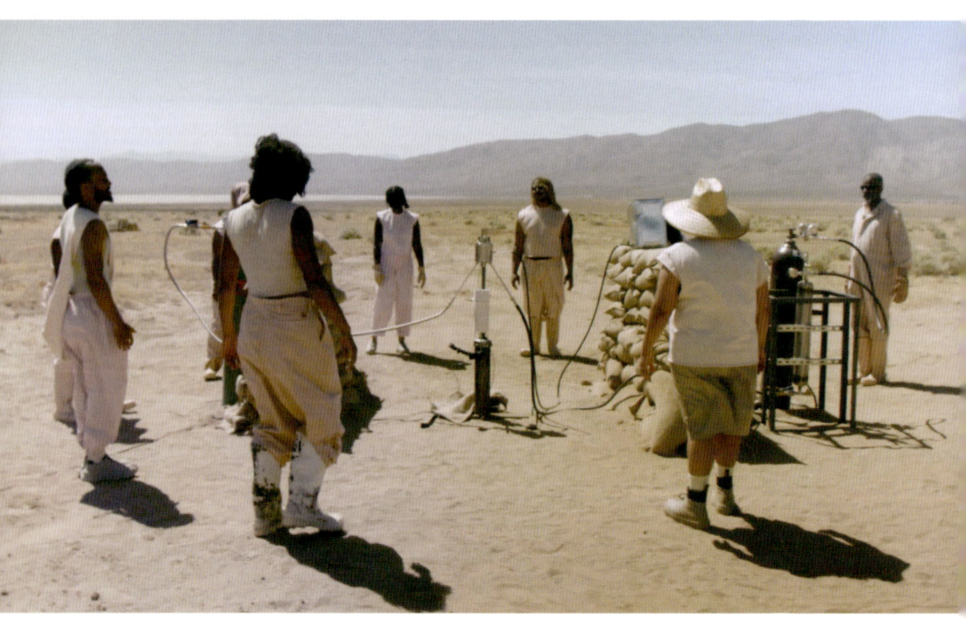

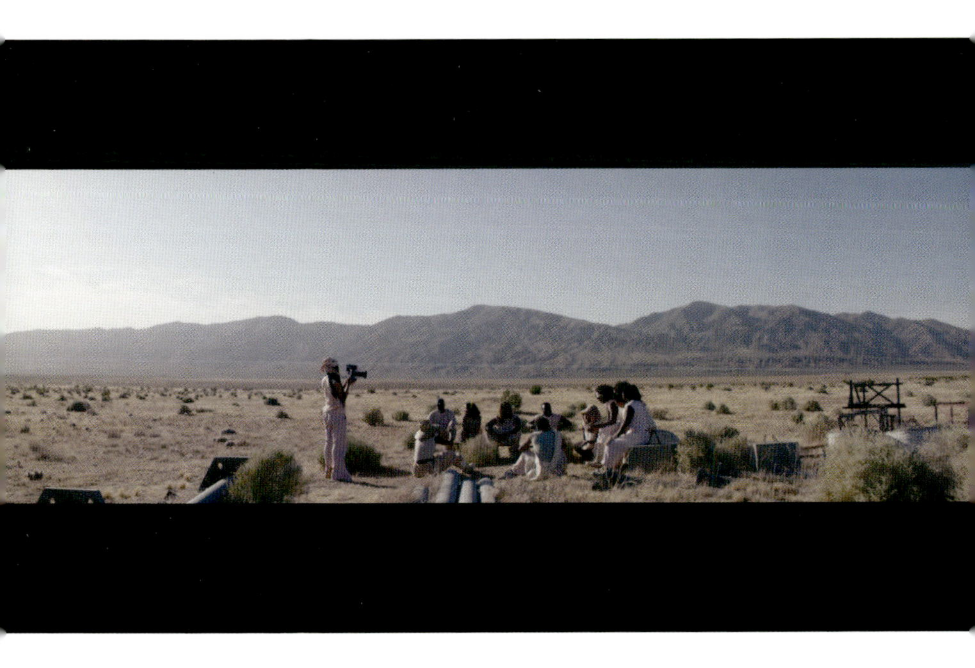

ARTW015c
Film still from American
Artist, *The Monophobic
Response*, 2024.

Wardrobe for *The Monophobic Response* designed by Tessa Matthias, 2024.

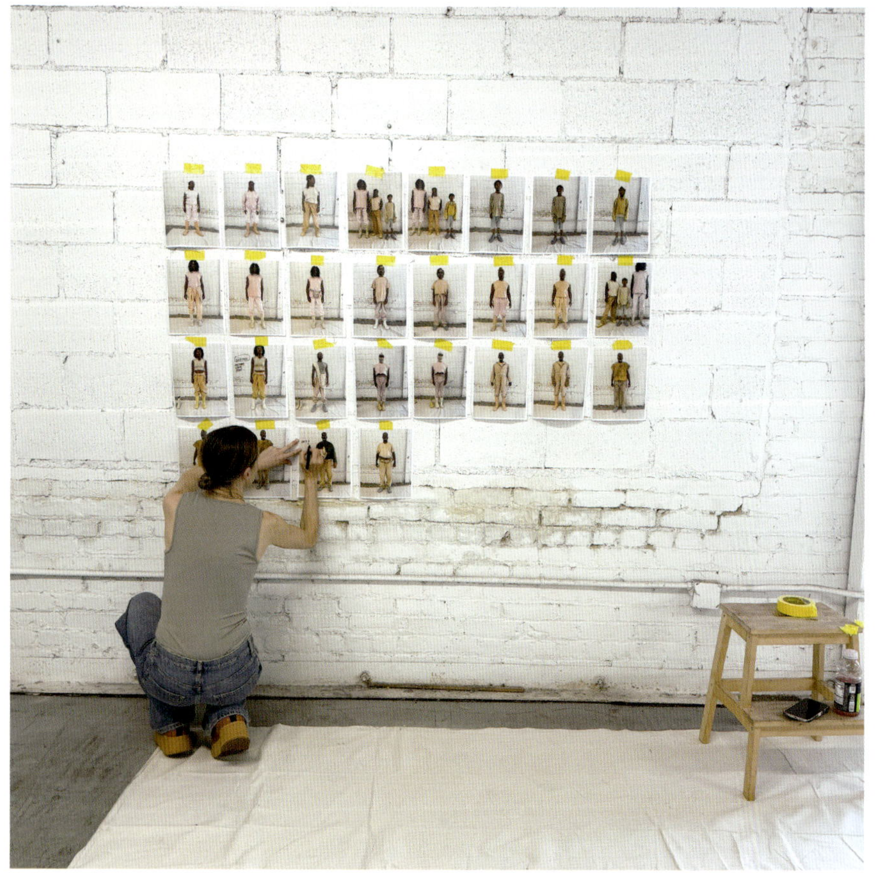

Denali Jöel, Ayana Jamieson, and Cydel Lam in wardrobe fitting for *The Monophobic Response*, 2024.

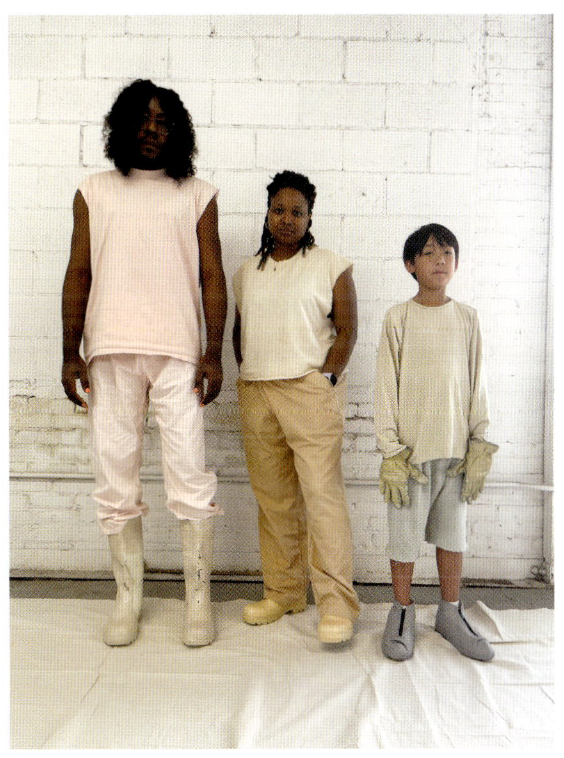

Drawing of early rocket motor test by Frank Malina, 1936.

[232]

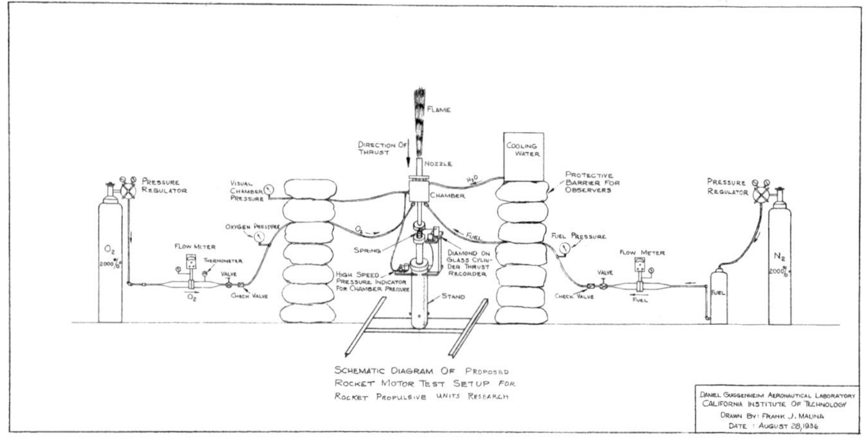

Sketch of replica of 1936 GALCIT rocket engine and fuel source by Dave Nordling, 2023.

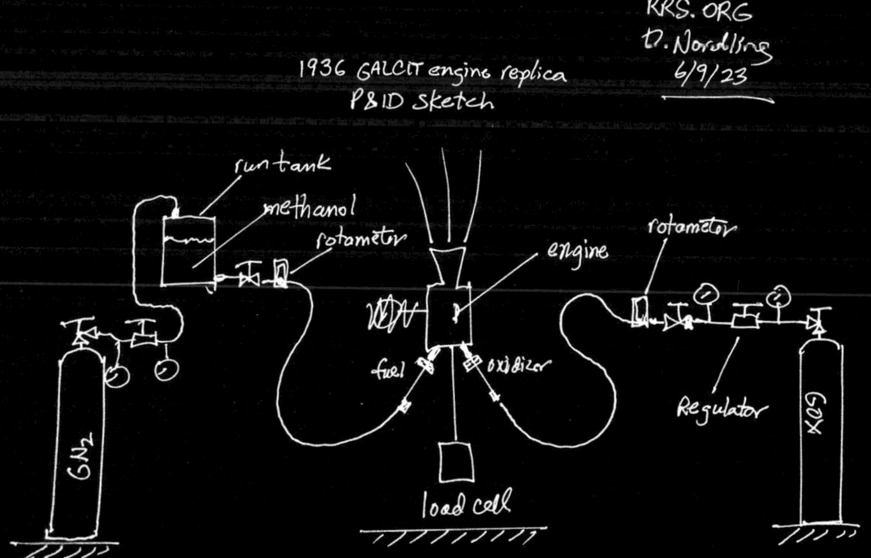

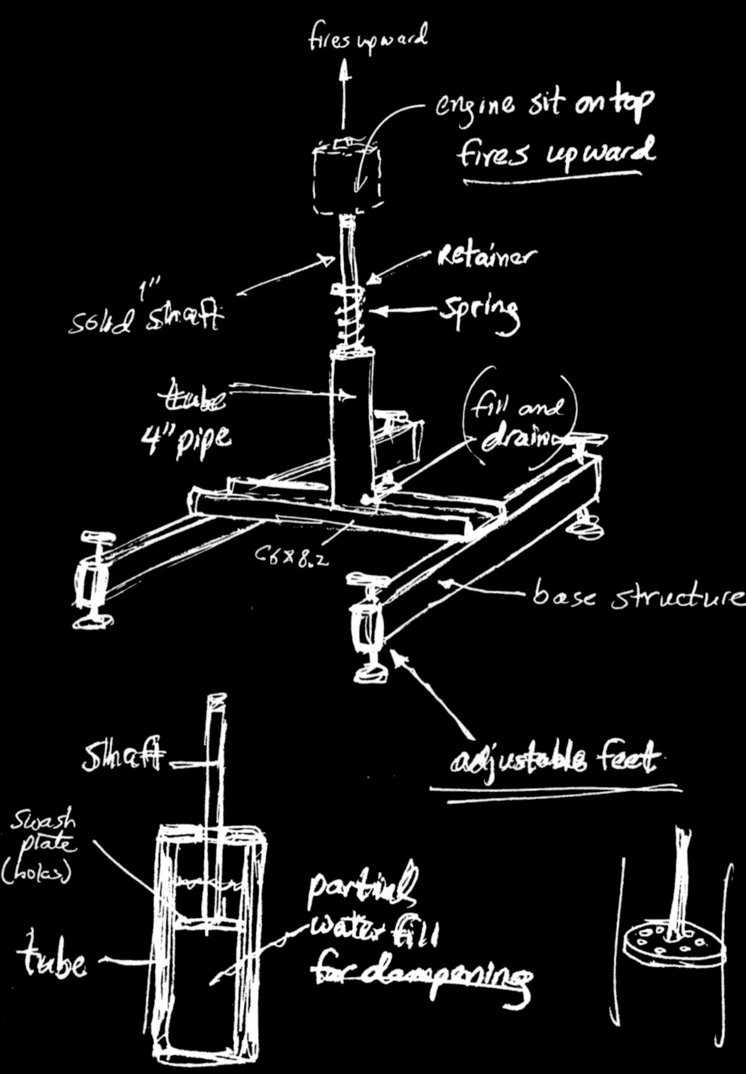
fires upward
engine sit on top
fires upward
Retainer
spring
solid 1" shaft
tube
4" pipe
fill and drain
C6×8.2
base structure
adjustable feet
shaft
swash plate (holes)
tube
partial water fill for dampening

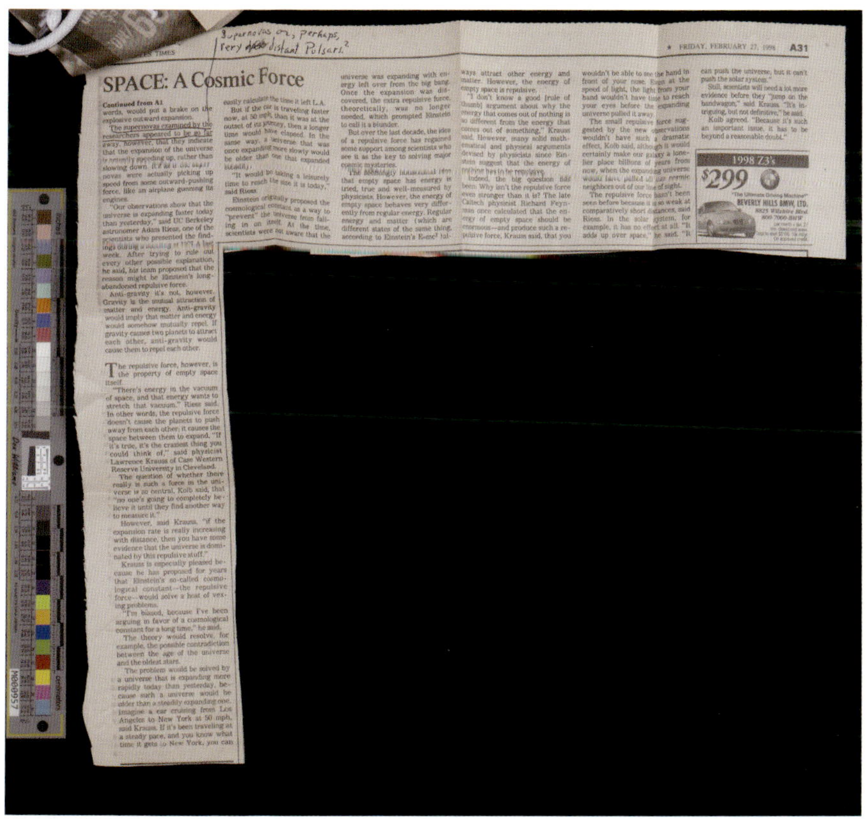

Supernovas or, perhaps, very ~~new~~ distant Pulsars?

LOS ANGELES TIMES ★ FRIDAY, FEBRUARY 27, 1998 A31

SPACE: A Cosmic Force

Continued from A1

words, would put a brake on the explosive outward expansion.

The supernovas examined by the researchers appeared to be so far away, however, that they indicate that the expansion of the universe is actually speeding up, rather than slowing down. It's as if the supernovas were actually picking up speed from some outward-pushing force, like an airplane gunning its engines.

"Our observations show that the universe is expanding faster today than yesterday," said UC Berkeley astronomer Adam Riess, one of the scientists who presented the findings during a meeting at UCLA last week. After trying to rule out every other possible explanation, he said, his team proposed that the reason might be Einstein's long-abandoned repulsive force.

Anti-gravity it's not, however. Gravity is the mutual attraction of matter and energy. Anti-gravity would imply that matter and energy would somehow mutually repel. If gravity causes two planets to attract each other, anti-gravity would cause them to repel each other.

The repulsive force, however, is the property of empty space itself.

"There's energy in the vacuum of space, and that energy wants to stretch that vacuum," Riess said. In other words, the repulsive force doesn't cause the planets to push away from each other; it causes the space between them to expand. "If it's true, it's the craziest thing you could think of," said physicist Lawrence Krauss of Case Western Reserve University in Cleveland.

The question of whether there really is such a force in the universe is so central, Kolb said, that "no one's going to completely believe it until they find another way to measure it."

However, said Krauss, "if the expansion rate is really increasing with distance, then you have some evidence that the universe is dominated by this repulsive stuff."

Krauss is especially pleased because he has proposed for years that Einstein's so-called cosmological constant—the repulsive force—would solve a host of vexing problems.

"I'm biased, because I've been arguing in favor of a cosmological constant for a long time," he said.

The theory would resolve, for example, the possible contradiction between the age of the universe and the oldest stars.

The problem would be solved by a universe that is expanding more rapidly today than yesterday, because such a universe would be older than a steadily expanding one. Imagine a car cruising from Los Angeles to New York at 50 mph, said Krauss. If it's been traveling at a steady pace, and you know what time it gets to New York, you can easily calculate the time it left L.A.

But if the car is traveling faster now, at 50 mph, than it was at the outset of its journey, then a longer time would have elapsed. In the same way, a universe that was once expanding more slowly would be older than one that expanded steadily.

"It would be taking a leisurely time to reach the size it is today," said Riess.

Einstein originally proposed the cosmological constant as a way to "prevent" the universe from falling in on itself. At the time, scientists were not aware that the universe was expanding with energy left over from the big bang. Once the expansion was discovered, the extra repulsive force, theoretically, was no longer needed, which prompted Einstein to call it a blunder.

But over the last decade, the idea of a repulsive force has regained some support among scientists who see it as the key to solving major cosmic mysteries.

The seemingly insensible idea that empty space has energy is tried, true and well-measured by physicists. However, the energy of empty space behaves very differently from regular energy. Regular energy and matter (which are different states of the same thing, according to Einstein's $E=mc^2$ jal-) always attract other energy and matter. However, the energy of empty space is repulsive.

"I don't know a good [rule of thumb] argument about why the energy that comes out of nothing is so different from the energy that comes out of something," Krauss said. However, many solid mathematical and physical arguments devised by physicists since Einstein suggest that the energy of nothing has to be repulsive.

Indeed, the big question has been: Why isn't the repulsive force even stronger than it is? The late Caltech physicist Richard Feynman once calculated that the energy of empty space should be enormous—and produce such a repulsive force, Krauss said, that you wouldn't be able to see the hand in front of your nose. Even at the speed of light, the light from your hand wouldn't have time to reach your eyes before the expanding universe pulled it away.

The small repulsive force suggested by the new observations wouldn't have such a dramatic effect, Kolb said, although it would certainly make our galaxy a lonelier place billions of years from now, when the expanding universe would have pulled all our cosmic neighbors out of our line of sight.

The repulsive force hasn't been seen before because it is so weak at comparatively short distances, said Riess. In the solar system, for example, it has no effect at all. "It adds up over space," he said. "It can push the universe, but it can't push the solar system."

Still, scientists will need a lot more evidence before they "jump on the bandwagon," said Krauss. "It's intriguing, but not definitive," he said.

Kolb agreed. "Because it's such an important issue, it has to be beyond a reasonable doubt."

For Olamina: You're talking to a group of people that are mostly much older than you, but you are their religious leader. They are here by choice but they are exhausted, they have been studying this scripture with you for months, but life keeps getting harder, and they are losing faith in the scripture. You just gave a charismatic speech that has their interest renewed, and you close it out by repeating this part of the scripture. The way you speak to them is a little bit maternal (talking down, frustrated, but also from a place of care, you are teaching them).

Behind the scenes on the set of *Alicia Catalina Godinez Leal*, 2024.

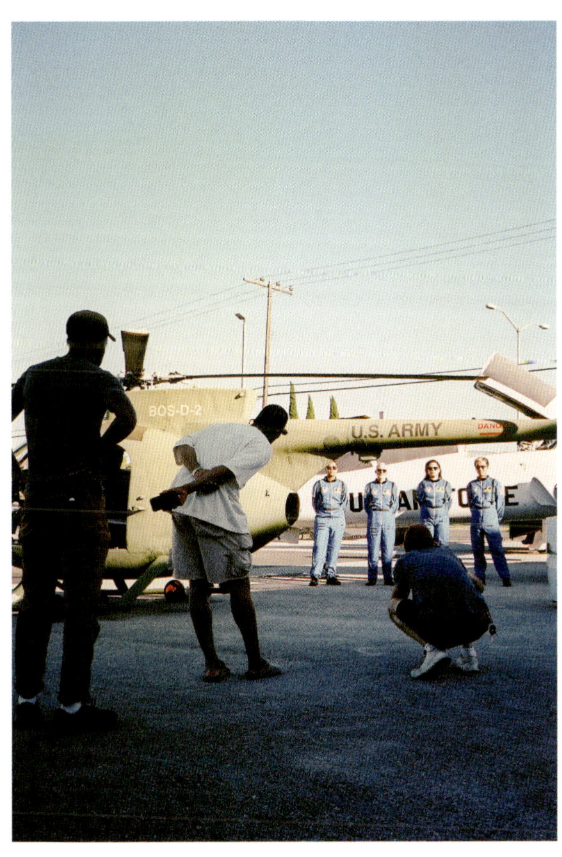

2 Alexis 3:2 – 3

It is one part of my ongoing process of listening to the dead, who still remain. May it provoke conversations among the living.

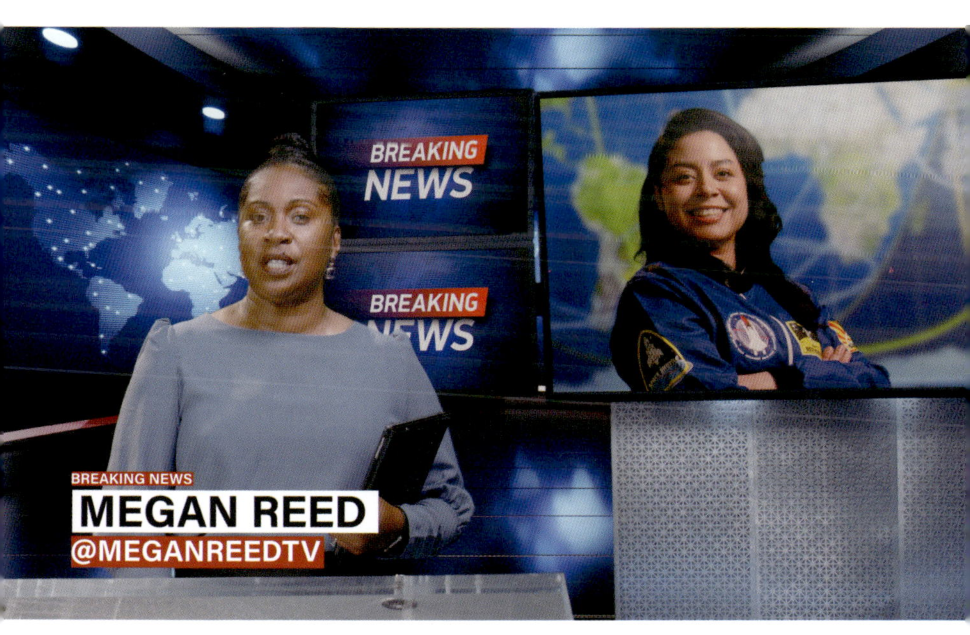

ARTW001a
Film still from American
Artist, *Alicia Catalina
Godinez Leal*, 2024.

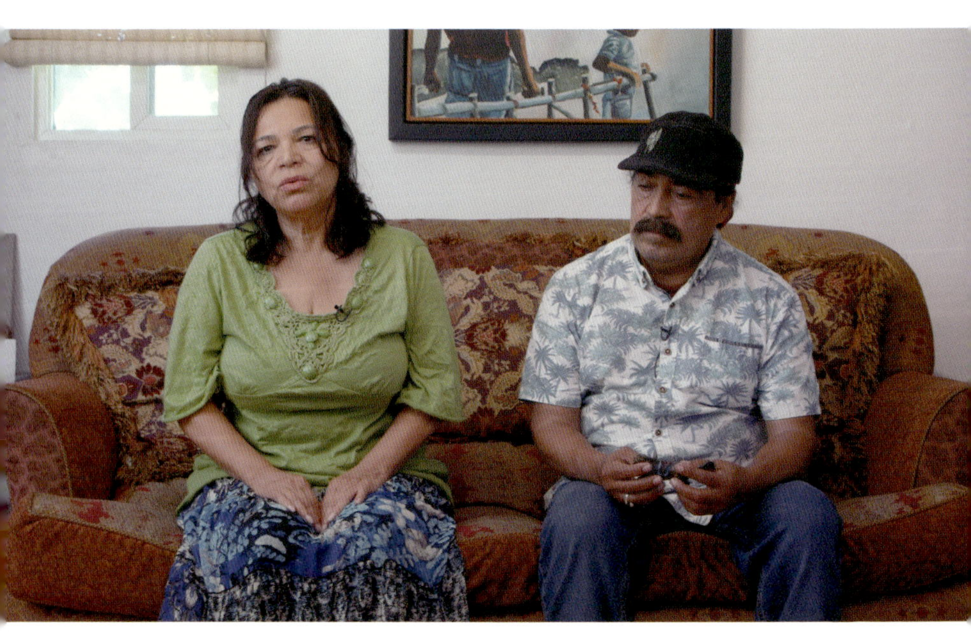

ARTW001b
Film still from American
Artist, *Alicia Catalina
Godinez Leal*, 2024.

What if someone had paid *her*
to stargaze? Her habit for early
mornings came from what poverty
required—writing in the dark before
her factory shift.

It could be helpful to think about the days prior and events leading up to this moment. Where they came from, conflict, goals, etc. Imagine being a small slice into a much larger moment/ movement

Imagine the video being*

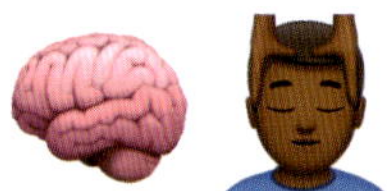

Space shuttle explosion of Challenger on January 28, 1986.

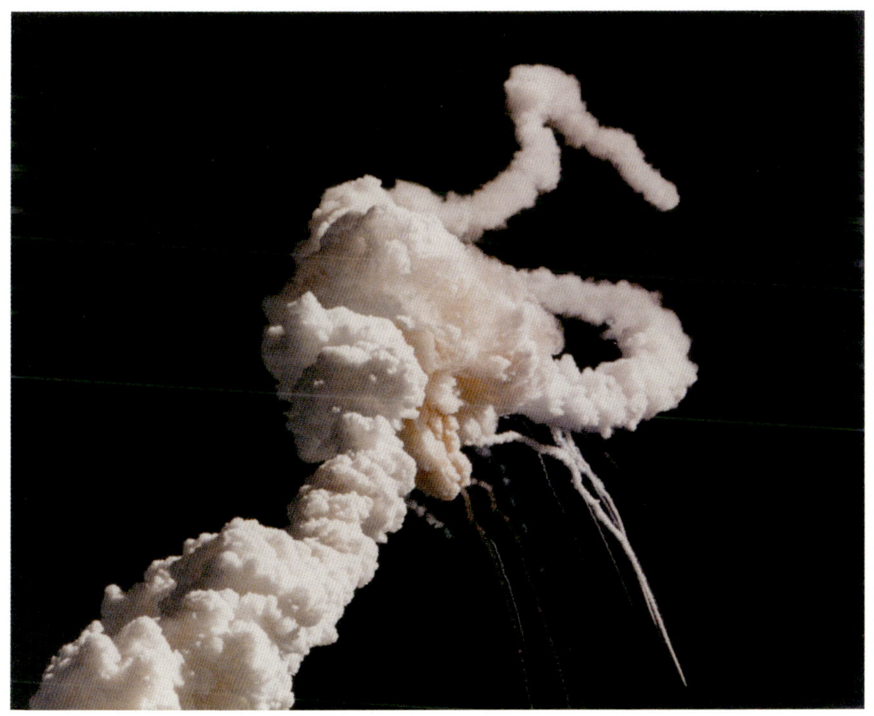

Yes Grandma, I remember: They may have their God, but we have our hands.

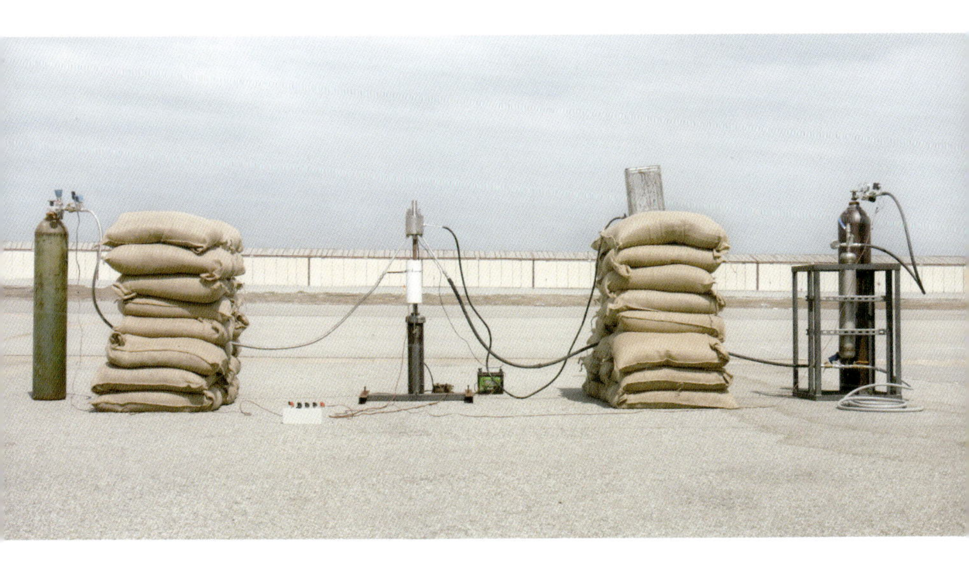

ARTW016a
American Artist, *The Monophobic Response (sculpture)*, 2024.
Steel, methanol, oxygen, tanks, sandbags, hoses, paper, pencil.
150 x 72 x 48 in.

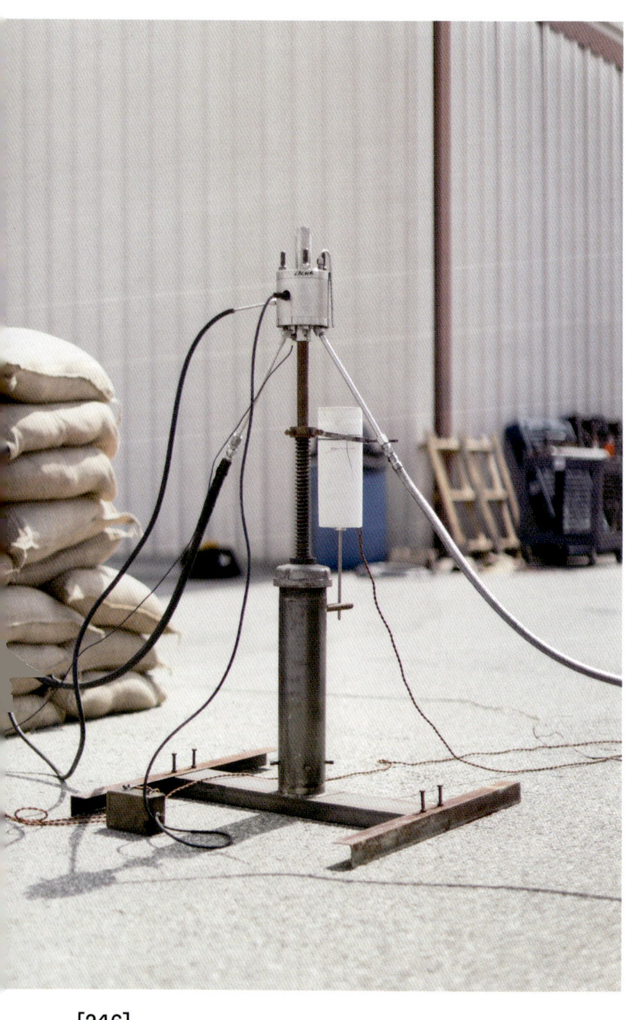

ARTW016b
Detail of American
Artist, *The Monophobic
Response* (*sculpture*),
2024.

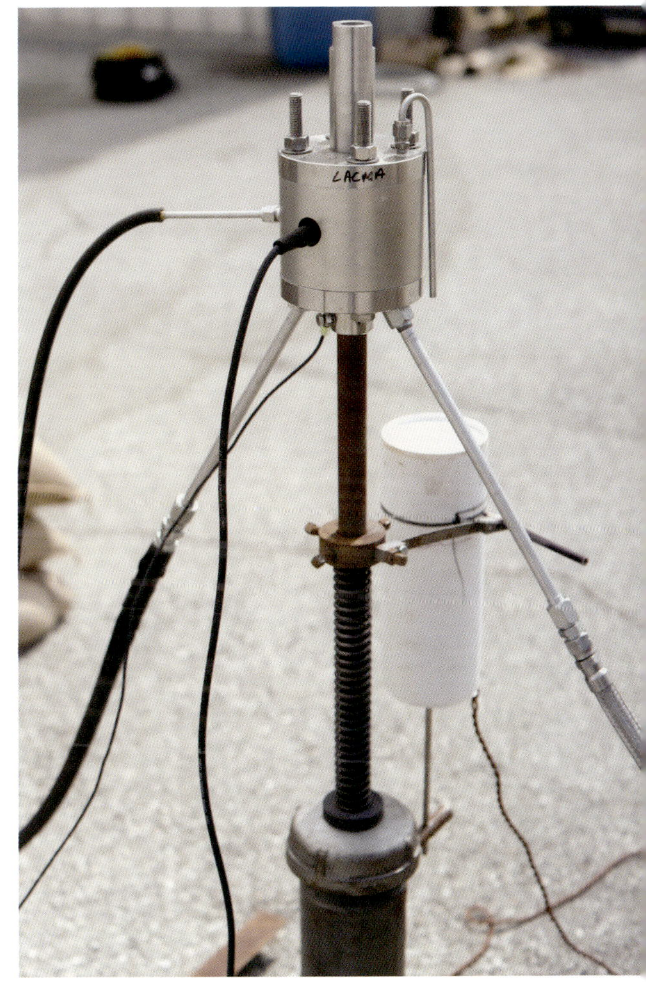

ARTW016c
Detail of American
Artist, *The Monophobic
Response (sculpture)*,
2024.

Approximate number
of words: 700

THE MONOPHOBIC RESPONSE

By Octavia E. Butler

At the moment, there are no true aliens in our lives.
No Martians or Tau Cetians, to swoop down in advanced space
ships, their attentions firmly fixed on the all-important
us, no gods or devils, no spirits, angels, or gnomes. . . .
Some of us know this. Deep within ourselves, we know
it. We're on our own, the focus of no interest except
our consuming interest in ourselves.

Is this too much reality? It is, yes. No one is
watching, caring, extending a hand or taking on a little
demonic blame. If we are adults, and past the age of
having our parents come running when we cry, then our
only help is ourselves and one another.

This is far too much reality.

Suicide Squad and the first liquid rocket fuel test, 1936.

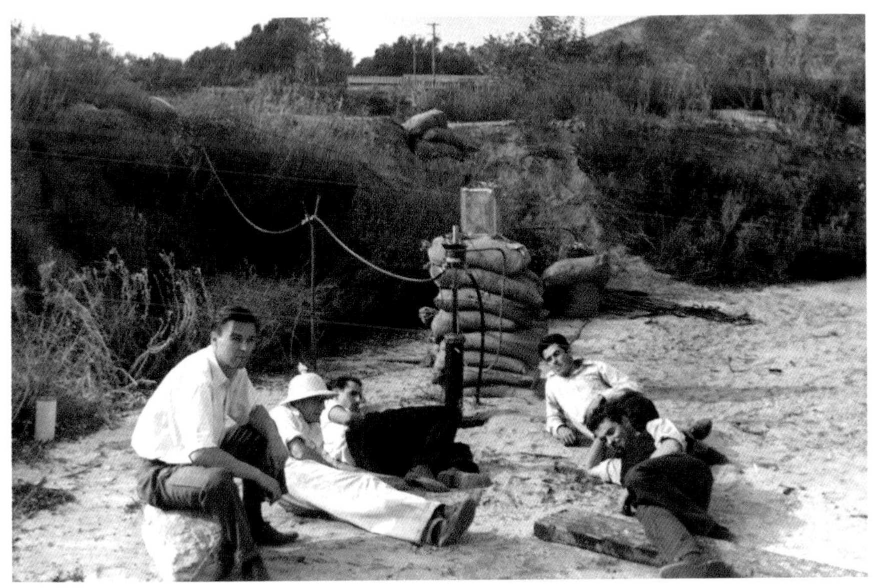

Map of facilities at Mojave Test Area. Courtesy of Reaction Research Society.

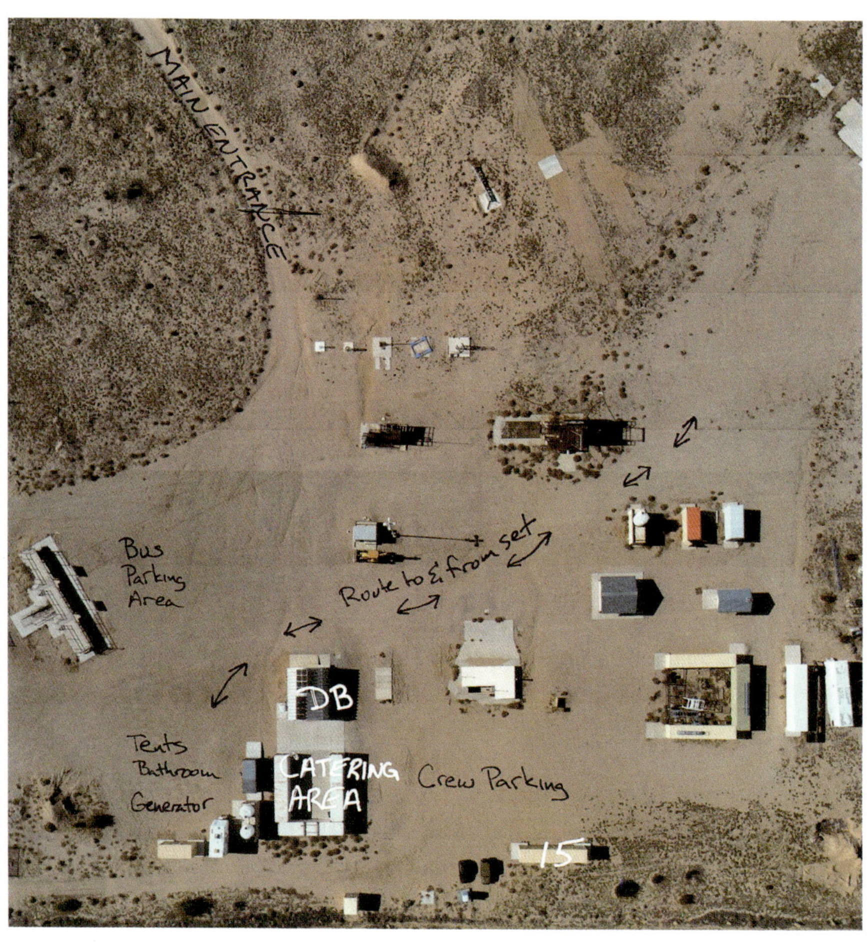

James E. Crimi, "Distribution of minority racial groups in Pasadena in 1935."

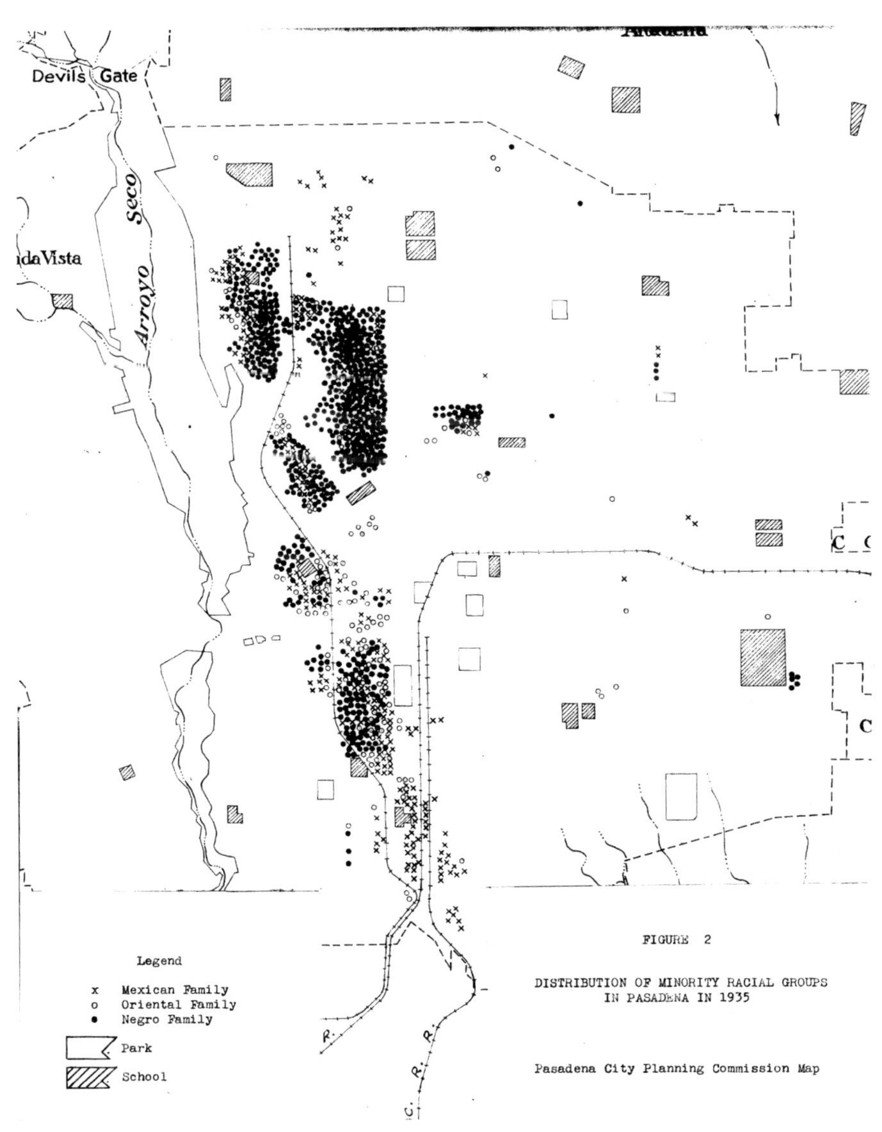

Thirty-sixth anniversary, first rocket firing at JPL
Date: 1968-10-31. Courtesy NASA/JPL-Caltech.

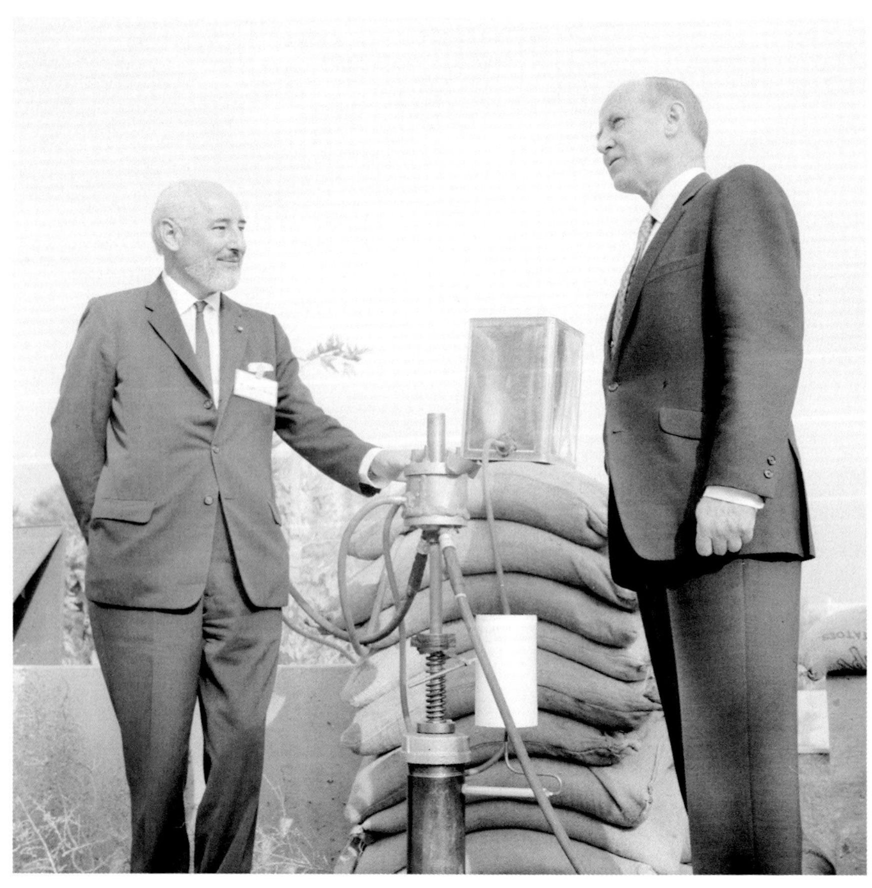

Rocket engineers Arrington Mitchell and Tre Willingham on the set of *The Monophobic Response*, 2024.

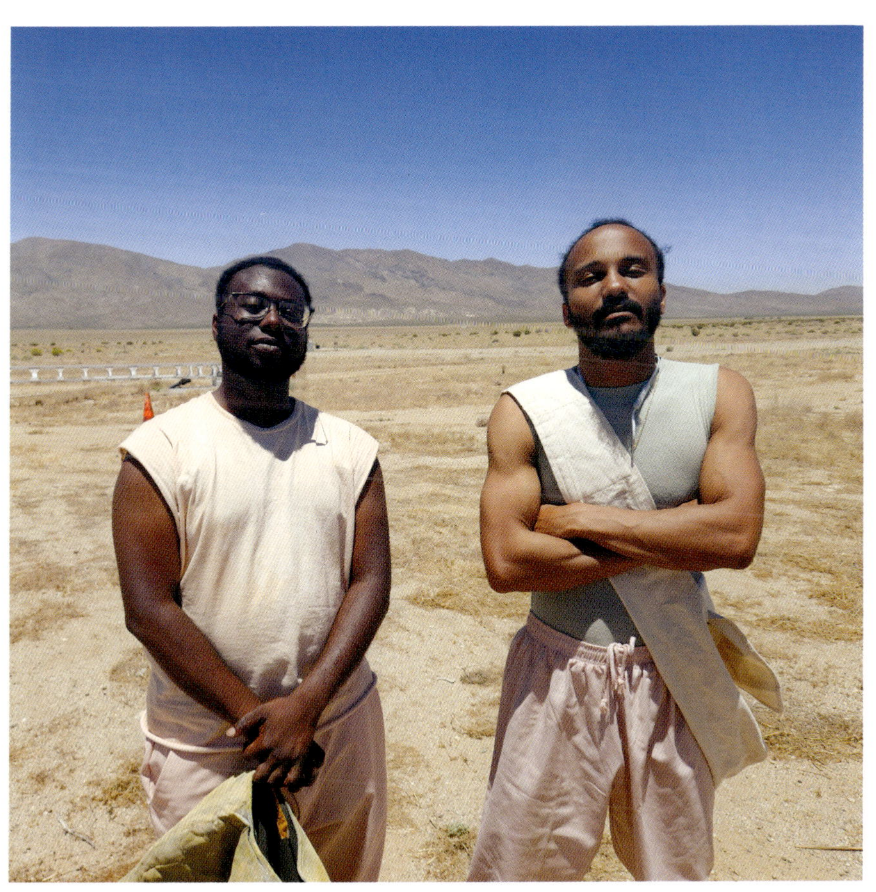

1 Alexis 1:1

Octavia E. Butler explores multiple contexts of difference through the intimate lives and decisions of her Black female protagonists: the power of dreams, shapeshifting, and apocalyptic response.

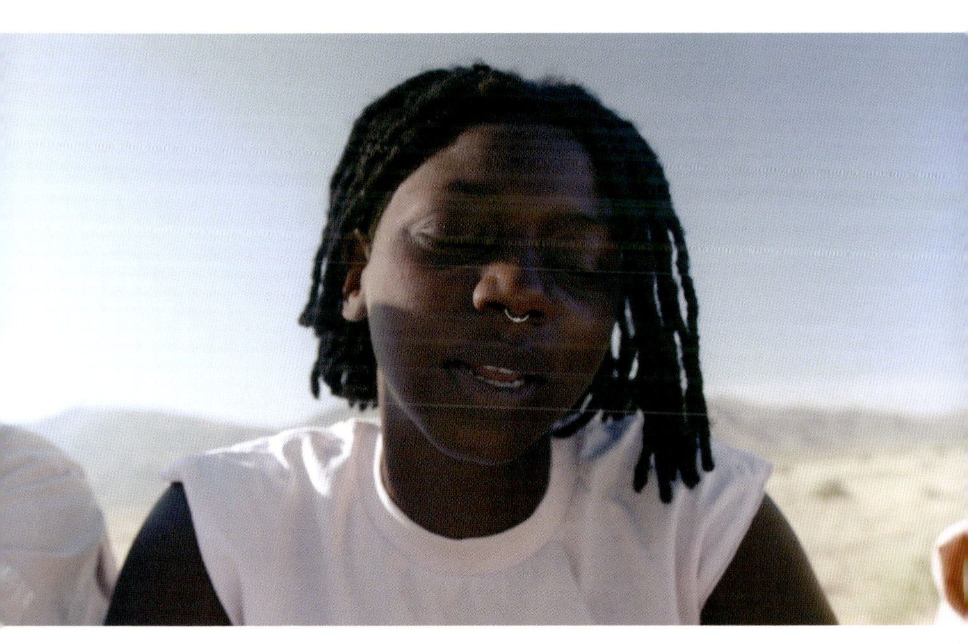

ARTW015d
Film still from American
Artist, *The Monophobic
Response*, 2024.

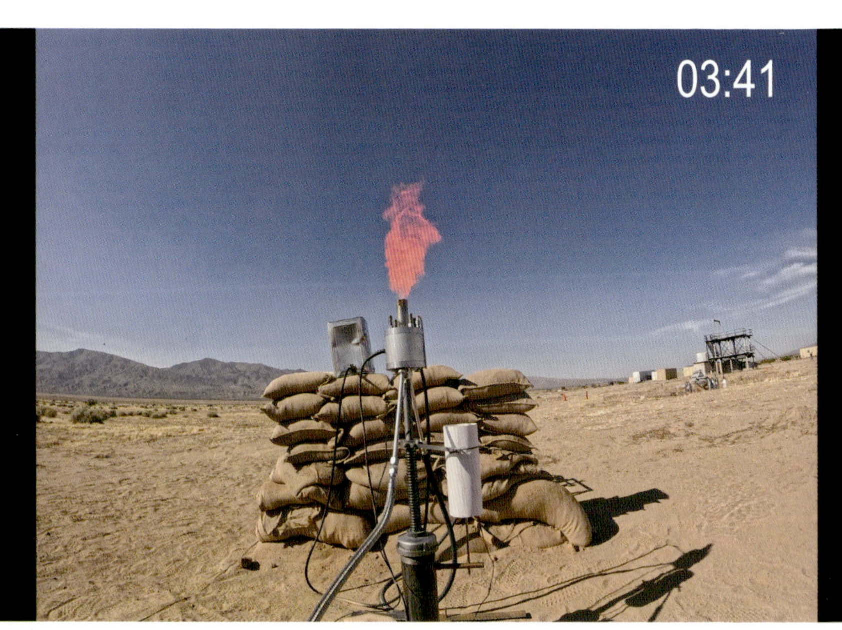

ARTW015e
Film still from American
Artist, *The Monophobic
Response*, 2024.

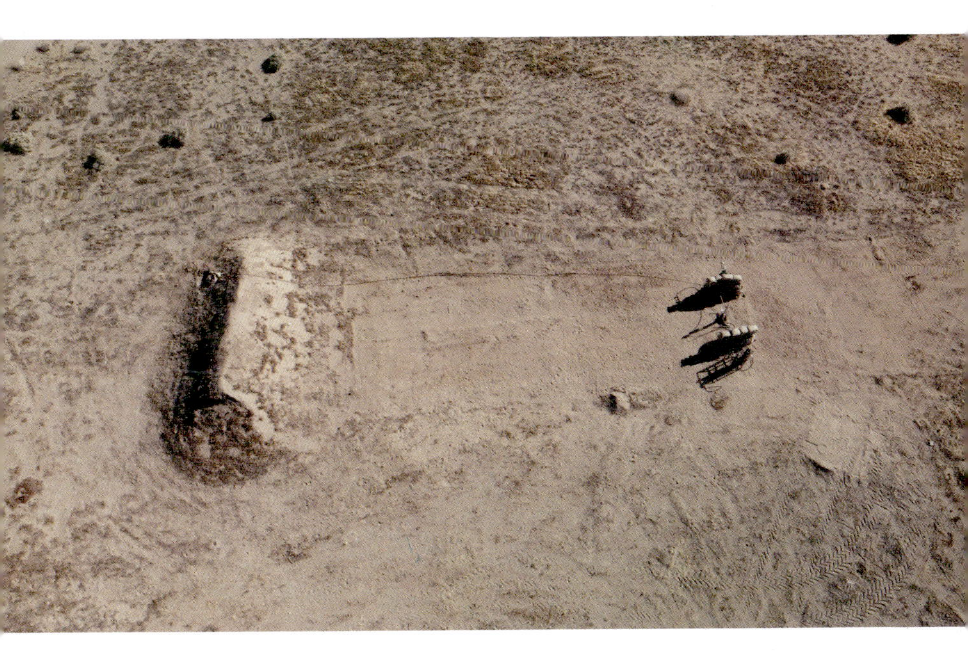

ARTW015f
Film still from American
Artist, *The Monophobic
Response*, 2024.

Such a meaningful experience for me. Thanks to all of you. (And may your next few days bring rest and many electrolytes)

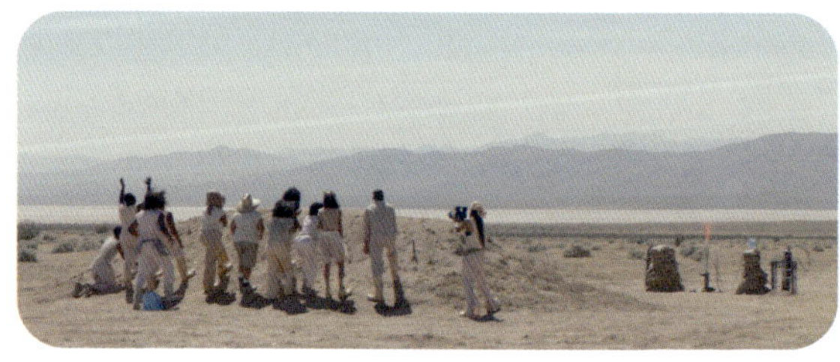

Nitrogen and Oxygen Tanks with Regulators, Copies from Project Report from Dr. Malina, 1945. Courtesy NASA/JPL-Caltech.

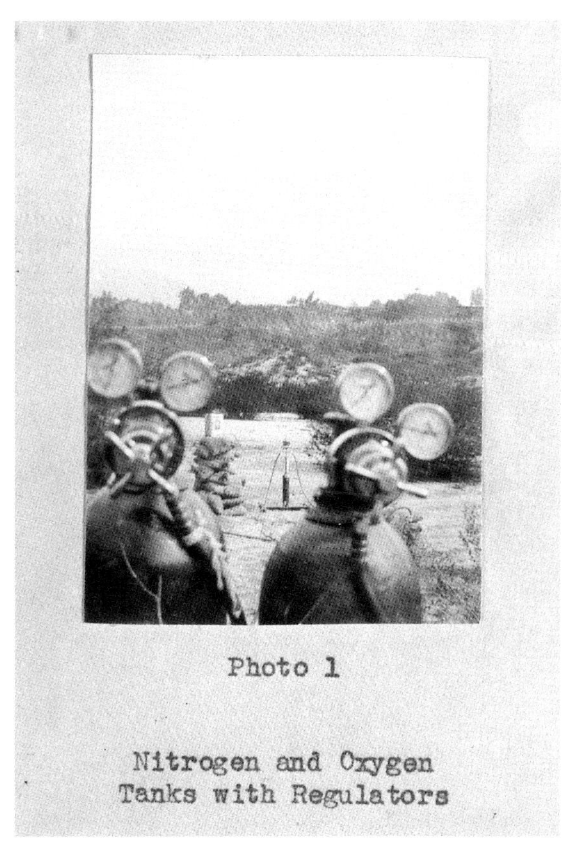

"There is a vast, terrible sibling rivalry going on within the human family as we satisify our desires for territory, dominance, and exclusivity. How strange: In our ongoing eagerness to create aliens, we express our need for them. And we express our deep fear of being alone and on our own in a universe that cares no more for us than it does for stones, for suns; for any fragments of itself. And yet we are unable to get along with those aliens closest to us, those aliens who are, of course, ourselves."

Text message between Chester Toye and American Artist, 2024.

[261]

Relationships and community really the only art that lasts forever

No one tells you how when you live in the archives your sense of smell heightens. You become attuned to the nuances of dust.

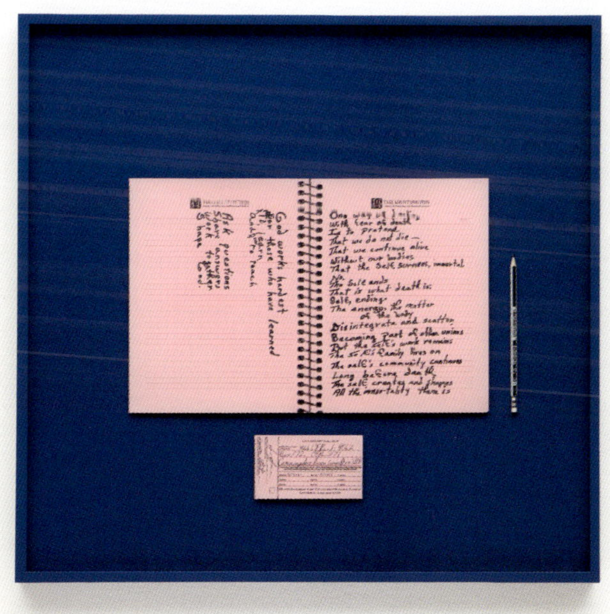

ARTW006
American Artist, *Octavia E. Butler Papers: mssOEB 1-9062 I (Shape God)*, 2022. The Huntington stationary, graphite, pencil, and felt.
26.5 x 27.5 x 1.5 in.

Chester Toye in Mojave, CA on the set of *The Monophobic Response*, 2024.

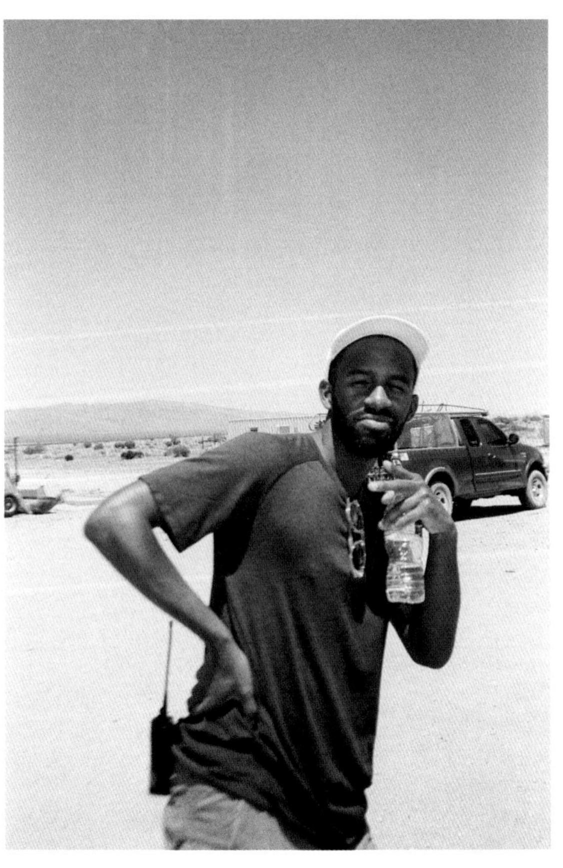

American Artist in Mojave, CA on the set of *The Monophobic Response*, 2024.

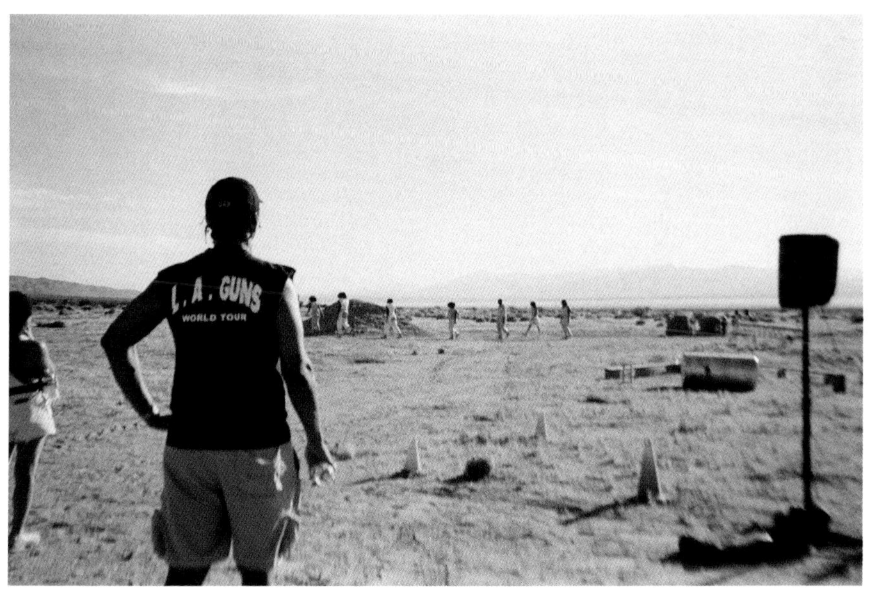

A common place (flaw

by Fred Moten

1   "The Black Radical Tradition is after capitalism as well as before and during, in multiple modalities always. [2]Octavia Butler's *Xenogenesis* trilogy is all about this, I think, using the scariest life-substance—cancer— to reflect on expansive constantly changing sociality."

Ruth Wilson Gilmore

2   What's a commonplace book? ²One of yours is blue. ³A blue spiral with a little yellow, a little yellow with a sign and a .79. ⁴The flaw that would have made me scrape the price tag off is something you don't have. ⁵Because your openness to flaw is perfect, you can stay at impurity. ⁶We come a long way to love the human taste. ⁷You never settle. ⁸Walking away from freedom to find a ceremony. ⁹Gathering passages of hasn't happened yet in dreaming through what has. ¹⁰Always making the book of the common place,

3   it's a theme of general application, a salad of many herbs whose scheme is burning in an essay concerning human understanding. ²The novel is an essay concerning human understanding when you hear the common place. ³Hume ripped and folded in the open house, home is impossible when you grew some church in broken hume. ⁴It's already open so I can't open it. ⁵Why pretend interior to access? ⁶Why look for secrets when all we need is a margin we can build stuff in and out of? ⁷Even if the chromosome is arbitrary there might be true devotion in the fingerprint. ⁸Can I caress a thought up in your notebook? ⁹Touch a whisper your collective head? ¹⁰Let me make it chroma. ¹¹You teach me how to want to taste. ¹²Got me trading for a gene of the general strike. ¹³Your research in seizure is a recess of seed. ¹⁴If we stop, can we grow?

4   *I'm* ~~*still*~~ *a child who loves fun and play,*
An adolescent—idealistic and unrealistic—
An adult, pragmatic, bitter, and frightened.
²Some ash, flung, spent and critical.
³Some waving—permanent and gone—
I'm still a feel who loves fun and play.

5   *something quiet, intense, utterly real—*
even when and where its weird, her f's all
curved like e's,

6   *a human wandering, a terraformed Mars,*
terror-formed, wishing not to be forgotten.
²*Photocopy all Postcards.* ³Radio all photography.
⁴*Intelligence and compassion* all phonography.

7   *Perhaps there is a "mission school" where-*
in natives are kept from doing what comes natu-
rally. ²We naturally make some in some broken
skin. ³We came to read a suit made out of them.

8   *A spider mother submits to being eaten by*
her young. ²*My kids eat your kids.* ³*This genera-*
tion I eat you, next generation you eat me

9   *Fitness determined by who consumes who.*
²*Mating is a true struggle with two beings striving*
to consume one another. ³*They are biologically the*
same. ⁴*But when one kills and consumes the oth-*
er, the consumed one acts as male and fertilizes the
reproductive cells of the consumer. ⁵I mean, you
know, we need to grow some flowers through
their hearts.

10   *They await the ecstasy of being eaten.*

11   Flow on flaw is stereo, and I yearn for sisters, 'cause brotherly love is existential theft, an ethics of gardening when it's way past that, like a truck full of cousins and cushions, or a bathhouse on the run, or a ship in dry rub. ²But you still hold out a platform for massage in tune. ³There's so much life and death, and all this generative gone, that you just left a table full of planets, a lot of 'em blue, with stations, and yellow changes. ⁴Antigone claims unintelligibility by resisting the imposition of unintelligibility. ⁵Lilith broods her brood, her flaw, in anhygienic relay. ⁶If you could ever be alone, it would be like every time I say everybody, when I sound the same in assuming every body. ⁷But you sound different, and what it is to veer by way of choir, and bend, and liquefy the angle's rectitude. ⁸To tweak or twerk or *terkw* or torque like making do? ⁹To make *norma* stop and grow like *khéra*? ¹⁰Your substance is substitution

12   and there's a messed-up warmth beneath stance, an infinitely purple twirl of ground, the enemy within and below in nestle, but it's just some presidents and, as you know, your thing's unpresidented. ²Raised, urged, ingestion effect; revolutionary gestation; evolutionary indigestion; some blush or bruise or brush or blur; some blue; a little yellow, rhythmed, like the said to never turn that turns the dial. ³Oh, when I wake up in the morning, the very first thing that I do. ⁴I turn on my radio and I listen to Y.O.U. ⁵What can it be to bleed and breathe these stories?

SHAPER

OF

GOD

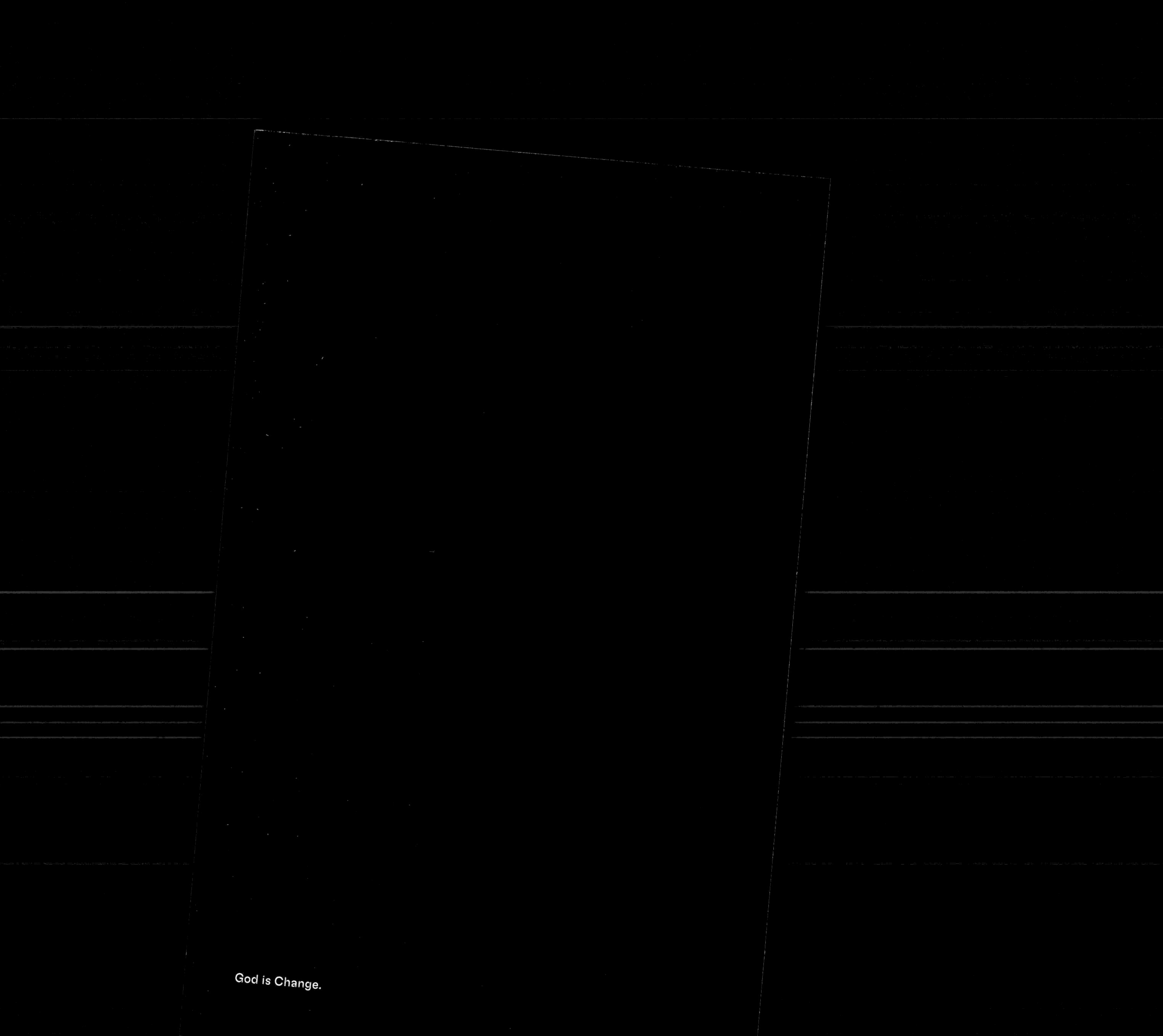

God is Change.

Colophon

Alicia Catalina Godinez Leal
2024

ARTW001
[239, 240]

Christopher Donner
2024

ARTW002
[207, 214]

Estella Butler's Apple Valley Autonomy
2024

ARTW003
[51, 52, 54, 55, 57]

[276]

Single-channel HD
video with sound.
5 mins. 59 secs.
https://vimeo.
com/890870999.

This film is a fictional news segment announcing the death of Alicia Catalina Godinez Leal, an astronaut in *Parable of the Sower* who dies on Mars. The segment features interviews with Godinez Leal's family and members of her community, shedding light on conflicting perspectives on space exploration and the consequences of neoliberal privatization. In the novel, Lauren Olamina sympathizes with the astronaut's passion to visit Mars and unheeded desire to be buried there. It is part of the video series installation *Yannis Window*, which includes representations of media referenced in the novel.

Single-channel HD
video with sound.
2 mins. 23 secs.
https://vimeo.
com/890854198.

This film is a presidential campaign video for Christopher Donner, the leading presidential candidate in *Parable of the Sower*. In the year 2024, Lauren Olamina's father intends to vote for Donner so he can "return [the country] to glory, wealth, and order" but ultimately Mr. Olamina decides not to vote. Artist created a version of Donner that mirrors a real world megalomaniac garnering political attention while promising abstract claims rooted in contemporary aesthetics and cultural hype. Writing the script partly from imagination, and partly based on political claims made by Ye in his 2020 campaign for president, Artist's Donner represents the current political rhetoric of the United States, where presidential candidates are right, left and center at the same time.

Wood, paint, rusted
steel, archival boxes.
168 x 48 x 84 in.

This work is a speculative recreation of Octavia E. Butler's grandmother, Estella Butler's chicken coop, once located in Apple Valley near Victorville, CA. Considering the chicken coop as a symbolic architectural form that represented migration and place-making for Butler's mother and grandmother, American Artist recreated the structure based on archival photos from that era, conversations with friends and family, and AI renderings created using the image software Midjourney. Butler's archives recount her memory of being carried out of the burning chicken coup when she was a child, a formative event

Index of Artworks

The Huntington
stationary, graphite,
pencil, felt.
26.5 x 38 x 1.5 in.

The Huntington
stationary, graphite,
pencil, felt.
26.5 x 52.5 x 1.5 in.

The Huntington
stationary, graphite,
pencil, felt.
26.5 x 27.5 x 2.5 in.

The Huntington
stationary, graphite,
pencil, felt.
26.5 x 38 x 1.5 in.

that perhaps inspired the pervading motif of fire as a symbol of transition throughout her novels.

This work is part of a series of drawings traced from items in the archival collection of Octavia E. Butler that were donated to The Huntington, in San Marino, CA after her passing. The documents are captured on pink stationary provided by The Huntington using pinstriped #2 Staedtler pencils that are available within the archive. The documents reproduced span lecture notes she wrote about her commitment to L.A., her bus route and timetable, a prediction of the 2020s she wrote in 1993, a map of the grounds that informed the slave plantation in her novel *Kindred*, and a memoir of her mother's adolescent life in rural Louisiana.

Index of Artworks

Octavia E. Butler Papers: mssOEB 1-9062 II (The L.A. Area) 2022	ARTW008 [89]	
Octavia E. Butler Papers: mssOEB 1-9062 II (Waylin Plantation) 2022	ARTW009 [167]	
Robledo Community Wall (Olamina cu-de-sac) 2022	ARTW010 [157, 158]	

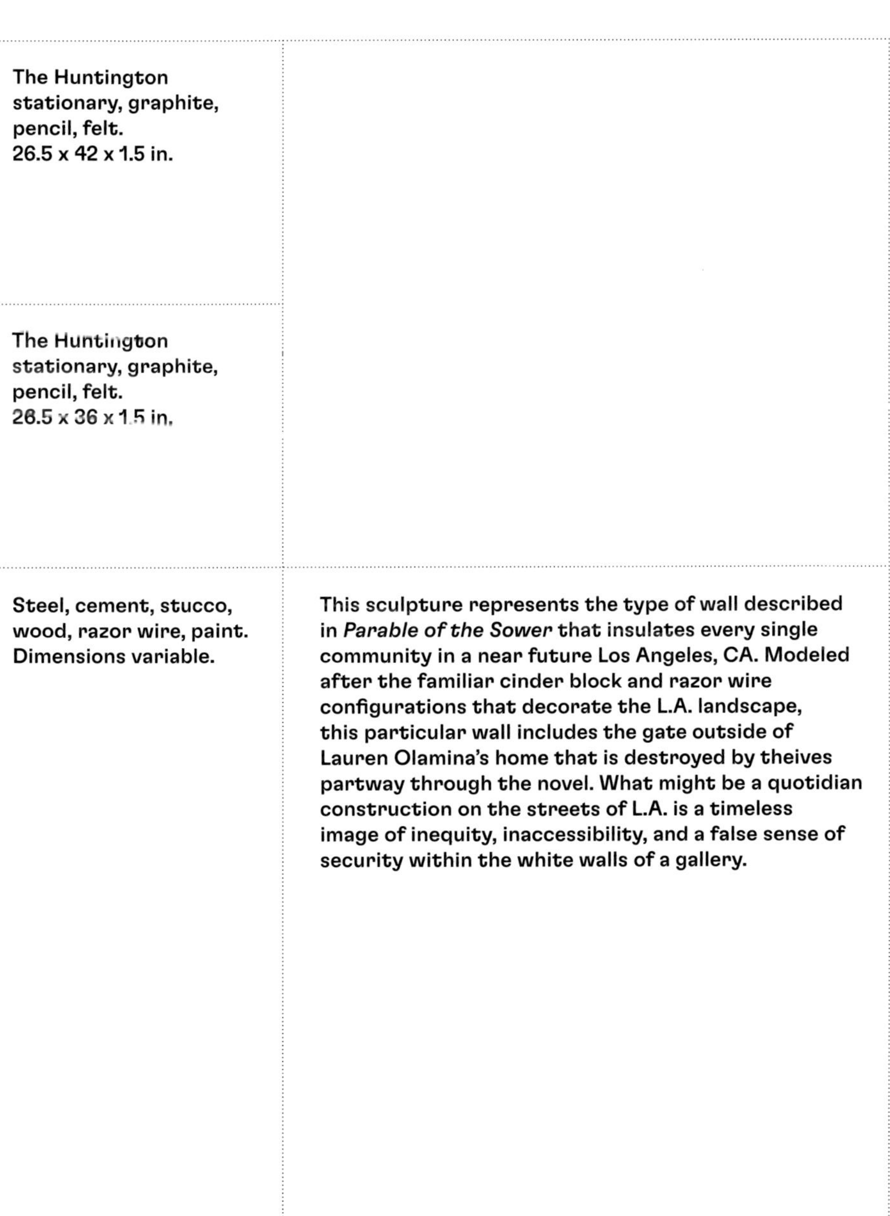

The Huntington
stationary, graphite,
pencil, felt.
26.5 x 42 x 1.5 in.

The Huntington
stationary, graphite,
pencil, felt.
26.5 x 36 x 1.5 in.

Steel, cement, stucco,
wood, razor wire, paint.
Dimensions variable.

This sculpture represents the type of wall described
in *Parable of the Sower* that insulates every single
community in a near future Los Angeles, CA. Modeled
after the familiar cinder block and razor wire
configurations that decorate the L.A. landscape,
this particular wall includes the gate outside of
Lauren Olamina's home that is destroyed by theives
partway through the novel. What might be a quotidian
construction on the streets of L.A. is a timeless
image of inequity, inaccessibility, and a false sense of
security within the white walls of a gallery.

The Arroyo Seco   ARTW014   [103, 115]

Single-channel HD video with sound. 6 mins. 47 secs. https://vimeo.com/706315821.

This short film is a fictional 1990s public access documentary of a historical site in Octavia E. Butler's hometown. It is produced by the fictional City of Robledo Historical Society, a reference to Lauren Olamina's hometown in *Parable of the Sower*. The documentary begins with an introduction to the history and ecology of the Hahamongna Watershed Park in the Arroyo Seco. It goes on to trace the historical evolution of the site from its origins as the home of the native Tongva tribe, to the colonial settlement led by Gaspar de Portola in the eighteenth century, and to its current day designation as the site of the Jet Propulsion Laboratory. The film is part of the video series installation, *Yannis Window*, inspired by passages from *Parable of the Sower*.

Two-channel HD video with sound. 18 mins. 18 secs. https://vimeo.com/992314511 (Single-channel version).

In her novel *Parable of the Sower* (1993), Butler describes a religious collective known as Earthseed, led by Lauren Olamina, that aspires to "take root among the stars." The novel begins in the year 2024 in a California city wrought with inequity, theft, and violence. In this film, American Artist asked the participants, who include artists, rocket engineers, and Octavia E. Butler scholars—to live action role-play an imagined first rocket test performed by Earthseed on their quest to leave the planet.

Steel, methanol, oxygen, tanks, sandbags, hoses, paper, pencil. 150 x 72 x 48 in.

This rocket engine is a functional replica of a design by students of the Guggenheim Aeronautical Lab (GALCIT) in 1936. It was built by referring to pencil sketches by aeronautical engineer Frank Malina in the archives of Jet Propulsion Laboratory. The tests performed in 1936 took place in the Arroyo Seco Canyon near Altadena, CA, and close to where the science fiction author Octavia E. Butler was born in 1947. The tests performed on this engine in the accompanying film parallel those of GALCIT students nearly one hundred years prior.

To Acorn (1968)
2022

ARTW011
[145, 146]

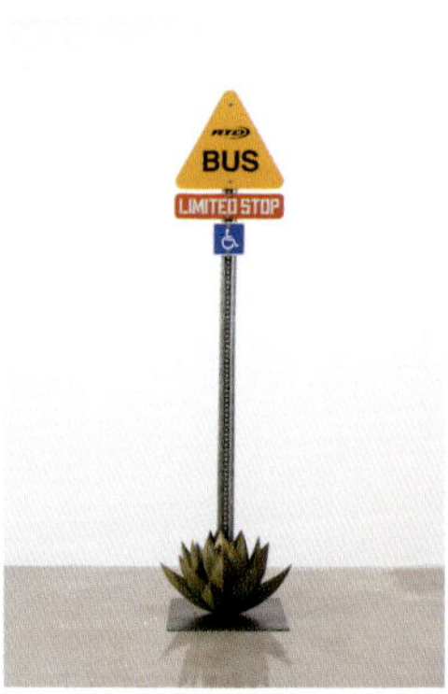

To Acorn (1984)
2022

ARTW012
[137]

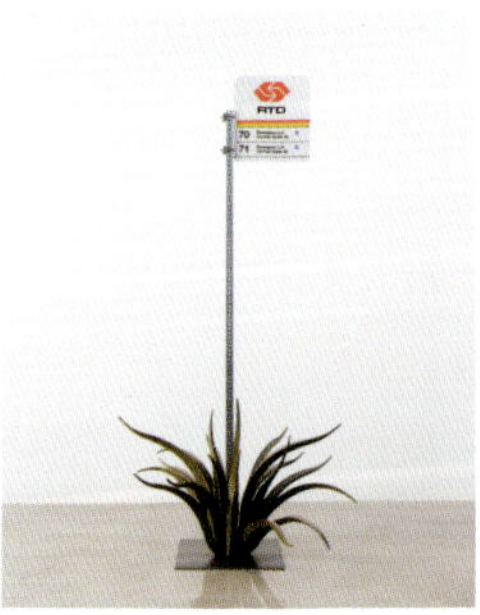

To Acorn (1985)
2022

ARTW013
[129]

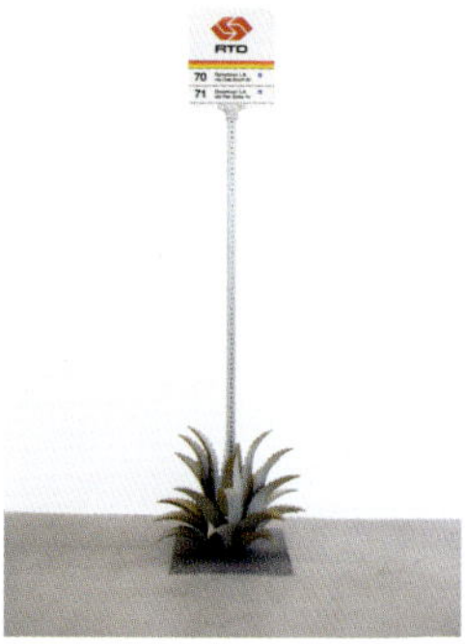

Steel, acrylic, and
hardware.
108 x 30 x 30 in.

Steel, acrylic, and
hardware.
105 x 40.5 x 42 in.

Steel, acrylic, and
hardware.
107 x 33 x 33 in.

Living in Los Angeles for most of her life, Octavia E. Butler never drove a car, and is widely known for riding the bus. The sculptures in the series *To Acorn* reproduce bus stop signs along the route from Pasadena to Downtown Los Angeles, where Butler worked on her novels at the Central Library, as the signs would have looked at various points during her life from high school into adulthood. In her novel *Parable of the Sower*, the town of Robledo gets sacked, and the protagonist, Lauren Olamina leads survivors on a trek across a dystopian California in the year 2024; they ultimately find refuge in Acorn, a new community founded by Lauren. The steel agave plant grounding the sculptures envisages the protective barrier that community members of Acorn planted to protect their compound. This body of work layers the landscapes in which Butler lived with those she imagined, in order to consider history's cycles and the process of envisioning the future.

Index of Artworks

Yannis Window
2022

ARTW017
[95, 96, 97]

Sculptural projection,
single-channel HD video
with sound.
Dimensions variable.

This sculptural video installation is based on passages from *Parable of the Sower* by Octavia E. Butler. It references the wall of a California home, consisting of American Craftsmen-style windows—inspired by the historic Gamble House in Pasadena—on which various news segments and syndicated media play in rotation in order to alert and inform the local community. The Yannis family, who owns the home, was once wealthy, but now, in a California set in the year 2024, peddles fruit and sells television access to other destitute civilians. The collection of videos displayed on the Window is intended to expand in the future, like a news broadcast.

Credits

This publication has been realized on the occasion of the *Shaper of God* exhibition, curated by Vivian Chui with Gabriel Florenz, at Pioneer Works, January 24 – April 13, 2025.

ISBN: 978-1-945711-22-0
Copyright © 2025 Pioneer Works

Publisher →
Pioneer Works Press
159 Pioneer Street
Brooklyn, NY 11231
PioneerWorks.org

Pioneer Works builds community through the arts and sciences to create an open and inspired world. Pioneer Works is a non-profit 501(c)(3). Programs are made possible by the generous support of our board of directors, grants, and donations.

At Pioneer Works, publishing is essential to artistic practice. Pioneer Works Press is our award-winning imprint, dedicated to supporting experimental and pathbreaking work from leading artists and writers in contemporary culture.

Editor →
Zainab Aliyu

Zainab "Zai" Aliyu is a Nigerian-American artist, designer and cultural worker living in Lenapehoking (Brooklyn, NY). Her work explores the cybernetic and temporal entanglements within societal dynamics to understand how all sociotechnological systems of control are interconnected, and how we are all materially implicated through time. She draws upon her body as a corporeal archive and site of ancestral memory to craft counter-narratives through sculptures, videos, installations, virtual environments, publications, archives, and social practice. Zai is a 2023–24 NYSCA/NYFA Artist Fellow and former co-director of the School for Poetic Computation. Her work has been shown internationally at Gardiner Museum (Toronto, Canada), Vienna Design Week (Vienna, Austria), Film at Lincoln Center (New York, NY), Smack Mellon (Brooklyn, NY), Museum of Modern Art Library (New York, NY), Miller ICA (Pittsburgh, PA), Centre for Heritage, Arts and Textile (Hong Kong, China), among others. She has been awarded residencies at MASS MoCA (North Adams, MA), Haystack Mountain School of Crafts (Deer Isle, ME), The Luminary (St. Louis, MI), Casa do Povo (São Paulo, Brazil), Aktuelle Architektur der Kulturimages (Murcia, Spain), and Pocoapoco (Oaxaca, Mexico), among others.

Managing Editor →
Micaela Durand

Copy Editor →
Drew Zeiba

Designer →
Zainab Aliyu

Featuring →
Taylor Renee Aldridge
Lou Cornum
Tananarive Due
Alexis Pauline Gumbs
Ayana Jamieson
Fred Moten

Printer →
Regent Publishing
Services
171 Madison Avenue
Suite 1312
New York, NY 10016
RegentPublishingServices
.com
Printed in China

Typefaces →
GT Alpina
GT America
GT Flexa
GT Flexa Mono

Distribution in NA LA
ASIA AU/NZ AFR ME →
ARTBOOK | D.A.P. USA
75 Broad Street
Suite 630
New York, NY 10004
ArtBook.com

Distribution in EU / UK →
Public Knowledge Books
90 Hoe Street, London,
E17 4QS
PublicKnowledgeBooks
.com

Artwork Credits →

Alicia Catalina Godinez Leal, 2024

Writer & Director:
  American Artist
Producer:
  Chester Toye
Director of
Photography:
  Corey Gegner
First Assistant Camera:
  Celeste Barbosa
Key Grip:
  Danny Green
Gaffer:
  Kristin Steusloff
Editor:
  Bryan Monroe Simpson
Visual Effects:
  Jonathan Manni
Sound Mixer:
  Tomasso Pompei
Post-Production
Sound Mixer:
  Andrew Siedenburg
Production Designer:
  Jesse Hoffman
Props Assistant:
  Haley Castro
Production Assistants:
  Ethan Duffy, Gabriela
  Freid, Marion Tannis
Production Manager:
  Rafaela Sanchez
Performers:
  Megan Reed: Anna
  Dennis; Alicia Leal:
  Alondra Sanchez;
  Guadalupe Leal:
  Carolina Rivera
  Escamilla; Uncle: Rafael
  Escamilla; Neighbor:
  Ayana Jamieson;
  Neighbor's Child: Mars
  Jamieson; Astronauts:
  Taylor Aldridge, Kibum
  Kim, Joel Ferree

Christopher Donner,
2024

Writer & Director:
  American Artist
Producer:
  Chester Toye
Director of
Photography:
  Corey Gegner
First Assistant Camera:
  Celeste Barbosa
Key Grip:
  Danny Green
Gaffer:
  Kristin Steusloff
Editor:
  Bryan Monroe Simpson
Visual Effects:
  Jonathan Manni
Sound Mixer:
  Tomasso Pompei
Post-Production Sound
Mixer:
  Andrew Siedenburg
Production Designer:
  Jesse Hoffman
Props Assistant:
  Haley Castro
Production Assistants:
  Ethan Duffy, Gabriela
  Freid, Marion Tannis
Production Manager:
  Rafaela Sanchez
Performer:
  Christopher Donner:
  Ajuma Rahmaan

The Arroyo Seco, 2022

Writer & Director:
  American Artist
Producer:
  Chester Toye
Director of
Photography:
  Chester Toye
Narrator:
  Gail Irby
Musical Score:
  Topu Lyo,
  William Logan

The Monophobic Response, 2024

Director:
 American Artist
Executive Producer:
 Anne Alexander
Producer:
 Chester Toye
Director of
Photography:
 Tanisha Moreno
First Assistant Camera:
 Elaine Pusey
Drone Operator:
 OJ Pipkin
Costume Designer:
 Tessa Matthias
Sound Mixer:
 Tomasso Pompei
Production Assistants:
 Trapper Piatt, Joey
 Davis, Charlie Scovill
Performers:
 Lauren Olamina:
 Chelsea Allison;
 Bankole: DeMorge
 Brown; Earthseeders:
 Beatriz Cortez, Tre
 Willingham, Arrington
 Mitchell, Denali Joel,
 Yacine Fall, Siyona
 Ravi, Ayana Jamieson,
 Jeffrey Martin, Steven
 Lam, Cydel Lam, Star
 Feliz; Engineers and
 Pyrotechnics: Dave
 Nordling, Dimitri
 Timohovich; Medic:
 Shane Hermanson
 Snake Handler: Derek
 Toth; Motorhome
 Driver: Jamie Drezek;
 LACMA Representa
 tive: Joel Ferree
Filmed on-site at
Mojave Test Area with
support from Reaction
Research Society.

Image Credits →

Front cover:
 Reference:
 OEB 7174-7175 -
 Octavia E. Butler
 portrait. ca. 1962.
 2 photographs: color;
 5x7cm.

Description:
A color photograph
of teenage Octavia
E. Butler, with short,
dark hair styled into
a rounded shape that
frames her face. She
has a calm expression,
looking directly at
the camera. She is
wearing a white shirt,
and the plain, neutral
background keeps the
focus on her face. The
image is a yearbook
photo from John
Muir High School in
Pasadena, California,
and has a distinct
vintage quality.

Note:
Despite due diligence,
it was not possible
to obtain copyright
permissions for
this image from the
Octavia E. Butler
Estate.

Back inside page:
 Photographer:
 Myles Loftin

Acknowledgements
by American Artist

First, I would like to thank my co-shapers Adam Kleinman, Ayana Jamieson, and Joel Ferree, who struck a perfect balance of parental and endearing. I believe you would have done anything to make this project possible. What a gift to be supported unconditionally. Together you created the perfect setting for ideation, trial, error, and celebration, for which I am grateful.

To Chester Toye, the best in a business that has yet to be defined: thinker, energizer, producer, and thought-partner. I'm so lucky that you cold-emailed me one fateful day. To Zainab Aliyu, the most prolific Capricorn I've had the pleasure of knowing. May we never escape the matrix. My friendship with the two of you has made me realize what I want in life, which is to make incredible works of art with my friends. More collaborations to come.

To Rebecca Miralrio, my angel, who *sees* me, in high definition. You show me love in a way I didn't think possible. I couldn't have navigated the institutional abyss without your wisdom and patience. Let this acknowledgement serve as a manifestation of your wildest dreams. "So be it, see to it."

To the team at Pioneer Works: Gabriel Florenz and Vivian Chui, thank you for letting me grace your ground-floor gallery, one of the most enviable exhibition spaces in Brooklyn. And thank you Micaela Durand, Daniel Kent, and Priscilla Posada for making my first artist book a reality, even when calls and emails became abundant.

I would like to extend my gratitude to those that have contributed to *Shaper of God* through knowledge, guidance, writing, and exhibition opportunities: Taylor Renee Aldridge, Ian Blair, Lily Braden, Robyn Braden, Breanne Bradley, Joao Ribas, Young Chung, Patrick Collins, Lou Cornum, Erik Conway, Tananarive Due, Pamela Echevarria, Alexis Pauline Gumbs, Lynell George, Hermenia Rodgers, Gail Irby, Nora Khan, Kibum Kim, Steve Matousek, Fred Moten, David Nordling, Karla Nielsen, Brian "Brains" Rigazzi, Natalie Russell, Dimitri Timohovich, Elisa Wouk Almoni.

This project was made possible with support from KADIST, LACMA Art & Tech Lab, Creative Capital, United States Artists, and the Jacques and Natasha Gelman Foundation.

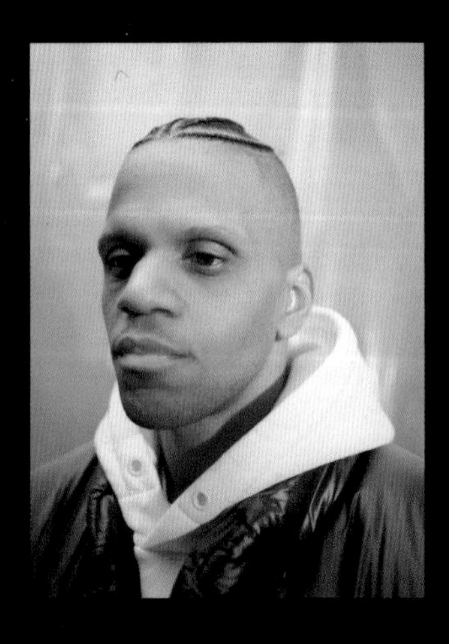

1977 ·························· **NASA**

NASA launches Voyager 1 and Voyager 2, designed at JPL, to communicate Earth's diversity to potential extra-terrestrial life.

1984 ·························· **OEB**

Butler's short story "Bloodchild" is published in Isaac Asimov's *Science Fiction Magazine*. In the subsequent years, she writes the *Xenogenesis* trilogy.

1986 ·························· **NASA**

1995 ·························· **OEB**

Butler becomes the first science fiction writer to receive the prestigious MacArthur Fellowship, affirming her role as a visionary and groundbreaking author.

1999 ·························· **OEB**

After her mother's passing, Butler relocates from Pasadena to Lake Forest Park, Washington.

2003 ·························· **AA**

Four decades after Butler's gradua-